Passion Narratives
and Gospel Theologies

Theological Inquiries

Studies in Contemporary Biblical and Theological Problems

General Editor
Lawrence Boadt, C. S. P.

PAULIST PRESS
New York • Mahwah • Toronto

Passion Narratives and Gospel Theologies

Interpreting the Synoptics Through Their Passion Stories

Frank J. Matera

PAULIST PRESS
New York • Mahwah

Library of Congress
Catalog Card Number: 85-62962

ISBN: 0-8091-2775-X

Published by Paulist Press
997 Macarthur Boulevard
Mahwah, New Jersey 07430

Printed and bound in the United States of America

CONTENTS

IN MEMORIAM

John F. Quinn
1922–1984

ABBREVIATIONS

AbhTANT	Abhandlungen zur Theologie des Alten und Neuen Testaments
AnBib	Analecta biblica
BETL	Bibliotheca ephemeridum theologicarum lovaniensium
BTB	Biblical Theological Bulletin
CBA	Catholic Biblical Association
CBQ	Catholic Biblical Quarterly
CBQMS	Catholic Biblical Monograph Series
EKK	Evangelisch-katholischer Kommentar
EvQ	Evangelical Quarterly
HTKNT	Herders theologischer Kommentar zum Neuen Testament
HTR	Harvard Theological Review
Int	Interpretation
JBL	Journal of Biblical Literature
JSNT	Journal for the Study of the New Testament
JSNTSS	Journal for the Study of the New Testament Supplement Series
JSOT	Journal for the Study of the Old Testament
JR	Journal of Religion
NIGTC	New International Greek Testament Commentary
NovT	Novum Testamentum
NRT	La nouvelle revue théologique
NTS	New Testament Studies
RB	Revue biblique
RevExp	Review and Expositor
RNT	Regensburger Neuen Testament
RSV	Revised Standard Version
SANT	Studien zum Alten und Neuen Testaments
SBLDS	Society of Biblical Literature Dissertation Series

SNTSMS	Studiorum Novi Testamenti Societas, Monograph Series
TST	Theologische Studien und Kritiken
WUNT	Wissenchaftliche Untersuchungen zum Neuen Testament
ZKT	Zeitschrift für katholische Theologie

Unless otherwise noted, all scriptural quotations have been taken from the Revised Standard Version of the Bible.

PREFACE

Although every book is an intensely personal project, it is inevitably written with the assistance of a community. Authors are forever indebted to colleagues and friends who help and encourage them. It is my pleasure to acknowledge those who have aided me.

I owe a debt of gratitude to my colleagues at St. John's Seminary in Brighton: Rev. John P. Galvin, Rev. John L. Sullivan, and Rev. Laurence W. McGrath, and to Dr. Susan Praeder of Boston College. Dr. Praeder and Fr. Sullivan read an early draft of the manuscript and offered many helpful insights. Father Galvin read several chapters at the beginning stages of composition. His suggestions were invaluable in helping me to structure the work. His continued interest in the project was a constant source of encouragement. Father McGrath read the entire manuscript in its final stages. He painstakingly checked the thousands of biblical references in this work. With his keen mind, he made invaluable suggestions and criticisms. No amount of gratitude is sufficient to thank him for devoting so much time to this manuscript.

The passion narratives have interested me since my days at Union Theological Seminary in Virginia. This book affords me an opportunity to acknowledge my professors at Union, especially Paul J. Achtemeier and Jack D. Kingsbury.

Several people have heard these ideas expressed in adult education sessions, clergy days, and seminary classes. I am grateful for the support I received from parishioners of St. Patrick's Church (Richmond, Va.), St. Joseph's Church (New Haven, Conn.), St. Rose's Church (Meriden, Conn.), St. Mary's Church (Clinton, Conn.), and St. Rita's Church (Hamden, Conn.), as well as from the priests of the archdiocese of Hartford and the students of St. John's Seminary, Brighton.

This book is dedicated to the memory of Father John F. Quinn, a friend and colleague for sixteen years. His untimely death during the summer of 1984 was an immeasurable loss for the church of Hartford and the parish of St. Rose. I hope that in some small way this book does honor to his love for scholarship and the Church.

INTRODUCTION

For since, in the wisdom of God, the world did not know God
through wisdom, it pleased God through the folly of what we
preach to save those who believe. For Jews demand signs
and Greeks seek wisdom, but we preach Christ crucified, a
stumbling block to Jews and folly to Gentiles, but to those who
are called, both Jews and Greeks, Christ the power of God and
the wisdom of God. For the foolishness of God is wiser than
men, and the weakness of God is stronger than men (1 Cor
1:21–25).

Christ redeemed us from the curse of the law, having become
a curse for us—for it is written, "Cursed be everyone who
hangs on a tree" (Gal 3:13).

The proclamation of Jesus' death and resurrection is the heart of the
Christian faith. In its Creed, the Church confesses:

For our sake he was crucified under Pontius Pilate;
he suffered, died, and was buried.
On the third day he rose again
in fulfillment of the Scriptures.

That Christians esteem the crucified Christ is apparent. The crucifix is
found in churches and homes and is even worn as jewelry. Christians
acknowledge without apology that Jesus Christ, the Son of God, suffered
and died on the cross. But in a world where crucifixion is no longer employed as a death penalty, it is necessary to explain the meaning of that
punishment.

To be sure, Christians have not forgotten or ignored the unspeakable sufferings which Jesus endured on the cross. Popular devotions such as the Stations of the Cross legitimately remind believers of the excruciating agony Jesus endured. But these devotions do not always come to grips with the central scandal of Christianity: the crucified Messiah, the suffering Son of God. How is it possible for the eternal Son of God to suffer as an ordinary man? How can one speak of a crucified Messiah? In a sense, Christians have become immunized to the shocking reality that the object of their faith is a crucified Messiah, the Son of God, who suffered as an ordinary mortal.

The word "crucifixion" passes our lips too easily; it should not. Crucifixion was the most barbaric and sadistic form of punishment known in the world of Jesus' day. Invented by the Persians, it was taken over by Alexander the Great and his successors, and from them it passed to the Romans who called the instrument used the *crux* ("cross").[1]

For the Romans, crucifixion was primarily a religious-political punishment "with the emphasis falling on the political side."[2] In particular, they employed crucifixion for rebellious foreigners, criminals and robbers, and slaves.[3] It was not a punishment for Roman citizens as Cicero reminded his audience when defending Rabirius: "But the executioner, the veiling of the head and the very word 'cross' should be far removed not only from the person of a Roman citizen but from his thoughts, his eyes and his ears."[4]

Crucifixion was a way for Rome to protect its citizens from brigands who roamed the countryside and to control the foreigners under its rule. In both instances this frightening punishment was intended to act as a deterrent to those who would upset the order of the Roman state. But in a particular way, crucifixion became known as the slave's punishment. As in the case of foreigners and criminals, it was practiced upon the large slave population of Rome to insure its compliance and to keep it from rebelling. So the Roman poet Plautus described crucifixion as the ultimate fate of every slave.[5] Valerius Maximus called it "the slave's penalty" and Tacitus "the punishment usually inflicted on slaves."[6]

It is no coincidence that in the Christ hymn of Philippians Paul writes:

who, though he was in the form of God,
did not count equality with God
a thing to be grasped

> but emptied himself,
> taking the form of a *slave*[7]
> being born in the likeness of men.
> And being found in human form
> he humbled himself and became obedient unto death,
> *even the death on a cross* (Phil 2:6–8).

Paul was aware that Jesus suffered crucifixion, the slave's punishment. Taking the form of a slave, Jesus died the death of a slave.

In sum, for the Romans crucifixion was a hideous form of punishment reserved for rebellious foreigners, criminals and robbers, and slaves. It was abhorrent to, and not intended for, Roman citizens. Cicero, in a well-known phrase, refers to it as the most cruel and disgusting penalty, *crudelissimum taeterrimumque supplicium.*[8]

But crucifixion was as abhorrent to the Jewish world as it was to the Roman world. In the time of Jesus, the Romans employed crucifixion to insure their domination over the Jewish populace. One might expect, therefore, that crucifixion would have become a symbol for Jewish resistance. This could not take place, however, because in the Jewish world yet another meaning, derived from Deuteronomy 21:22–23, attached itself to this fearsome penalty.

> And if a man has committed a crime punishable by death and
> he is put to death, and you hang him on a tree, his body shall
> not remain all night upon the tree, but you shall bury him the
> same day, for a hanged man is accursed by God; you shall not
> defile your land which the Lord gives you for an inheritance.

This, of course, is the text to which Paul alludes in Galatians 3:13. He and his contemporaries interpreted the expression "hangs on a tree" in terms of crucifixion.

This was not the original meaning of the text. In its historical setting, this text from Deuteronomy referred to persons who had been put to death by stoning or decapitation and then were hung upon a tree as a means of defiling their corpses. But by the period of the New Testament the text was assuming a new meaning. From material found at Qumran it appears that the expression "hang upon a tree" was being employed for crucifixion.[9]

A case in point is the Temple Scroll. I quote from the translation provided by Joseph Fitzmyer.[10] The underlined words refer to Deuteronomy 21:22–23.

> If a man has informed against his people, and has delivered his people up to a foreign nation and has done evil to his people, you shall hang him on the tree and he shall die. On the evidence of two witnesses and on the evidence of three witnesses, he shall be put to death, and they shall hang him [on] the tree. If a man has committed a crime punishable by death and has fled to the midst of the Gentiles and has cursed his people and the children of Israel, *you shall hang him* too *on* the *tree* and he shall die. Their bodies *shall not pass the night on the tree, but you shall indeed bury* them *that very day, for what is hanged upon the tree* is *accursed by God* and men; *and you shall not defile the land which* I am *giving to you for an inheritance*. . . .

It appears that the Essene community viewed the crimes of treason and flight from due process, in capital cases, as meriting crucifixion.[11]

The expression "hang upon a tree" is also found in the New Testament and clearly refers to Jesus' crucifixion. In Acts 5:30 Luke writes, "The God of our fathers raised Jesus whom you killed by hanging him on a tree" (see also Acts 10:39). At other times the cross is referred to as a tree. In Acts 13:29 Luke writes, "And when they had fulfilled all that is written of him, they took him down from the tree, and laid him in a tomb." And the author of 1 Peter notes, "He himself bore our sins in his body on the tree, that we might die to sin and live to righteousness" (1 Pet 2:24). In brief, the cross could be referred to as a tree, and the expression "to hang upon a tree" could be understood as referring to crucifixion. When this occurs, it is difficult not to think of the text from Deuteronomy 21:22–23 with its judgment that one hanged upon a tree is cursed.

Those who preached the message that God saved the world through the death and resurrection of Jesus faced a double obstacle. To the Jewish world the crucified Messiah was a contradiction in terms: an oxymoron. The argument against Jesus' messiahship runs thus. Deuteronomy 21:22–23 teaches that one who is hanged on a tree is cursed. Jesus was hanged on a tree; he was crucified. Therefore, Jesus was cursed. But if Jesus was cursed he cannot be the Messiah since the Messiah is God's anointed. So Paul acknowledges: "We preach Christ crucified, *a stumbling block to Jews* and folly to Gentiles" (1 Cor 1:23).

In the Greek world, Christian missionaries faced another problem. The story of a Son of God who died upon the cross contradicted the Greek philosophical notion of God who cannot suffer. Furthermore, the very idea of a god enduring the ignominious death of a slave was repulsive to Greek sensibilities. The argument against Jesus' divine sonship runs thus. Gods are immortal and are free from suffering. Jesus of Nazareth suffered a death reserved for slaves, criminals, and political rebels. Therefore, Jesus of Nazareth cannot be the Son of God. Again Paul writes, "But we preach Christ crucified, a stumbling block to Jews and *folly to Gentiles*" (1 Cor 1:23).

It would appear that no matter where Christians preached, the message of the crucified Messiah and Son of God would not find a sympathetic audience. The proclamation seems to contradict itself and to defy all rules of logic be they Jewish or Greek. It is not surprising, then, that in some quarters Jesus' death by crucifixion was downplayed. This seems to be part of the problem Paul encountered at Corinth, Galatia, and Philippi. It may also explain some of the reasons why Mark found it necessary to write his Gospel. In face of this kind of retreat from the cross Paul writes, "But far be it from me to glory except in the cross of our Lord Jesus Christ, by which the world has been crucified to me, and I to the world" (Gal 6:14).

The Gospel passion narratives are an attempt to deal with the scandal of the cross in a responsible manner. More than simple historical reports, they are profound theological documents which interpret Jesus' suffering and death upon the cross. Part of their purpose is to help the believer see and accept the scandal of a crucified Messiah. They attempt to answer why the Messiah died upon the cross. They endeavor to show that the passion was God's will for Jesus the Messiah and that Jesus obediently accepted it.

This study deals with the passion narratives of the Synoptic Gospels: Matthew, Mark, and Luke. It is not an historical study, that is, it does not try to reconstruct the historical events which actually occurred.[12] That is an important and worthwhile project, one requiring finely tuned historical skills and demanding another book. The goal of this project is more modest. It is to study each passion narrative in terms of the particular evangelist's theology. This study is redactional and literary in nature. It places the historical question "What actually happened?" in brackets and deals with each passion story as the particular evangelist presents it. In so doing, it hopes to elucidate the theological point of view proper to each writer.

Too often in the past, however, the passion narratives have been studied apart from their respective Gospels. To some extent this is understandable since they form such clearly defined units within the Gospels. But this approach results in a truncated version of the story, one which tells the climax but not the beginning and development. It is like listening to an aria but not the many musical movements which prepare for it. To be sure, one will always enjoy the aria, but it will not be completely appreciated until it is set into the wider context of the scene, the act, the opera. The passion narratives must also be set into their wider contexts. Consequently, an important element of this study are the sections devoted to each evangelist's Gospel theology. These chapters take major themes from the passion narrative, melodies if you will, and show how each evangelist develops them in the rest of the Gospel. In this way I hope to demonstrate the relationship between the theology of the particular passion narrative and the theology of the Gospel in which it is found.

I have thought it necessary to say something about the sources each evangelist employed in composing his narrative. This is an important question for contemporary scholarship, especially for the Gospels of Mark and Luke. To be sure one can read the passion narratives without such knowledge, and I suppose most people do. But I suggest that information about the sources each evangelist employed aids the thoughtful reader toward a deeper appreciation of these documents.

The structure of this book is rather simple. Three chapters are devoted to each of the Synoptic Gospels. In the first, I provide an overview of the passion narrative and discuss the question of sources. In the second, I offer a commentary on the particular passion story. In the third, I examine four themes from the passion narrative and show how each one is developed in the rest of the Gospel.

Chapter One

THE PASSION ACCORDING TO MARK: OVERVIEW

Few writings in the New Testament have received more attention in the twentieth century than the Gospel of Mark.[1] With the rise of the historical critical method in the nineteenth century, scholars became convinced that Mark was the first Gospel to be written. That century, so interested in composing a life of Jesus, examined this Gospel with greater interest than any other since it believed it was the most historically reliable of the four Gospels.[2] In the twentieth century, the interests of scholars changed, and new methods of Gospel criticism arose. But scholars remained fascinated with the earliest Gospel, and they applied the new methods of form,[3] redaction,[4] and literary criticism[5] to it. In fact, these methods usually surfaced first in the study of Mark's Gospel. As a result, the study of Mark has benefited from a steady stream of scholarly publications.

What is true of the Gospel in general applies especially to its passion narrative. Most scholars view it as the earliest of the Gospel passion narratives and as a source, or the source, for the accounts found in Matthew and Luke, and perhaps even John. As a result, studies of the passion narratives usually begin with the Gospel of Mark. How did the account grow and develop? How reliable is the information it relates? What theology does it proclaim? Scholars have asked such questions for more than half a century. Although there is no unanimity, there are certain clear directions and trends.

I.

THE THEOLOGICAL CHARACTER OF MARK'S NARRATIVE

Martin Dibelius, a pioneer in the study of the passion narratives, identified Christology as a major concern in Mark's passion story when he stated that there are two high points in Mark's account: Jesus' confession before the Sanhedrin (14:62) and the centurion's confession (15:39) that Jesus was truly God's Son.[6] Since that time most students of the passion have recognized the Christological importance of Mark's narrative, even if they do not agree upon the precise nature of Mark's Christology.

That Jesus of Nazareth was crucified by the Roman state as a messianic pretender, allegedly as a political insurgent, is apparent from the charge placed over the cross: ''The King of the Jews'' (15:26).[7] Although authors argue about the historical worth of Mark's passion narrative, nearly all concede the accuracy of this fact: that Jesus was condemned as the King of the Jews, a messianic pretender. But it was precisely the charge that Jesus was the King of the Jews which became the focus of Mark's passion Christology. His narrative is an attempt to explain the paradox of the crucified Messiah. In other words, Mark's passion deals with the same problem that vexed Paul's readers at Corinth: ''For Jews demand signs and Greeks seek wisdom, but we preach *Christ crucified,* a stumbling block to Jews and folly to Gentiles'' (1 Cor 1:22–23).

The Marcan passion is a relentless account of how the crucified Messiah was abandoned by his followers and seemingly forsaken by God. It poses the paradox that the crucified Jesus is God's royal Messiah.[8] Thus the two high points of the passion as identified by Dibelius, Jesus' confession before the Sanhedrin and the centurion's cry, proclaim what everything else in the narrative apparently belies: Jesus was the Son of God.

Read in isolation, the passion narrative of chapters 14–15 provides a remarkable story which forms a literary unit. That the liturgy can employ the narrative as a unit confirms this fact. One of the achievements of contemporary scholarship, despite its lack of agreement about Mark's sources, is its insistence upon reading Mark's passion narrative as part of his wider Gospel theology. In fact, this is the reason that the source question, which I shall discuss below, has been so important for scholars. They seek to isolate the earliest passion narrative in order to see how Mark edited it in light of his Gospel theology. The investigation of the passion narrative is, in effect, a study of Gospel theology.

In this presentation of the passion, I attempt to relate the story of Jesus' death to Mark's wider Gospel theology by showing that throughout the Gospel the evangelist prepares for themes found in the passion. The four themes I have chosen are: (1) Jesus' royal sonship, (2) the abandonment of Jesus by his disciples, (3) the destruction of the temple, (4) Jesus' view of the future expressed in the kingdom, the Son of Man, and the coming persecution.[9]

II.
THE QUESTION OF SOURCES

At the beginning of this century, Karl Ludwig Schmidt, Martin Dibelius, and Rudolf Bultmann undertook a thorough analysis of the Gospel material. Their discipline, known as form criticism, sought to classify that material in light of its literary form or type. In doing so, each of them examined the passion narrative. Schmidt viewed the passion account as formally different from the other material in the Gospel. It presented, he said, a continuous story, whereas the rest of the Gospel consisted of independent pericopes, i.e., small units of material, which the evangelist-editor strung together like pearls on a string. Dibelius concurred with Schmidt and wrote, "And that is exactly what differentiates the Passion story from the gospel tradition as a whole, i.e., its early composition as a connected narrative."[10] Both Dibelius and Schmidt argued that Mark received the passion story as a continuous narrative and, except for a few minor additions, incorporated it, as found, into his Gospel. Thus both authors gave support to an earlier statement of Martin Kahler that the Gospels are passion narratives with extended introductions.

Bultmann's approach was slightly different. He also believed that Mark inherited an earlier passion account, an account most scholars refer to as the pre-Marcan passion narrative. But unlike Dibelius and Schmidt, he did not maintain that the passion, as found in Mark, is that narrative. Instead, he suggested that the Marcan passion was composed of separate units such as the anointing at Bethany, the prophecy of the betrayal, the Last Supper, the agony in Gethsemane, and Peter's denial. In addition to these units of tradition, there was a primitive narrative "which told very briefly of the arrest, the condemnation by the Sanhedrin and Pilate, the journey to the cross, the crucifixion and death.''[11] This brief, continuous narrative was the pre-Marcan passion narrative around which the several other units of tradition gravitated. Thus Bultmann agreed that there was a pre-Marcan passion narrative, but he disagreed with Dibelius and Schmidt as to its scope.

Although more than sixty years old, the approaches of these three scholars continue to influence the discussion of how Mark's passion narrative grew and developed. The majority of scholars still concur with Bultmann, Dibelius and Schmidt that Mark inherited some kind of passion narrative. But the extent of that pre-Marcan passion narrative remains a point of debate.[12]

Most scholars follow in the footsteps of Bultmann. They view Mark's passion narrative as the result of a primitive narrative enhanced by later traditions. In devising their hypotheses, they have sought to unravel how the passion tradition grew and how Mark edited or redacted it for his own needs. Most theories understand Mark as an active editor who molded and altered the traditions he received. Some authors, such as Schreiber, W. Schenk, L. Schenke, Dormeyer, Linnemann, and Kelber would also view him as a creative theologian who was the master of the traditions he received.

Over and against this approach, especially that which views Mark as a creative theologian, is the work of Rudolf Pesch.[13] Standing in the tradition of Martin Dibelius, he understands Mark as a conservative editor more concerned to maintain the tradition as he found it than to change or alter it. With this view of the evangelist, Pesch proposes a startling hypothesis that challenges the majority opinion. He argues for a pre-Marcan passion narrative that begins not with the crucifixion account, or Jesus' arrest, or his triumphal entry into Jerusalem, but with Peter's confession at Caesarea Philippi (8:27–30). Pesch, in his massive two-volume commentary, states that this narrative derives from the Aramaic-speaking community of Jerusalem, was composed for catechetical purposes, and can be dated before the year 37. It presents Jesus' passion as the passion of the Son of Man. Pesch maintains that Mark made few editorial changes to the original account. Because of this, and because of the age of the account, he sees it as an historically reliable document.

The account consists of 8:27–33; 9:2–13, 30–35; 10:1, 32–34, 46–

52; 11:1–23, 27–33; 12:1–17, 34c–37, 41–44; 13:1–2; 14:1–16:8.[14]
Pesch finds that he can divide it into thirteen sections, each of which
consists of three parts.[15] For example, section one is made up of 8:27–
30, 8:31–33, and 9:2–8. The reader will notice that my own structuring
of chapters 14–15 follows a similar pattern. Although Pesch's views
have not been widely accepted, his analysis of the passion is replete with
a wealth of information that no one can afford to overlook. In my opinion, his hypothesis also has the advantage of relating chapters 14–15 to
a substantially large portion of Mark's Gospel since he sees the passion
beginning at 8:27.

By way of summary, the works of Bultmann, Schmidt and Dibelius
set in motion two important lines of investigation. On the one hand, in
the spirit of Bultmann, several authors have sought to recover a shorter,
pre-Marcan passion narrative embedded in the present account.[16] The
more adventuresome of these explorations, it seems to me, have not succeeded and are not likely to convince students of Mark. On the other
hand, in the spirit of Dibelius, Pesch views Mark as a more conservative
editor who did not tamper with the traditions he received. While Pesch's
position is a corrective to the more adventuresome types, I feel that he
underestimates Mark's own contribution to the passion narrative.

In the chapter which follows, I examine Mark's passion narrative
as found in chapters 14–15. I do not make any attempt to isolate a pre-
Marcan passion account. Nor do I maintain that the passion, as found,
is the simple creation of Mark. In my view, the evangelist inherited traditions, most of which are difficult for the scholar to isolate from one
another. Mark may even have inherited an earlier passion narrative. But
I submit that the final composition of Mark's narrative reflects both his
style and theology as manifested in the rest of the Gospel.[16] Therefore,
I endeavor to relate the passion story to the entire Gospel in order to show
the convergence of passion narrative and Gospel theology.

Chapter Two

THE PASSION ACCORDING TO MARK: COMMENTARY
Mark 14:1–15:47

I.

THE PLOT TO DESTROY JESUS, 14:1–11

Mark's passion story opens with three incidents which foreshadow the death of Jesus: the plotting of the chief priests and scribes, the anointing at Bethany, and the betrayal by Judas. The evangelist arranges the incidents in a sandwich fashion[1] so that the two outer stories of plotting and betrayal contrast with the central story of generosity and love. This technique occurs several times in Mark's Gospel, and it encourages the reader to draw the kind of contrast noted above.

A. The Plot (14:1–2)

In these verses, Mark sets the passion within a precise time frame and identifies Jesus' opponents, thereby connecting the passion to what has preceded. He begins by placing the passion events within the context of the Passover. Jesus will die during the feast which celebrates Israel's national redemption. The implications for the meaning of Jesus' death are evident. That death will bring about a new redemption.

The Revised Standard Version (RSV) says that "it was now two days before the Passover and the feast of Unleavened Bread." The Greek text, however, is not so precise. A more literal translation would read

12

"It was the Passover and the feast of Unleavened Bread after two days (*meta duo hēmeras*)." The Greek betrays the inclusive Jewish mode of reckoning days by which "after two days" can mean the next day. Thus, the plot to destroy Jesus occurs on Wednesday since the next day ("after two days") would be Thursday, the day of the Last Supper. With this starting point, I construct the following chronology from Mark's narrative.[2]

Sunday	Jesus enters Jerusalem (11:1–11). Verse 11 closes this day.
Monday	Jesus curses the fig tree and cleanses the temple (11:12–19). Verse 19 closes this day.
Tuesday	Jesus teaches in Jerusalem (11:20–13:37). 11:20 opens this day; there is no formal closing to the day.
Wednesday	The religious leaders plot against Jesus (14:1–11).
Thursday	Jesus celebrates the Last Supper, and he is arrested (14:12–72). Verse 12 suggests a different day.
Friday	Jesus is crucified (15:1–47). Verse 1 indicates the beginning of the day, verse 42 the close of the day.
Saturday	This is the Jewish sabbath (16:1a).
Sunday	The women find the tomb empty (16:2b–8).

This chronology shows that the brief statement of time in 14:1 ties the passion narrative to earlier events in the Gospel, more specifically to Jesus' Jerusalem ministry (11:1–13:37). In addition, it demonstrates how important the passion is to Mark. In this short book of sixteen chapters, the last seven deal with the final week of Jesus' life.

Mark also ties the passion narrative to the rest of the Gospel when he mentions the religious leaders: the chief priests and the scribes. The evangelist names both of these groups several times during his narrative. The scribes (the lawyers and theologians of the day) appear from the beginning of the story. For example, the crowds contrast the authoritative teaching of Jesus with the teaching of the scribes which lacks such authority (1:22). When Jesus forgives the sins of a paralytic, the scribes believe he has blasphemed (2:6–7). When he eats with sinners, they again criticize him (2:16). Later, they accuse him of being possessed by Beelzebul (3:22), and still later they and the Pharisees complain that Jesus' disciples do not observe the traditions of the elders (7:5). In the first half of the Gospel, therefore, Mark establishes a conflict between Jesus and the scribes which comes to a climax in the passion.

In the second half of the Gospel, the chief priests, a sort of consistory of advisors to the high priest, appear. Jesus mentions them and the scribes in his first (8:31) and third (10:33) passion predictions as the ones who will reject him and condemn him to death. In 11:18, after Jesus cleanses the temple, the chief priests and the scribes seek (*ezētoun*) a way to destroy him. In 11:27 the chief priests, scribes and elders come to him and ask by what authority he does such things. Jesus responds with the parable of the vineyard (12:1–11), after which Mark writes, "And they tried (*ezētoun*) to arrest him, but feared the multitude, for they perceived that he had told the parable against them; so they left him and went away." The plot of the scribes and chief priests in 14:1 becomes the third time that the leaders seek (*ezētoun*) to destroy Jesus. There is a consistent narrative line in Mark's story, from the opposition in Galilee, to the passion predictions, to the Jerusalem ministry, to the final plot to destroy Jesus.

The religious leaders seek to arrest Jesus by stealth/deceit (*en dolō*) in order to kill him. By speaking of deceit, Mark may be alluding to a number of psalms in which deceit (*dolos*) is a characteristic of those who persecute the righteous sufferer (Pss 10:7; 35:20; 52:2).[3] If so, he casts Jesus as the ultimate righteous sufferer. The intention to kill (*apokteinōsin*) Jesus connects the plot to all three of Jesus' passion predictions (8:31; 9:31; 10:34) as well as to the parable of the vineyard (12:7–8). In all of these texts, Jesus foretells that the religious leaders will kill him.

Although brief, these opening verses (14:1–2) are pregnant with meaning. They connect the passion with the first part of the Gospel story, and they show that although the passion results from the evil plotting of human beings, it still fulfills God's plan. Consequently, although the religious leaders decide not to destroy Jesus during the feast, lest there be a tumult among the people, Jesus dies on the very day of Passover because God wills it so.[4]

B. Anointed for Death (14:3–9)

The presence of this story, after the plotting of the religious leaders, provides a striking contrast between those who would destroy Jesus and a woman who manifests extravagant love for him. By locating the incident at Bethany, Mark ties the passion to the rest of his Gospel, since Bethany is Jesus' headquarters during his Jerusalem ministry (11:11–12).

The story is shrouded in anonymity. Mark does not identify the woman or those who object to her action. Later tradition, however, calls her Mary, the sister of Lazarus (Jn 12:3), and identifies those who oppose her as the disciples (Mt 26:8) and then Judas (Jn 12:4).

For some readers, the story is disturbing because of Jesus' remark, "For you always have the poor with you, and whenever you will, you can do good to them; but you will not always have me." On first hearing, Jesus seems to manifest a fatalistic attitude toward poverty: it is inevitable and will never be eradicated. But this is not the point of the saying or of the narrative. Verse 7 is an allusion to Deuteronomy 15:11, "For the poor will never cease out of the land; therefore I command you, you shall open wide your hand to your brother, to the needy and to the poor, in the land." This is a text which summons Israel to attend to the poor of the land. Jesus does not counsel a fatalistic attitude toward poverty. Rather, by alluding to Deuteronomy, he reminds his followers of their responsibility to care for the poor after his death.[5] At the same time, he commends the woman because she recognizes what no one else does: Jesus is about to die. Her action is an anointing for burial, and her good deed serves as a prophetic sign which points to his death.

At the end of the Gospel other women will go to the tomb to anoint Jesus (16:2), but they will not find his body. The anointing by the anonymous woman now, therefore, hints at the resurrection which makes further anointing of Jesus' body impossible.

In addition, there may also be a royal motif here. By anointing Jesus' head, the woman recalls Old Testament scenes in which Saul (1 Sam 10:1) and Jehu (2 Kgs 9:6) were anointed kings in a similar fashion.[6] The presence of a royal motif at this point would be in harmony with Mark's wider theology since he views Jesus as a king on other occasions. At Jesus' entry into Jerusalem (11:1–10), Mark portrays him as the messianic King, and in chapter 15, he presents the condemned and crucified Christ as the King of the Jews.

The most distinctive aspect of Mark's account, however, comes in the final verse: ''And truly, I say to you, wherever the Gospel is preached in the whole world, what she has done will be told in memory of her.'' The word Gospel(*euaggelion*) connects this incident to the rest of Mark's narrative in which the word Gospel plays an important role. For Mark the Gospel is the *message of the kingdom* which Jesus preached: ''Jesus came into Galilee, preaching the Gospel of God, and saying, 'The time is fulfilled, and the kingdom of God is at hand; repent, and believe in the Gospel' '' (1:14–15). But the Gospel, because of Jesus' death and resurrection, can also mean the *good news about Jesus.* Thus Mark begins his story, ''The beginning of the Gospel of Jesus Christ, the Son of God'' (1:1). Here he understands Gospel as both the message of Jesus and the story about Jesus. Because of this relationship between Jesus and the Gospel, the Gospel can also stand *for* Jesus.[7] On two occasions, Mark explicitly makes this connection: ''For whoever would save his life will lose it; and whoever loses his life *for my sake and the Gospel's will save it*'' (8:35), and, ''Truly, I say to you, there is no one who has left house or brothers or mother or father or children or lands, *for my sake and for the Gospel,* who will not receive a hundredfold now in this time . . .'' (10:29).

When Mark has Jesus say, ''wherever the Gospel is preached in the whole world, what she has done will be told in memory of her,'' he understands Gospel both as the message of Jesus and the message about Jesus. That saving message about Jesus includes, according to Mark, not only Jesus' death and resurrection but the course of his life, his public ministry. It is this insight which inspired Mark to write the first Gospel, a new genre of literature for Christians, in which he unites the message of Jesus' death and resurrection with the traditions of his public life.

Finally, the evangelist indicates the universal aspect of the Gospel when he says, ''wherever the Gospel is preached in the whole world'' (see 13:10 for a similar universal outlook). Jesus' message, and the message about Jesus, are not confined to a single race or nation. In making this point, Mark implicitly points to the universal aspect of Jesus' redemption. The Son of Man has come ''to give his life as a ransom for many'' (10:45).

This brief incident, in which an unknown woman anoints Jesus for burial, is related to the whole of Mark's story and highlights the significance of Jesus' death.

C. *Judas' Betrayal (14:10–11)*

The betrayal by Judas forms another contrast with the anointing of Jesus. While the woman pours three hundred denarii worth of ointment upon Jesus, Judas betrays him. Mark does not offer any motive for Judas' betrayal. The religious leaders promise to give him money, but money does not appear to be his motivation (cf. Mt 26:15 where it is). Although he does not offer an explanation for Judas' behavior, Mark focuses upon the freedom of his act and so on the enormity of the crime (cf. Jn 13:2 which points to the role of Satan).

This incident is connected to the rest of the Gospel by the identification of Judas as one of the twelve and the use of the word betray (*paradidōmi,* literally "hand over") which has an important theological meaning in the second Gospel. Judas is one of the twelve because Jesus chose him to be with him, to be sent out to preach, and to have authority to cast out demons (3:13–19; 6:7). As one of the twelve, Judas is given the secret of the kingdom of God (4:10–12) and receives teaching that no one else does (9:33–37; 10:32–34). There is no way to measure his crime. But the paradox is that only such an intimate, not a stranger or enemy, can betray Jesus. Thus Mark warns all of his readers, who count themselves as Jesus' disciples, that they are capable of the most heinous crime.

The second way that Mark connects this story to the rest of the narrative is by the word betray/hand over (*paradidōmi*). In Mark's Gospel there is a line that runs from the handing over of John the Baptist, to the handing over of Jesus, to the handing over of Jesus' disciples. After John is handed over (RSV translates "arrested"), Jesus begins his public ministry (1:14–15). During his public ministry, he predicts that he will be handed over to suffering and death (9:31; 10:33), and in the passion narrative he is (14:10,11,18,21,41,42,44; 15:1,10,15). But Jesus also predicts that what happens to him will happen to his disciples: "for they will deliver you up to councils; and you will be beaten in synagogues; and you will stand before governors and kings for my sake, to bear testimony before them" (13:9). The betrayal by Judas at this juncture is the culmination of a theme which runs throughout Mark's Gospel.

II.
THE LAST SUPPER, 14:12–25

Mark describes the Last Supper in three scenes: the preparations for the Passover meal (14:12–16), the announcement of the betrayer (14:17–21), and the institution of the Eucharist (14:22–25). Scholars debate whether or not Jesus' Last Supper with his disciples was a Passover meal, and many point out that Mark's account contains few, if any, elements from the Passover ritual. But there is no doubt that Mark intends his readers to understand this scene as a Passover meal.

The feast of Passover occurs during the spring, on the fifteenth day of the Jewish month Nisan, which usually falls in the month of April. On that feast, Israel recalls her deliverance from Egypt (Ex 12). At the time of Jesus, Jews came from all of Israel, and beyond, to celebrate the feast in Jerusalem. Because of the character of the feast, national feelings and a desire for liberation reached a fever pitch. Consequently, the Roman governor, who usually resided at Caesarea on the Mediterranean coast, came to Jerusalem with a contingent of soldiers in order to prevent any uprising.

Passover was more than a commemoration of the past. It looked to the future and aroused a profound sense of eschatological expectation, that is, hope for God's final and definitive salvation. A targum (an interpretative, Aramaic paraphrase of the Old Testament) on Exodus 12:42, for example, speaks of four nights when Yahweh delivers his people. The first was when he overcame the night of chaos and created the world. The second was when he appeared to Abraham who was one hundred years old and Sarah who was ninety to bring about the marvelous birth of Isaac. The third was when he appeared in Egypt and delivered Israel from bondage. But the fourth night is yet to come. It will occur at the end of time, when Yahweh accomplishes his final salvation. That night will come at Passover.[8]

It is not difficult to see the relationship between Passover and the death of Jesus. For the first Christians, the majority of whom were Jewish, Jesus' death was the fourth night, God's final and definitive act of redemption. By placing Jesus' Last Supper and death in the context of this feast, Mark and the other evangelists do more than recall the time of Jesus' death, they interpret it in the light of the feast which celebrates

Israel's freedom and redemption. Jesus' passion, death, and resurrection become the Christian Passover.

A. *Preparations for the Meal (14:12–16)*

The feast of Unleavened Bread began with Passover and continued for seven days (Ex 12:14–20). In order to recall the plight of their ancestors and to purify their homes during the feast, the Israelites did not eat leavened bread for seven days. Thus the feast of Passover and the feast of Unleavened Bread were associated with each other.

The lambs for the Passover supper were slain during the afternoon of the fourteenth day of Nisan (Thursday according to Mark) and eaten that evening. Since the Jewish calendar reckons the beginning of a new day at sundown, the fifteenth day of Nisan (Passover) began that evening, Thursday.

Lambs slain	Thursday afternoon	14 Nisan
Passover supper	Thursday evening	15 Nisan
Passover	Friday	15 Nisan
Sabbath	Friday evening	16 Nisan

According to Mark and the other Synoptic writers, Jesus celebrated the Last Supper on the eve of Passover (Thursday evening) and was crucified on Passover day (Friday). While our calendar calculates this as two separate days (Thursday and Friday), the Jewish calendar sees it as one day (sunset to sunset, 15 Nisan). Mark emphasizes this twenty-four hour period that extends from sunset to sunset by the phrase *kai opsias genomenēs* ("and when it was evening") which occurs at the beginning of the Last Supper (14:17) and at the conclusion of the crucifixion (15:42).

The preparations for the Passover meal are similar to those for Jesus' triumphal entry into Jerusalem (11:1–6). Both accounts point to Jesus' prophetic foreknowledge. He knows where the colt will be found (11:2) and where the Passover will be celebrated (14:15). The disciples find everything just as Jesus tells them (11:16), and the passion occurs just as Jesus predicts (8:31; 9:31; 10:33–34). There is a similar story in 1 Samuel 10:1–9 where the prophet Samuel gives the young Saul a number of signs to assure him that the Lord has anointed him "prince over his heritage" (1 Sam 10:1). The two incidents in Mark belong to the same genre; they are stories which highlight the prophet's foreknowledge. So Mark establishes that Jesus enters the passion aware of what lies ahead of him.

In this scene, Jesus identifies himself as "the Teacher." At first hearing, it seems a banal description but in Mark's Gospel the title occurs several times (4:38; 5:35; 9:17, 38; 10:17, 20, 35; 12:14, 19, 32; 13:1), and teaching appears as one of Jesus' primary activities (1:21, 22; 2:13; 4:1, 2; 6:2, 6, 34; 8:31; 9:31; 10:1; 11:17; 12:14, 35; 14:49). When Mark identifies Jesus in this story as the Teacher, he recalls a favorite theme: Jesus is the one who teaches with authority. Mark implies that the passion is Jesus' last and greatest teaching.

B. Prediction of the Betrayer (14:17–21)

With the arrival of evening, Jesus sits with the twelve to eat the Passover meal. In the midst of the meal, he employs the prophetic amen formula (RSV translates *amen* as "truly") to announce his betrayer. The designation of the betrayer as "one who is eating with me" recalls the plight of the righteous sufferer,[9] in the psalms of lament, who is betrayed by his friend. "Even my bosom friend in whom I trusted, who ate of my bread, has lifted his heel against me" (Ps 41:9; also see Ps 55:12–14). They ask Jesus, "Is it I?" But Jesus does not identify the betrayer, even when he says, "It is one of the twelve, one who is dipping bread into the dish with me," since the dish is the common bowl into which all would be dipping their bread.

Mark does not explain why Judas betrays Jesus, but he suggests that the betrayal happens because the Scriptures foretell it: "For the Son of Man goes as it is written of him . . . ." Precisely what Scripture passages he has in mind Mark does not say. It may be that he interprets Jesus' passion as part of a pattern revealed in the psalms of lament. Or, he may have a specific text in mind such as Psalm 41:9 or Psalm 118:22–23, the text which concludes the parable of the vineyard: "The very stone which the builders rejected has become the head of the corner; this was the Lord's doing, and it is marvelous in our eyes" (12:10b–11). Whatever the answer, this passion saying makes clear that even the betrayal is part of God's plan for the Son of Man.

In the passion the plan of God and the wickedness of human beings intersect. Immediately after saying that the betrayal is in accordance with Scripture, Jesus utters a prophetic woe which endows the betrayer with full responsibility: ". . . but woe to that man by whom the Son of Man is betrayed! It would have been better for that man if he had not been born." The betrayal presents a mystery which defies explanation; Judas' action accords with Scripture yet derives from human freedom.

By announcing the betrayal in the context of a meal with the twelve, Jesus exposes the nature of Judas' crime. The twelve are Jesus' chosen disciples and, as their number suggests, they represent the twelve tribes of Israel to whom he announces the arrival of God's kingdom (1:14–15). The meal, as the next section makes clear, points to the messianic banquet God will share with the elect in heaven. The essence of the betrayal is the breaking of table fellowship with Jesus. It is a crime of which every disciple, and *only a disciple,* is capable.

C. The Eucharist (14:22–25)

Having predicted the betrayal, Jesus explains the significance of his death. First, he blesses, breaks, and gives bread to his disciples, identifying it as his body.[10] The gestures are similar to those he performed at the feeding of the five thousand and the four thousand (6:41; 8:6), but this time they interpret Jesus' death. His body will be broken and given for them. Body should not be interpreted too narrowly, as though it referred merely to a part of Jesus. In the Semitic mentality the body (*soma*) refers to the whole person.[11] Jesus gives his entire self to his disciples in his death.

Next Jesus identifies wine with his blood, relating it to the blood of the covenant poured out for many. The wording "blood of the covenant" is the same as that found in Exodus 24:8 where Moses takes blood and sprinkles it upon the people of Israel, thereby ratifying the Sinai covenant. By calling his blood the blood of the covenant, Jesus says that his death will establish a covenant between God and the people gathered round him (Jesus). The final phrase, "poured out for many," may be an allusion to the Suffering Servant described in Isaiah 53. "Therefore I will divide him a portion with the great, and he shall divide the spoil with the strong; because he poured out his soul to death, and was numbered with the transgressors; yet bore the sin of *many,* and made intercession for the transgressors'' (53:12). The literary contacts are not strong, and it is not clear if Mark has this text in mind. But it is evident that Jesus' death has a universal significance for Mark, a point emphasized in 10:45: ''For the Son of Man also came not to be served but to serve, and to give his life as a ransom for many.''

According to Mark, Jesus' death has redemptive value and establishes a covenant people. Furthermore, Jesus knows that his death will not end in defeat. Thus he pronounces a second amen saying in which he looks beyond death. ''Truly, I say to you, I shall not drink again of the fruit of the vine until that day when I drink it new in the kingdom of God'' (14:25). The kingdom of God is a familiar theme in Mark's Gospel. It is the content of Jesus' teaching (1:15; 4:11,26,30), and Jesus is confident that it will arrive soon with power (9:1). By this saying, he prophesies that his death will result in the coming of that kingdom.

To summarize: Jesus interprets his death as a total giving of self for all that will establish a covenant and bring about the kingdom of God. Mark implies that each time his readers celebrate the Eucharist, they anticipate this kingdom and celebrate the saving death of their Lord.

III.
AT THE MOUNT OF OLIVES, 14:26–52

The supper ends and the scene changes to the Mount of Olives where Jesus prays in the garden of Gethsemane and then is arrested. The Mount of Olives plays an important role in Mark's story. In chapter 13, Jesus delivers a long discourse ''as he sat on the Mount of Olives opposite the temple'' (13:3). Although only Peter, James, John and Andrew are present, it is evident from the last verse of the chapter that the discourse is directed to Mark's entire community: ''And what I say to you I say to all: Watch'' (13:37). The command to watch is integral to the entire discourse in which Jesus instructs the four disciples about the signs that precede the destruction of the temple and his return as the exalted Son of Man. The same word occurs three times in this section when, in the garden of Gethsemane, Jesus instructs Peter, James and John to watch (14:34,37,38) while he prays.

Jesus' hour of suffering and trial begins on the Mount of Olives. His suffering prefigures the persecution predicted for the disciples in

13:9–13. Mark draws a comparison between the passion of Jesus begun at the Mount of Olives, and the passion of his followers predicted from this same place. The section may be divided into three parts: three prophecies (14:26–31); the agony in the garden (13:32–42); Jesus' arrest and the flight of the disciples (14:43–52).

A. *Three Prophecies (14:26–31)*

This section contains three prophecies which highlight Jesus' prophetic foreknowledge and explain why the passion happens as it does. In the first (14:27), Jesus tells the disciples that they will "all fall away." In back of the words "fall away" stands the Greek *skandalizein* which, in Mark, has the sense of fall away from faith (4:17) or cause others to sin (9:42–48). Jesus explains that the disciples will fall away from him because Scripture (Zech 13:7) foresees their failure, "I will strike the shepherd, and the sheep will be scattered." This text comes from an oracle found in Zechariah 13:7–9 in which Yahweh's shepherd is struck by the sword in order to scatter the sheep, that is, the people of Israel. Mark interprets the text so that the shepherd refers to Jesus and the sheep to the disciples. When Jesus, the shepherd king of Israel, is struck, his sheep, the disciples, will be scattered.

Who strikes the shepherd? The text from Zechariah reads, "Strike the shepherd, that the sheep may be scattered." But Mark writes, "*I* will strike the shepherd, and the sheep will be scattered." The mystery of the passion becomes terrifying. It is God who strikes the shepherd. It is God who delivers up his own Son (see 9:31 where the passive voice may imply the action of God). Once more human freedom and the divine plan intersect. The disciples will fall from faith and must take responsibility for their actions, but their free choice coincides with the divine purpose.

The second prophecy (14:28), however, shows that the failure of the disciples will not result in separation from Jesus: "But after I am raised up, I will go before you to Galilee." After his resurrection, Jesus will gather the scattered sheep of his flock. The angel at the empty tomb repeats these words to the woman, "But go, tell his disciples and Peter that he is going before you to Galilee; there you will see him, as he told you" (16:7). In Mark's Gospel, the inability of the disciples to understand Jesus' message and their failure to follow him to the cross form a major theme. But this failure does not result in separation from Jesus since he reestablishes the relationship between himself and the disciples at Easter, making clear that discipleship is a gift from above.

Why Galilee? In Mark's Gospel there is an opposition between Jerusalem and Galilee. The first is the place of Jesus' death, the second the land of his ministry. Jesus is from heathen Galilee (1:9); he does not belong to the official circles of Jerusalem. In Galilee he begins to preach the Gospel (1:14–15), and Galilee becomes the center of his ministry (1:28,39; 3:7; 7:31). By going ahead of (*proaxō,* 14:28; 16:7) the disciples to Galilee, the risen Lord brings them back to the beginnings of his own ministry so that they can walk, once more, the path of discipleship. This time, however, they will trod that path in the light of Jesus' death and resurrection. They will walk in the way of discipleship, a path which leads to the cross. Discipleship becomes a never ending journey from Galilee to Jerusalem.

Because they have not yet experienced these events, the disciples do not understand Jesus' words. Peter protests that even if all should fall away (*skandalizein*), he will not. The others say the same. Throughout the Gospel, Mark presents Peter as a spokesman for the others (8:29; 9:5; 10:28; 11:21; 13:3). But now Peter separates himself from the rest. Already the community of disciples is disintegrating![12]

Despite Peter's protestations of loyalty, Jesus utters his third prophecy. Peter will deny him (14:30). It is also the fourth of Jesus' *amen* sayings in chapter 14 (see vv. 9,18,25).

By the conclusion of this chapter two of Jesus' predictions come to pass. The disciples abandon him (14:50) and Peter denies him (14:68,70). The third prediction finds its fulfillment in 16:7. There can be no doubt that Jesus is an authentic prophet. There can be no insinuation that the passion caught him unprepared.

B. *Jesus' Prayer and the Disciples' Failure (14:32–42)*

This scene has a three-part structure. In vv. 32–38 Jesus and the disciples come to Gethsemane, an olive orchard on the Mount of Olives. Jesus takes three of them and goes off to pray. When he returns, he finds the disciples asleep. In vv. 39–40 he prays once more, but when he returns he again finds them sleeping. Finally, in v. 41 the same events occur. The words pray (14:32,35,38,39), watch (14:34,37,38) and sleep (14:37,40,41) dominate the story and point to its major themes. There is a strong contrast between Jesus who prays and accepts the Father's will, and the disciples who sleep and eventually flee at the moment of his arrest.

The first of these three sections (14:32–38) is the most detailed. It consists of three parts. In the first (14:32–34), Jesus takes Peter, James and John with him and becomes distressed and troubled before them. The choice of these three is important because they were witnesses of Jesus' power when he raised Jairus' daughter (5:35–43). They were present at the transfiguration (9:2–13). And they, with Andrew, were privy to Jesus' apocalyptic discourse on the Mount of Olives (13:3–37) in which he spoke of his parousia as the glorious Son of Man (13:24–27). The disciples who witnessed Jesus' glory now see him in weakness and fear. In the presence of the three, he manifests terror and dread as he faces death. His words, "My soul is very sorrowful (*perilypos*)," come from two psalms of lament (Pss 42:5,11; 43:5) in which the righteous sufferer expresses similar sentiments when afflicted by his adversaries. The Gethsemane scene acts as a counterbalance to Jesus' transfiguration, and it implies that no one can fully understand Jesus without accepting him as the suffering Son of Man, as well as the glorious Son of God.

In the second subsection (14:35–36), Jesus withdraws from the three and prays to his Father. He addresses God with the Aramaic word *Abba,* which the Greek translates as father, but which has the more intimate sense of papa (the same word occurs in Rom 8:15 and Gal 4:6). Scholars, especially Joachim Jeremias,[13] have pointed out that such an intimate relationship with God is unheard of in the Jewish literature of Jesus' day that scholars are aware of. Such an address implies a unique sense of sonship on the part of Jesus with God. It is evident that Jesus undergoes the passion as more than a righteous sufferer; he suffers as God's Son. Mark returns to this theme at the end of chapter 15 where the centurion confesses that Jesus is the Son of God.

Jesus, acknowledging that all things are possible to God (see 10:27 where he uses a similar phrase), asks his Father to let the hour pass and to remove this cup.[14] The hour and the cup refer to Jesus' suffering. In his apocalyptic discourse, Jesus tells the four disciples to watch and pray because no one knows, not even the Son, the day or the hour when the events described in that discourse will take place (13:32–37). The passion is the hour of final, eschatological suffering for Jesus. It foreshadows the events mentioned in his apocalyptic discourse.

The cup points to Jesus' death. When James and John ask him for the seats at his right and his left (10:35–37), Jesus responds, ''Are you able to drink the cup that I drink, or to be baptized with the baptism with which I am baptized?'' (10:38). The imagery points to the passion. In this moment of dread, Jesus would avoid the passion, provided it accorded with God's will (''yet not what I will, but what thou wilt'').

In the final subsection (14:37–38), Jesus returns and finds the three disciples asleep. He addresses Peter, the representative of the others, and asks why they sleep rather than watch and pray. The dialogue recalls Jesus' parable at the end of the apocalyptic discourse in chapter 13. There (13:34–37), he compares the coming of the final hour with the unexpected arrival of the master of the household. ''Watch therefore . . . lest he come suddenly and find you asleep'' (13:35–36). The disciples do not watch during Jesus' hour of agony, and he finds them asleep.

The second scene (14:39–40) is briefer. Jesus prays, and, returning, he finds the three asleep a second time. Mark writes that ''they did not know what to answer him.'' The phrase echoes that found in the transfiguration account when Peter did not know what to say (9:6) because he and the other disciples were exceedingly afraid. Mark encourages the reader to understand the accounts of the transfiguration and the agony in light of each other.

In the final scene (14:41–42), Jesus finds the disciples asleep for the third time. But while they have slept he has found the courage to accept the Father's will. He announces that the hour has come and that the Son of Man is betrayed into the hands of sinners. This Son of Man saying forms a climax to several sayings about the suffering Son of Man which run through the second half of Mark's Gospel (8:31; 9:12,31; 10:33; 14:21). In all of these, Jesus predicts his betrayal. Now that the hour of passion and betrayal arrives, terror and dread no longer grip Jesus. Prayer and vigilance have prepared him for the hour.

C. Jesus' Arrest and the Disciples' Flight (14:43–52)

At the beginning of this section, Jesus predicted that the shepherd would be struck and the sheep would be scattered. Now that prediction comes to pass. Having failed to pray and watch for the hour, the disciples scatter at Jesus' arrest. There are two major divisions to this part. The first (14:43–46) features Judas and the arresting party, the second

(14:47–52) focuses upon the reactions to Jesus' arrest. The word seize (*kratein*) runs throughout the narrative (14:44,46,49,51). With the seizure of Jesus in Gethsemane, the attempt to arrest (*kratein*) him, first mentioned in 12:12, is realized.

Judas arrives with an arresting party from the chief priests, the scribes and the elders: the three groups who form the Sanhedrin, the Jewish high council. The chief priests and the scribes, according to 14:1, seek to arrest Jesus. According to 14:10, Judas had gone to the chief priests to betray Jesus. In the rest of the narrative all of these groups play an important role (14:53,55; 15:1,3,10,11,31), since Mark places the primary responsibility for the death of Jesus upon the Jewish leaders.

Judas approaches Jesus saying, Rabbi (Master), and kisses him. In the rest of the Gospel, Rabbi is a title of honor by which the disciples acknowledge that Jesus is their teacher, the one with whom they cast their lot. For example, Peter calls Jesus Rabbi, both on the mount of transfiguration (9:5) and after the cursing of the fig tree (11:21). The use of the title here highlights Judas' treachery, as does the kiss which accompanies it.

The kiss of the betrayer has several counterparts in the Old Testament.[15] Jacob, pretending to be Esau, kisses his father Isaac (Gen 27:26–27), an action which the rabbis interpreted as an act of deceit.[16] Absalom, in an effort to undermine the authority of his father David, kisses those who do obeisance to him (2 Sam 15:5). Joab slays Amasa with a sword as he kisses him (2 Sam 20:9–10). And the Book of Proverbs teaches, "Faithful are the wounds of a friend; profuse are the kisses of an enemy" (27:6). After Judas' kiss, the arresting party "laid hands on him," thereby fulfilling Jesus' words, "the Son of Man is betrayed *into the hands of* sinners" (14:41).

Except for the behavior of Jesus, the reaction to Jesus' arrest is utter confusion. A bystander draws a sword and strikes the high priest's servant (14:47). All of the disciples flee (14:50) and a young man, fearful of arrest, runs away naked (14:52). The flight of the disciples fulfills Jesus' prophecy about the scattering of the sheep (14:27) and recalls the chaotic flight described in Jesus' apocalyptic discourse (13:14–20). The incident of the naked young man is not meant to be interpreted humorously or symbolically. It simply emphasizes the panic which characterizes the moment.[17]

Jesus defends himself. He complains that they treat him as a robber, although he taught openly in the temple. The word for robber (*lēstēs*) can also mean a political revolutionary. It occurs two other times. During the cleansing of the temple, Jesus complains that the temple has been turned into a den of robbers (11:17). He does not say who the robbers are, but there is a strong implication that he is referring to the religious leaders.[18] At the crucifixion, Jesus is crucified between two robbers (15:27), a circumstance which casts him in the role of a brigand and revolutionary. Mark invites the reader to make a choice. Who are the real criminals? Jesus or his persecutors?

Having defended himself, Jesus does not resist arrest. He says, "let the Scriptures be fulfilled." His words are part of a wider theme in Mark which affirms that Jesus' suffering and death are in accordance with Scripture (9:12; 14:21). The picture of Jesus abandoned by all of his friends has a model in those psalms which portray the righteous sufferer.[19] "I am the scorn of all my adversaries, a horror to my neighbors, an object of dread to my acquaintances; those who see me in the street flee from me" (Ps 31:11; also see, Pss 38:11; 88:8). From this point forward, Jesus will play a more passive role. Having foretold the passion and prepared for it, he now endures it.

IV.

THE TRIAL OF JESUS AND PETER'S DENIAL, 14:53–72

The events of this section, especially the trial of Jesus, present scholars with some of the most difficult questions occasioned by the New Testament. Both Jews and Christians point out that the trial, as portrayed in Mark, violates the fundamental laws necessary for a legal trial according to Jewish jurisprudence. For example, that the trial takes place at night on the eve of Passover and that Jesus is condemned to death on the day of the trial violate several prescriptions of Jewish law found in the Mishna. The historical problem is complicated because our knowledge of Jewish law derives primarily from the Mishna, a work codified toward the end of the second century A.D. There are no extant documents that can provide an exact knowledge of the Jewish legal system operative at the time of Jesus.[20]

The historical question of Jesus' trial is of immense importance to both Christians and Jews since accusations about the Jewish responsibility for Jesus' death have often led to anti-Semitism. As I indicated in the introduction, the primary purpose of this study is to read the text on the literary level. Therefore, I shall not attempt to reconstruct the historical events of Jesus' trial. Such an undertaking is a major task better reserved for another book.[21]

It is important to distinguish between the historical events of Jesus' trial and the evangelists' interpretation of them. In the past the lack of such distinction has sometimes promoted anti-Semitism. Mark's text is grounded in history, but that history is interpreted in the light of the resurrection. Mark's point of departure is that Jesus was condemned to death as the Messiah. In order to highlight this, he arranges the trial scene to climax in Jesus' confession before the high priest (14:62). Consequently, Mark provides a theological interpretation of the events rather than an indifferent, historical report.

The trial scene consists of three subsections: the handing over of Jesus to the religious leaders (14:53–54), the trial before the Sanhedrin (14:55–65), and Peter's denial (14:66–72). These stories establish a deliberate contrast between Jesus, who confesses his messiahship before the entire Sanhedrin, and Peter, who denies Jesus three times before a maid and some bystanders. Mark joins these two incidents, trial and denial, by his sandwich arrangement. The account of Peter's denial (14:54,66–72) encloses the account of Jesus trial (14:55–65). This arrangement gives the impression that the two events take place simultaneously. *As* Jesus makes his confession, Peter denies him.

Several elements of the trial reflect the passion of the righteous sufferer as portrayed in the psalms of lament. I quote some of the texts.[22]

> Ps 22:16—"Yea, dogs are round about me; a company of evildoers encircle me."
>
> Ps 31:13—"Yea, I hear the whispering of many—terror on every side!—as they scheme together against me, as they plot to take my life."
>
> Ps 54:3 —"For insolent men have risen against me, ruthless men seek my life; they do not set God before them."
>
> Ps 71:10—"For my enemies speak concerning me, those who watch for my life consult together."
>
> Ps 86:14—"O God, insolent men have risen up against me; a band of ruthless men seek my life, and they do not set thee before them."

In quoting these passages, I do not suggest that Mark had all of them in mind. But it does appear that he, and those before him who spoke of the passion, understood the trials of Jesus in light of what happened to the righteous sufferer portrayed in the psalms of lament.

A. *Jesus Is Handed Over (14:53–54)*

The arresting party brings Jesus to the chief priests, the scribes and the elders. The chief priests formed an advisory board to the high priest and assisted him in the daily running of the temple. The scribes were the theologians and lawyers of the day, drawn primarily from the sect of the Pharisees, one of the more progressive parties. The elders belonged to the landed gentry, the old and established families around Jerusalem. The Sadducees, a conservative and priestly party, filled their ranks. Representatives from these groups formed a council of seventy, headed by the high priest. They governed the people in religious and political affairs to the extent that the Romans allowed. Mark could hardly express the confrontation more sharply: the rabbi from heathen Galilee faces the highest council of the land.

Peter follows (*akolouthein*) Jesus at a distance (*apo makrothen*), even into the courtyard of the high priest where he sits warming himself with the guards. At other points in Mark's narrative, the verb to follow is used in relationship to discipleship. For example, Peter and Andrew leave their nets and follow Jesus (1:18). And when Jesus talks about the demands of discipleship, he says, ''If any man would come after me, let him deny himself and take up his cross and follow me'' (8:34). Here, despite Peter's boldness, the verb suggests an anti-disciple theme. Peter follows Jesus, but at a distance (*apo makrothen*), thereby associating himself with the kinsmen of the righteous sufferer who stand afar off, (*apo makrothen,* Ps 37:12, Greek text) from him. By standing with Jesus' persecutors, Peter begins the process of denying his master.

B. *The Trial (14:55–65)*

The trial scene is one of the most difficult texts in Mark's Gospel because there does not seem to be any continuity between the accusations of the witnesses and the question of the high priest. False witnesses accuse Jesus of threatening to destroy the temple and build another not made by hands (14:58). The high priest then asks Jesus if he is the Christ (i.e., the Messiah), the Son of the Blessed (14:61). What is the relationship between these two texts? I examine this section as three units: the false witnesses (14:55–59), the high priest's questions (14:60–64), and the mocking of Jesus (14:65).

The first unit describes the search for witnesses and their testimony against Jesus (14:55–59). Mark makes it clear that those who come forward are false witnesses and that their testimony does not agree. But what they testify is important for understanding the trial. "We heard him say, 'I will destroy this temple that is made with hands, and in three days I will build another, not made with hands.' " This charge that Jesus is a temple destroyer occurs a second time at the crucifixion, when the passers-by deride Jesus as a false messiah, saying, "Aha! You who would destroy the temple and build it in three days, save yourself, and come down from the cross!" (15:29–30) There appears to be a connection between the charge that Jesus is a temple destroyer and his messianic claims.

Although the evidence is not conclusive, there are some texts from this period which suggest a hope that a new temple will be built in the final age.[23] In 1 Enoch (90:28–29), a work written in the second century B.C., the author writes:

> Then I stood still, looking at the ancient house [the temple] being transformed: All the pillars and all the columns were pulled out; and the ornaments of that house were packed and taken out together with them and abandoned in a certain place in the South of the land. I went on seeing until the Lord of the sheep brought about a new house, greater and loftier than the first one, and set it up in the first location which had been covered up—all its pillars were new, the columns new, and the ornaments new as well as greater than those of the first, (that is) the old (house) which was gone. All the sheep were within it.[24]

The literature of this period does not specify the Messiah as the builder of the new temple, but a targum on Isaiah 53:5 does. "He will build the temple which was profaned because of our transgressions and delivered up because of our sins."[25] Similarly, a targum on Zechariah 6:12 reads, "And you shall say to him, 'Thus says the Lord of hosts, this man, Messiah is his name. He will be revealed and will be exalted, and he will build the temple of the Lord.' ''[26] The problem for scholars is that it is difficult to date these texts. They may contain traditions from the time of Jesus, but they were collected after that period. Like the trial scene in Mark, however, these texts suggest a connection between Messiah and temple. When the false witnesses claim that Jesus said he would destroy the old temple and build a new one, they imply that he claims to be the Messiah.

The high priest's question (14:60–64) is the second unit of this section. The high priest makes the connection between temple and Messiah when he asks Jesus to respond to the accusations. Jesus remains silent. His silence recalls the silence of the righteous sufferer as pictured in the psalms of lament. "I am dumb, I do not open my mouth; for it is thou who hast done it" (Ps 39:9, also see Ps 38:12–14). The high priest asks a second question, this time drawing out the implications of the temple charge, "Are you the Christ, the Son of the Blessed?" The question brings together the two most important Christological titles of Mark's Gospel: Messiah (Christ) and Son of God. Messiah is the content of Peter's confession at Caesarea Philippi (8:29), and Son of God will be the centurion's confession after Jesus' death (15:39). Both titles occur in the opening of the Gospel where Mark identifies Jesus for his readers: "The beginning of the Gospel of Jesus Christ, the Son of God" (1:1).

Jesus responds with a prophecy, "I am; and you will see the Son of Man seated at the right hand of Power, and coming with the clouds of heaven." His answer consists of two scriptural texts. The first is from Daniel 7:13, "I saw in the night visions, and behold, *with the clouds of heaven there came one like a Son of Man,* and he came to the Ancient of Days and was presented before him." Here the one like a Son of Man refers to an eschatological figure who comes with the power of God at the end of time. The second text is Psalm 110:1, a royal psalm which announces the power of judgment given to God's anointed, the king. As quoted by Mark it reads: "The Lord said to my Lord: '*Sit at my right hand,* till I make your enemies your footstool.' '' Jesus prophesies that he will return at the end of time in his capacity as the royal Son of Man[27] to execute judgment upon those who now judge him.

The high priest understands the meaning of Jesus' words because he immediately tears his garments and labels the prophecy blasphemy.

Scholars debate the precise nature of the blasphemy. But it seems to consist in Jesus assuming to himself the divine prerogative of judgment. The rest of the Sanhedrin agrees with the high priest, and "they all condemned him as deserving death." The last phrase echoes Jesus' third passion prediction, "and they will condemn him to death" (10:33).

The mockery of Jesus as a prophet (14:65) is the final unit in this section. It is the first of three mockery scenes in Mark's passion narrative. The second occurs in 15:16–20 where the Roman soldiers mock Jesus as the King of the Jews. The third comes in 15:27–32 where the religious leaders, the passers-by, and the criminals deride him as the Messiah King who cannot save himself.

By saying "some began to spit on him" Mark does not specify who mocks Jesus. But the placement of the mockery, immediately after the judgment of condemnation, suggests that members of the Sanhedrin engage in this cruel sport. In doing so, they fulfill part of Jesus' third passion prediction, "and they will mock him, and spit upon him" (10:34).

The leaders mock Jesus as a prophet because of his Son of Man prophecy. The scene is filled with irony since, at the precise moment they deride Jesus as a false prophet, one of his prophecies, the denial of Peter, is being fulfilled! The implications are clear. Jesus' Son of Man prophecy will also be fulfilled, and the judges will be judged.

C. Peter's Denial (14:66–72)

Mark returns to the story of Peter's denial begun in v. 54. Peter's three denials divide the text into three units: 14:66–68; 69–70a; 70b–72. In the first, the high priest's maid looks at Peter and identifies him as one who was *with* the Nazarene, Jesus. Peter makes his first denial and moves to the gateway. The word "with" recalls 3:14 where Jesus "appointed twelve, to be *with* him, and to be sent out to preach." By saying that he does not understand what the maid means, Peter, in effect, denies that he belongs to the twelve. At the end of this unit, some manuscripts add, "and the cock crowed." The text may have been added later in light of Jesus' prediction that Peter would deny him three times before the cock crowed *twice*. But if the text is authentic, there may be a connection with Jesus' warning in 13:35, "Watch therefore—for you do not know when the master of the house will come, in the evening, or at midnight, or at *cockcrow,* or in the morning." Peter fails in his moment of trial because he did not watch and pray with Jesus in Gethsemane.

In the second unit (14:69–70a), the maid speaks to the bystanders, saying, "This man is one of them." This time Peter's denial is not as dramatic, but the danger mounts because now more people than the maid know of Peter's relationship to Jesus. Although the denial is simpler, it is made before a group, thereby increasing its gravity.

The third denial (14:70b–72) is the most dramatic of all. The by-standers identify Peter as a Galilean. As noted above, Galilee is the land of Jesus (1:9,14) and the homeland to which the risen Lord returns (16:7). The first Christians were called the sect of the Nazarenes (Acts 24:5). Cursing and swearing, Peter denies any association with Jesus the Galilean, the one from Nazareth (1:24; 10:47; 16:6). Immediately, the cock crows.

Peter's denial fulfills Jesus' prophecy (14:30), and it marks the abandonment of Jesus' last disciple. Judas betrays him. The other disciples flee, and Peter denies him. Jesus endures the most severe part of his passion alone. At the climax of his suffering he will even experience the absence of God, leading him to cry, "My God, my God, why hast thou forsaken me?" (15:34). The abandonment of Jesus by the disciples is a major theme in Mark which I shall examine in the next chapter.

Peter's denial must have been a great embarrassment to the Church. But the earliest community refused to conceal the story, and, by retelling it Christians learned an important lesson: the most intimate companions of Jesus and the highest Church officials are capable of betraying him.

V.
JESUS, THE KING OF THE JEWS, 15:1–20A

Chapter 15 marks a major division in the passion story. The religious leaders deliver Jesus to the Romans (15:1) who crucify him as the King of the Jews. It is important to recall that crucifixion is a Roman penalty reserved for criminals, runaway slaves and political insurgents. That Jesus suffered crucifixion indicates that Roman authorities put him to death. That he was crucified as the King of the Jews (15:26) suggests that the Romans viewed him as a political insurgent who challenged their authority.

Although scholars debate the point, it does not appear that the Jews, during this period, had the right to exercise capital punishment.[28] Thus, in John's Gospel the religious leaders say to Pilate, "It is not lawful for us to put any man to death" (18:31). Moreover, if the Jews could have exercised the right of capital punishment, they would have carried it out by stoning the offender. This would apply especially to the case of Jesus which ended with the verdict of blasphemy (14:64), since Leviticus 24:16 reads, "He who blasphemes the name of the Lord shall be put to death; all the congregation shall stone him." Although Mark and the other evangelists place the burden of responsibility upon the religious leaders, Jesus suffered death at the hands of the Romans.

The events of this chapter occur during the course of a day which Mark divides into periods of three hours. The religious leaders deliver Jesus to Pilate early in the morning, *prōi,* 6:00 A.M. (15:1). At the third hour, 9:00 A.M., the Romans crucify Jesus (15:25). There is darkness over the whole land from the sixth to the ninth hour, 12:00–3:00 P.M. (15:33). At the ninth hour, 3:00 P.M., Jesus cries out and dies (15:34–37). Finally, when evening comes, 6:00 P.M., Joseph of Arimathea removes Jesus' body from the cross and buries it (15:42–46). In addition to this time scheme, Mark highlights Jesus' kingship, mentioning the title King (King of the Jews/King of Israel) no less than six times (15:2,9,12,18,26,32). This is remarkable considering that the title does not occur anywhere else in the Gospel.

The first twenty verses consist of three sections: the religious leaders deliver Jesus to Pilate (15:1–5); Pilate releases Barabbas and sentences Jesus to crucifixion (15:6–15); the soldiers mock Jesus as the King of the Jews (15:16–20a). The title, King of the Jews, occurs in all three sections (15:2,9,12,18) and serves as a leitmotif for the material.

A. *Jesus Delivered to Pilate (15:1–5)*

Mark emphasizes the responsibility of the religious leaders by saying that the chief priests, with the elders and scribes, led Jesus away and delivered him to Pilate. By delivering (*paradidōmi*) Jesus to Pilate, the religious leaders fulfill Jesus' third passion prediction (10:33–34): "and they will condemn him to death, and deliver him to the Gentiles." The third passion prediction becomes the stage script for the events of the passion.

and the Son of Man will be delivered to the chief priests and the
    scribes, cf. 14:53
and they will condemn him to death, cf. 14:64
and deliver him to the Gentiles, cf. 15:1
and they will mock him, and spit upon him, cf. 15:16–20a
and scourge him, cf. 15:15
and kill him, cf. 15:20b–39
and after three days he will rise, cf. 16:1–8

The trial before Pilate begins abruptly with the procurator asking
Jesus if he is the King of the Jews. His question is similar to the inquiry
of the high priest.

14:61   Are you the Christ, the Son of the Blessed?
15:2   Are you the King of the Jews?

However, whereas the high priest phrases his question in religious language, Pilate's inquiry stresses the political side of the issue since a Jewish messiah would be a political challenge to the Romans. Mark implies
that the religious leaders accuse Jesus, before Pilate, of the same basic
charge: messianic pretentions. But whereas they used religious language
in the trial (Messiah/Son of the Blessed), they employ political terminology (King of the Jews) before Pilate.

Although Jesus answers the high priest's question directly (14:62),
he leaves Pilate with an evasive response.

14:62   I am, and you will see the Son of Man . . .
15:2   You have said so.

Jesus' answer is neither an outright denial nor a clear affirmation of the
title King of the Jews. He is the true King of the Jews inasmuch as he is
the Messiah, the Son of the Blessed. But he does not claim the title outright because of the political connotations associated with it.[29] The rest
of the chapter will demonstrate the nature of Jesus' kingship and the real
meaning of the title.

Pilate asks Jesus a second question. It also parallels a question of
the chief priest.

14:60   Have you no answer to make? What is it that these men
         testify against you?
15:4   Have you no answer to make? See how many charges
         they bring against you.

In the trial before the Sanhedrin, false witnesses make the accusations.
In the trial before Pilate, the religious leaders do the same. Mark lets the
reader draw the implication from this parallel: the religious leaders are
now in the situation of being false witnesses. As in the trial before the
Sanhedrin, Jesus, the righteous sufferer, remains silent.

14:61   But he was silent and made no answer.
15:5   But Jesus made no further answer.

Pilate asks no further questions. Instead, Mark says that "Pilate wondered" (*thaumazein*). The expression implies a religious wonder such as
occurs in the presence of the holy (see 5:20). The same word occurs in
15:44 where Pilate wonders at Jesus' sudden death. The reaction is one
of amazement before a divine event.

Inasmuch as this scene presents Jesus standing before the Roman
governor, it recalls Jesus' apocalyptic discourse in chapter 13 where he
tells the disciples, "But take heed to yourselves; for they will deliver
you up to councils; and you will be beaten in synagogues; and you will
stand before governors and kings for my sake, to bear testimony before
them" (13:9). At his hour of trial Jesus provides a model of endurance
for the community of his disciples. Disciples of Jesus must be prepared
to do the same.

B. The Release of Barabbas (15:6–15)

In this section, Mark mentions the crowd for the first time since the
arrest of Jesus in Gethsemane (14:43). He portrays the crowd in a neutral
light. It comes to ask Pilate for the release of a prisoner in honor of the
feast. By contrast, Mark presents the priests as the true villains with a
parenthetical remark: "For he [Pilate] perceived that it was out of envy
that the chief priests had delivered him up" (15:10). The chief priests
are the primary evildoers in Mark's eyes. In 15:1 he names them first,

and then says that the scribes and elders were *with* them. And in 15:31 he pictures them mocking Jesus with the scribes.

Pilate twice calls Jesus the King of the Jews (15:9,12). The phrase, "whom *you* call the King of the Jews" (15:12), reveals that he does not believe the charge. But since the people consider Jesus a popular leader, Pilate supposes that they will ask for him. Instead, prompted by the priests, they cry for Barabbas, a rebel who committed murder during the insurrection. As a result, Pilate delivers (*paredōken*) Jesus to be crucified as a political rebel. In Mark's view, however, the real rebel is not Jesus but the group of priests who stir up the crowd to ask for Barabbas.

This section ends with Pilate delivering Jesus to be crucified. The word deliver (*paradidōmi*) occurs three times in vv. 1–15. The religious leaders deliver Jesus to Pilate out of jealousy (15:1, 10). And Pilate, to satisfy the crowd, delivers Jesus to crucifixion (15:15). This is the completion of a theme begun in 1:14 when John the Baptist is delivered up (RSV reads arrested). Jesus predicts that he, the Son of Man, will be delivered into the hands of men (9:31), to the chief priests and the scribes (10:33), and that one of his own will betray (*paradidōmi*) him (14:18, 21). With the crucifixion, the betrayal of the Son of Man which leads to his being handed over to the religious leaders and to Pilate comes to fulfillment.

C. *The Mockery (15:16–20a)*

Before being crucified, Jesus is mocked by the Roman soldiers. This is the second of three mockeries (14:65; 15:27–32). It is an ironic scene in which a cohort of soldiers (six hundred men, one-tenth of a legion) mock Jesus as the King of the Jews. Mark brackets the scene by two references to crucifixion.

> 15:15b.   He delivered him to be crucified.
>   [The Mockery]
> 15:20b.   And they led him out to crucify him.

By this sandwich arrangement the evangelist emphasizes that the one who is crucified is the King of the Jews.

Although brief, the scene is carefully structured.

15:17.   they *clothe* him in a *purple cloak*
15:18.   they salute him as the King of the Jews
15:19.   they do him mock homage
15:20.   they *strip* him of the *purple cloak*

The two references to the purple cloak bracket the mock homage of Jesus as the King of the Jews, forming yet another sandwich arrangement. Like the first mockery (14:65), the scene is intensely ironic. Although the soldiers do not realize it, what they say and do is true, but on a level they do not comprehend. Jesus is the King of the Jews, and he is worthy of their homage. But he is not the kind of king they suppose. He will manifest his kingship when he returns upon the clouds of heaven as the royal Son of Man (14:62). For now, his kingship is hidden in suffering and shame. He will reign from a cross.

This mockery is a further fulfillment of Jesus' third passion prediction (10:34): "they will mock him, and spit upon him." In this scene, the soldiers do precisely that: "And they struck his head with a reed, and spat upon him, and they knelt down in homage to him."

Verses 1–20a form an important introduction to Jesus' crucifixion since they present him as the King of the Jews. After reading them, the reader should understand that Jesus will die as a king. This surely reflects the historical fact that the Romans crucified Jesus because they viewed him as a political threat, a messianic pretender, the King of the Jews. This was a great embarrassment to the first followers of Jesus. On the one hand, his kingship did not seem to fulfill the royal messianic expectations of the Old Testament. On the other hand, his crucifixion categorized him as just another political rebel. But as the first believers meditated upon these events, they slowly understood the deeper meaning of Jesus' kingship.[30] He is king in a most unexpected way. During his earthly life his kingship is hidden in suffering and shame, but at the end of the ages he will return as the transcendent king, the royal Son of Man. Then all will recognize him as the Son of God.

VI.
Crucifixion and Death, 15:20b–39

These verses form the heart of the passion story. Many commentators argue that the earliest account of the crucifixion can be found in them. On first hearing, the section is straightforward and simple, and it is not surprising that some scholars see the nucleus of an eyewitness account here, perhaps that of Simon of Cyrene. But the simplicity of the narrative should not conceal the theological character of the material. As in the rest of Mark's passion story, the evangelist interprets these events theologically and relates them to the rest of his Gospel.

Psalm 22 plays an important role in this section. In v. 24, the dividing of Jesus' garments and the casting of lots is told in the language of Psalm 22:18. In v. 34 the great cry of Jesus comes from the opening words of the psalm (22:1). In addition to these explicit references, many authors see several allusions to the psalm, and a few argue that the passion narrative developed around the psalm.[31] Although this position has not met wide acceptance, it does highlight how important Psalm 22 was for the first Christians in their interpretation of Jesus' death. Below, I list some possible allusions to Psalm 22 in this section, as well as the two explicit citations already noted.

MARK 15		PSALM 22	
24	(garments)	18	(garments)
27	(two thieves surround Jesus)	12,13,16	(bulls, lions, dogs, surround me)
29	(wag their heads)	7	(wag their heads)
31	(cannot save self)	8	(let God save him)
32	(reviled)	6	(scorned)
34	(great cry)	1	(great cry)
39	(centurion's cry, universal salvation)	27–31	(universal salvation)

When the Church sought to understand the meaning of Jesus' death, it went to the psalter.[32] There, in the person of the righteous sufferer, it found a model by which to interpret the events of the passion. The first Christians saw in the psalms, especially Psalm 22, messianic prophecies pointing to Jesus' passion and death. For the Church, the righteous sufferer of the psalms was none other than the Messiah: Jesus.

I divide this section into three parts: the crucifixion (15:20b–27), the mockery (15:29–32), and the death of Jesus (15:33–39).

A. *The Crucifixion (15:20b–27)*

This is the simplest part of the passion account. Mark narrates several events connecting them by the conjunction *kai* (''and'') to the point of being monotonous. In addition, although the RSV and most translations employ the past tense, Mark relates the crucifixion almost exclusively in the present tense, thereby giving a sense of immediacy and vividness to his account.

> And they lead him out . . .
> And they compel a passer-by . . .
> And they bring him to a place called Golgotha . . .
> And they offered him wine . . .
> And they crucify him . . .
> And they divide his garments . . .
> And they crucified him . . .
> And the inscription of the charge against him read . . .
> And with him they crucify two robbers.

It is no surprise that many see the remnants of an eyewitness account here.

Crucifixions took place outside the city walls. Therefore, the soldiers led Jesus out (15:20b), a fact which the author of Hebrews recalls: ''So Jesus also suffered outside the gate in order to sanctify the people through his own blood'' (Heb 13:12). That Jesus died outside the city intensifies the shame of his death since it separates him from the people of Israel. In the Old Testament, blasphemers were stoned outside of the camp (Lev 24:14; Num 15:35,36). Jesus, accused of blasphemy by the Sanhedrin (14:64), dies the shameful death of crucifixion outside the capital city of his people.[33]

The Romans compel a passer-by to carry Jesus' cross. Who was Simon of Cyrene? Acts 6:9 speaks of a synagogue in Jerusalem composed of former slaves, Cyrenians, and Alexandrians. And Acts 11:20 says that some men from Cyprus and Cyrene were among the first to preach the Lord Jesus to the Greeks in Antioch. It may be that Simon was a Hellenist, a Greek-speaking Jew, who resided in Jerusalem[34] or who was present there for the feast (see Acts 2:10). Later, Simon probably became a Christian since the narrative speaks of his sons, Alexander and Rufus (see Rom 16:13 where the same or another Rufus is mentioned), as if they were known to the original readers. If Simon was a Hellenist, this is a significant fact since Mark directs his Gospel to Greek-speaking Christians who are not Jews. In addition, the first person to confess Jesus as the Son of God is a Gentile, the centurion (15:39).

Mark preserves the Aramaic name of the place where Jesus was crucified (Golgotha) and translates it for his Greek audience as "the place of a skull." According to some Church Fathers, the skull of Adam was buried there. While this provides suggestive symbolism, the name probably refers to the skull formation of the hill.

The attempt to give Jesus wine mingled with myrrh is an act of kindness which finds its origin in Proverbs 31:6: "Give strong drink to him who is perishing, and wine to those in bitter distress." Later Jewish tradition also referred to this. "To him, who was on the way to be executed, was given a tiny piece of frankincense in a cup of wine in order to numb his senses" (Babylonian Talmud, tract *Sanhedrin* 43a).[35] Jesus refuses this act of kindness so that he can endure his suffering fully conscious. He does not drink from the cup of men in order that he might fully drink from the cup of his Father (10:38; 14:36).

The dividing of Jesus' garments, like his execution outside of the city, is a further act of shame and humiliation. Jesus dies naked before the view of all. Only later, in the light of Psalm 22, did the Church understand that God foreordained even this humiliating act: "they divide my garments among them, and for my raiment they cast lots" (Ps 22:18).

Mark notes that it was the third hour (9:00 A.M.) when they crucified Jesus. The three hour periods which divide this day may be Mark's way of showing that the crucifixion follows a divine plan. Each event happens with a regularity that is divinely decreed.[36]

The inscription with the charge against Jesus, "The King of the Jews," would have been a cause for shame among the first believers. It proclaims that Jesus dies as a political insurgent. In addition, he is crucified with two robbers. As mentioned above, the Greek word for robber *(lēstēs)* can also refer to a political rebel. If it does so here, the two crucified with Jesus may have been insurgents arrested at the time of the uprising associated with Barabbas (15:7). Crucifying Jesus between the two *lēstēs* would be a further humiliation calculated to associate him with robbers and political rebels.

The believer who reads about these events, in the light of the resurrection, understands their deep irony. Although the title King of the Jews is meant to humiliate Jesus, it has become a title of honor. Jesus is truly a king. The robbers at his right and left are his royal attendants. They occupy the seats of honor which James and John sought when they asked, "Grant us to sit, one at your right hand and one at your left, in your glory" (10:37). At that time Jesus answered, "You do not know what you are asking. Are you able to drink the cup that I drink, or to be baptized with the baptism with which I am baptized?" (10:38). The reader of the passion now knows what Jesus meant. The seats of honor in his kingdom belong to those who suffer with him.

B. The Mockery (15:29–32)

According to Mark 15:25, Jesus is crucified at the third hour (9:00 A.M.). At the sixth hour (12 noon) darkness covers the whole land (15:33). Between these two periods a number of people mock the crucified Jesus. The description of this mockery is highly stylized and recalls several motifs from the trials of the righteous sufferer. In addition, it focuses upon the nature of Jesus' messiahship and the meaning of salvation.

The mockery consists of three parts. In the first (15:29–30) the passers-by blaspheme (*eblasphēmoun*; RSV reads derided) Jesus by calling him a temple destroyer, and they challenge him to save himself by coming down from the cross. In the second (15:31–32a), the chief priests take up where the first mockery leaves off, saying that although Jesus saved others, he cannot save himself. They also challenge him to descend from the cross so that they can *see* and thus believe that he is the Messiah, the King of Israel. Finally, those crucified with Jesus revile him (15:32b), but Mark does not report what they say. Thus all levels of society mock the crucified Jesus, from ordinary folk to religious leaders to common criminals.

Mark says that the passers-by blasphemed Jesus by wagging their heads and challenging him to descend from the cross. The act of wagging one's head is a form of mockery found in several Old Testament texts (2 Kgs 19:21; Job 16:4; Ps 109:25; Is 37:22; Jer 18:16; Lam 2:15; Sir 12:18). It also occurs in Psalm 22:7: "All who see me mock at me, they make mouths at me, they wag their heads." The taunt of the mockers, "Aha," is the same as that directed at the righteous sufferer in the psalms of lament (Pss 35:21; 40:15; 70:3).[37] It is clear that Mark portrays Jesus as this innocent sufferer. By taunting him as a temple destroyer, the passers-by recall the charge from the trial (14:58) and the time when Jesus cleansed the temple (11:15–17).

But why does Mark refer to these words and actions as blasphemy? At the beginning of the Gospel, Jesus said, "all sins will be forgiven the sons of men, and whatever blasphemies they utter; but whoever blasphemes against the Holy Spirit never has forgiveness, but is guilty of an eternal sin" (3:28–29). In the next verse Mark explains, "for they had said, 'He has an unclean spirit' " (3:30). In Mark's view, blasphemy means contradicting God's action, attributing evil to good, or good to evil. By their taunts the passers-by contradict God's action, challenging Jesus to save his life, even though he said "for whoever would save his life will lose it; and whoever loses his life for my sake and the Gospel's will save it" (8:35). If Jesus should try to save his life by descending from the cross, he would lose it and contradict God's will. But this is precisely what the bystanders challenge him to do. They tempt him to contradict God's way of salvation; they blaspheme.

The mockery of the chief priests and scribes continues what the bystanders say. But it adds a new dimension by referring to Jesus' miraculous power, "He saved others; he cannot save himself." The word save (sōzein) recalls the occasions when Jesus did save others by his powerful deeds (3:4; 5:23, 28, 34; 6:56; 10:52). The irony of the present situation is that the priests and scribes are correct, but they do not realize the full implications of what they say. Jesus cannot save himself; only God can save him. If he tries to save himself, he will lose his life (8:35). But if he endures to the end, he will be saved (13:13), "for all things are possible with God" (10:27), and "all things are possible to him who believes" (9:23). The religious leaders do not understand this because they do not comprehend the full meaning of faith. Faith is not a matter of seeing in order to believe, but of trusting to the point of death.

As in the trial, Mark draws a relationship between the temple charge and Jesus' messiahship by having the religious leaders call him the Messiah, the King of Israel. But just as the passers-by do not believe that Jesus can destroy the temple and build a new one, so the religious leaders do not believe that he is the Messiah, the King of Israel. Irony reigns supreme. By his death, Jesus makes the old temple obsolete, thereby showing that he is the messianic king.

C. *Jesus' Death (15:33–39)*

During the first three hours of crucifixion, Jesus' persecutors mock him. But during the last three hours (12:00 noon to 3:00 P.M.), darkness covers the whole land. It is difficult to define the precise meaning of this darkness. Many authors point to the text of Amos 8:9, " 'And on that day,' says the Lord God, 'I will make the sun go down at noon, and darken the earth in broad daylight.' " Others note that Jesus spoke of darkness as a sign which would precede the coming of the Son of Man: "But in those days, after that tribulation, the sun will be darkened, and the moon will not give its light" (13:24). A note of judgment characterizes both texts. Perhaps the three hours of darkness at Jesus' death signify God's response to the mockery and the impending judgment which Jesus' death will bring. Another suggestion, offered by Ernest R. Martinez,[38] interprets the darkness in terms of the ninth plague which afflicted the Egyptians at the time of the exodus (Ex 10:21–23). Then darkness covered the entire land of Egypt. According to Martinez, the darkness at the crucifixion should be interpreted in terms of Mark's exodus imagery, so present in the scene of the Last Supper. Just as darkness once announced the salvific event of the exodus, so it proclaims God's new salvific action in Jesus.

At the conclusion of the darkness, Jesus cries out the opening words of Psalm 22, "Eloi, Eloi, lama sabachthani?" which means, "My God, my God, why hast thou forsaken me?" Confusion follows. Some of the bystanders misunderstand *Eloi* (the Aramaic word for God) for Elijah and foolishly think that Jesus calls the prophet for help. As they try to keep him alive by giving him sour wine to drink, Jesus dies with a loud cry. As a result of his death, the temple curtain is torn from top to bottom and the centurion confesses that Jesus was the Son of God.

What is the sense of Jesus' cry? In light of the whole Gospel and of the centurion's confession, it would be a mistake to interpret it as a cry of despair. The great cry comes from Psalm 22, a psalm of lament. The psalm, however, does not end in despair, but in victory. Beginning with v. 22 the psalmist triumphantly proclaims, "I will tell of thy name to my brethren; in the midst of the congregation I will praise thee." Then the psalm concludes,

> All the ends of the earth shall remember
> and turn to the Lord;

and all the families of the nations
shall worship before him.
For dominion belongs to the Lord,
and he rules over the nations.
Yea, to him shall all the proud of the earth bow down;
before him shall bow all who go down to the dust,
and he who cannot keep himself alive.
Posterity shall serve him;
men shall tell of the Lord to the coming generation,
and proclaim his deliverance to a people yet unborn,
that he has wrought it'' (Ps 22:27–31).

Jesus' cry is not born of despair inasmuch as it comes from a psalm rooted in victory and trust.

But it would be erroneous to interpret the cry as merely a victory shout. The anguish of the righteous sufferer is real, and so is the anguish of Jesus. In the beginning of the psalm, the psalmist complains that he experiences the absence of God: ''Why art thou so far from helping me, from the words of my groaning? O my God, I cry by day, but thou dost not answer; and by night, but find no rest'' (22:1b–2). It is this absence of God, not despair, that Jesus experiences upon the cross. One of his chosen apostles has betrayed him. Peter has denied him; the others have fled. False witnesses have risen against him. The Sanhedrin has condemned him. The Gentiles, as well as his own people, have mocked him. Jesus stands alone because everyone has forsaken him. And in the depth of this abandonment, Jesus even experiences the absence of his Father. But like the psalmist, he remains confident: ''Yet thou art holy, enthroned on the praises of Israel. . . . Yet thou art he who took me from the womb; thou didst keep me safe upon my mother's breast. . . . But thou, O Lord, be not far off!'' (Ps 22:3, 9, 19). Trust, despite the absence of God, characterizes Jesus' cry.

The bystanders either misunderstand Jesus' cry as a last desperate call to Elijah for help, or they mockingly attribute such a desperate cry to Jesus. The Greek text is not clear. But in an action reminiscent of Psalm 69:21, they try to revive Jesus with sour wine: ''They gave me poison for food, and for my thirst they gave me vinegar to drink.'' But what the bystanders do not understand is that Elijah cannot come because he has *already* come in the person of John the Baptist. This is what Jesus tells Peter, James and John after the transfiguration: "And he said to them, 'Elijah does come first to restore all things. . . . But I tell you that Elijah has come, and they did to him whatever they pleased, as it is written of him' " (9:12–13). Because the bystanders, and the people they represent, did not accept John, they do not receive Jesus. At this crucial moment, therefore, they misunderstand, and perhaps mock, Jesus' great cry of trust.

Jesus utters a loud cry and the curtain of the temple is torn from top to bottom. Once more, the Greek text is not clear. The loud cry may be a second, wordless cry, or Mark may be referring to the cry of Psalm 22. In either case, Jesus dies with a loud cry which causes the temple curtain to tear.

There were two curtains in the temple. One separated the holy of holies from the holy place (Ex 26:31–35) while the other hung at the entrance of the temple (Ex 26:37). Mark does not specify which curtain was torn.[39] If he means the larger curtain which hung at the entrance, the outer curtain, the tearing of that curtain might symbolize the destruction of the temple, an important theme in the Gospel (13:2; 14:58; 15:29). But if Mark means the curtain separating the holy of holies from the holy place, the inner curtain, the symbolism is more positive. That curtain served to conceal God's glory: "and the veil shall separate for you the holy place from the most holy" (Ex 26:33b). By the death of Jesus, God's glory shines forth to all humanity, Gentile as well as Jew. It is most appropriate, then, that the first person to confess Jesus as the Son of God is the Roman centurion, a Gentile. Since Mark does not specify which curtain he means, he probably intends the reader to interpret the tearing of the curtain as a symbol which has both positive and negative connotations. The death of Jesus brings an end to the old temple cult. In doing so, it renders God's glory accessible to all humanity.

When the centurion sees that Jesus died in this way, that is, with a loud cry, he confesses that Jesus was the Son of God. This confession is the high point of the Gospel, and I shall return to it in the next chapter. Here I simply indicate that this is the fourth, major declaration of Jesus' sonship. The first occurs at the beginning of the Gospel (1:1) where Mark calls his story "the Gospel of Jesus Christ, the Son of God." The second and the third come at the baptism (1:11) and the transfiguration (9:7) when the Father declares that Jesus is his beloved Son. But this is the only confession by a human character in the story that Jesus is the Son of God. As I shall show in the next chapter, its occurrence here is of central importance for Mark's Christology.

VII.
THE WOMEN AND THE BURIAL OF JESUS, 15:40–47

All of the Gospel passion narratives conclude with a story of Jesus' burial. The significance of this episode should not be underestimated. The burial of Jesus puts the seal upon his death. It signifies that he truly died. That the burial of Jesus was important to the first Christians, we know from an ancient creed found in 1 Corinthians 15:3–7: "For I delivered to you as of first importance what I also received, that Christ died for our sins in accordance with the Scriptures, that he was *buried*, that he was raised on the third day in accordance with the Scriptures. . . ." If Christians were to proclaim the resurrection, they had to establish, beyond all doubt, that Jesus truly died. It is the burial of Jesus, attested to by witnesses, which establishes this fact.

This unit may be divided into three sections: the women looking at a distance (15:40–41); the burial of Jesus (15:42–46); the women watching (15:47). Mark employs his sandwich technique to arrange this material. References to the women watching (*theōrousai*, 15:40 . . . *etheōroun*, 15:47) surround the story of the burial (15:42–46). The women witness the death of Jesus and ascertain the place of his burial. They serve as reliable witnesses, and on Sunday they go to the correct tomb (16:1–8), because they witnessed Jesus' burial.

A. The Women (15:40–41)

The women look *from afar* just as Peter followed Jesus from afar (14:54). Mark may not mean this in a negative manner, however, since it probably would have been impossible for women, given the customs of the time, to approach closer. But the fact that they are present, and that the disciples are not, should not escape the reader. The women take the place of the disciples. They followed Jesus from Galilee. They served his needs. And they went up with him to Jerusalem. But what they have done, and what the disciples have failed to do, is to remain with Jesus at his death.

Mark says that there were many women but names only three: Mary

Magdalene, Mary the mother of James and of Joses, and Salome. None of them appears earlier in the narrative. At the conclusion of the burial story, the two Marys appear once more (15:47), and in the account of the empty tomb all three women are present. Mark makes these women the chief witnesses to Jesus' death, burial and resurrection, an astounding fact in a man's world.

B. The Burial (15:42–46)

With the burial of Jesus, the crucifixion day begun at the trial before Pilate (15:1), and marked off in periods of three hours (15:25, 33, 34), comes to a conclusion (15:42). Joseph of Arimathea, a respected member of the council (*bouleutēs*), probably not the Sanhedrin, petitions Pilate for Jesus' body. Mark describes Joseph's behavior as courageous, because the request could be construed as an act of rebellion, inasmuch as Jesus was condemned as a political insurgent. Like the women, Joseph does what the disciples should have done. The disciples of John the Baptist buried the body of their master (6:29), but the disciples of Jesus do not.

When Joseph approaches Pilate, the governor is amazed that Jesus has died already (*ethaumasen ei ēdē tethnēken*; RSV translates the Greek "wondered if he were already dead"). Pilate's reaction is the same as when he first encountered Jesus (15:5). Mark may intend a double meaning here. On the one hand, the quickness of Jesus' death amazes Pilate, since a crucified person often lived for several days. But on the other, Pilate's reaction betrays a sense of awe before the holy. At the trial he stood amazed at Jesus' silence. Now he stands amazed at this unusual death.

To ascertain if Jesus has died, Pilate summons the centurion. His presence reminds the reader that Jesus is the Son of God. This is no ordinary burial; it is the burial of God's royal Son.

C. The Women (15:47)

As Joseph buries Jesus, the women watch. The words watch, see, and look occur throughout the latter part of the passion narrative. The chief priests and scribes say, "that we may see and believe" (15:32). The centurion "saw that he thus breathed his last" (15:39). The women were "looking on from afar" (15:40). And Mary Magdalene and Mary the mother of Joses "saw where he was laid" (15:47). But the centurion and the women see more than the priests and scribes because they believe that despite his suffering and death Jesus was the Son of God.

CONCLUSION

The Marcan passion presents Jesus as the royal Son of God. It is a story in which Jesus is gradually abandoned by all of his followers and at the moment of death even experiences the absence of God. The leaders of the people plot against him. Judas betrays him. The disciples forsake him. Peter denies him. And he is mocked as Prophet, King and Messiah. In the depths of his agony, Jesus cries out, "My God, my God, why hast thou forsaken me?" But he does not surrender his trust in the Father, because he knows that he will return as the glorious Son of Man upon the clouds of heaven to judge his judges. Moreover, he will go to Galilee and gather his scattered flock after his resurrection. When he finally dies, the curtain of the temple is torn and a Gentile soldier recognizes who he was; he was truly the royal Son of God.

The Marcan passion develops several themes:(1) Jesus' royal sonship; (2) the abandonment of the disciples; (3) the role of the temple; (4) Jesus' expectation of future vindication. All of these, moreover, form a part of Mark's wider story. In order to appreciate their full meaning in the passion narrative, it is necessary to examine them in the rest of the Gospel. In the next chapter, I investigate each of them and show how all reach their climax in Mark's passion narrative. By doing this, I hope to demonstrate the coherence of Mark's passion narrative and his Gospel theology.

Chapter Three

MARK'S GOSPEL THEOLOGY

At the conclusion of the last chapter, I listed four themes which characterize Mark's passion narrative. I also suggested that to appreciate the full meaning of the passion narrative, the reader should study these themes as they are found throughout Mark's entire Gospel. By doing this the reader discovers how each of them culminates in Mark's passion story. In this chapter I investigate four themes: (1) Jesus' royal sonship; (2) Jesus and the disciples; (3) Jesus and the temple; (4) Jesus and the future. I will show how each prepares for and culminates in the passion narrative.

I.
Jesus' Royal Sonship

At three points, during the passion narrative, Mark highlights Jesus' sonship. In the garden of Gethsemane, Jesus prays to God, ''Abba, Father, all things are possible to thee; remove this cup from me; yet not what I will but what thou wilt'' (14:36). At the trial before the Sanhedrin, when the high priest asks, ''Are you the Christ, the Son of the Blessed?'' Jesus responds, ''I am'' (14:62). And immediately after Jesus' death, the centurion confesses, ''Truly this man was the Son of God'' (15:39). In addition, there are six instances when Jesus is called King of the Jews or King of Israel (15:2,9,12,18,26,32). Although the title is found upon the lips of Jesus' opponents and constitutes the inscription over the cross, I indicated that Mark intends the reader to see the irony of the situation. Jesus is a King, though not the kind of king his persecutors accuse him of pretending to be.

This data raises two important questions. First, what, if any, is the

51

relationship between the designation of Jesus as King and as God's Son? Why does chapter 15 culminate with the confession that Jesus is the Son of God, even though the title King dominates the chapter? Second, why does the centurion confess that Jesus is the Son of God? How is he able to recognize what has been hidden from all of the other characters in the story? To answer these questions, it is necessary to grasp the first part of Mark's story. In other words, it is not sufficient to read the passion narrative as an independent unit. The passion must be read as part of Mark's total story.

A. Who Is Jesus? (1:1–13)

Nothing is more important for a story than the beginning. The beginning sets the tone for everything that follows. The narrator introduces the characters of the story and provides the reader with important information for understanding them. To overlook the beginning is to miss the note which sets the tone for everything that follows. This is especially so for Mark's Gospel.[1]

Mark's story of Jesus[2] begins with a verse which identifies, for the reader, who Jesus is: ''The beginning of the Gospel of Jesus Christ, the Son of God.'' From the outset of the story Mark makes the reader privy to inside information of which the characters within the story will be ignorant. Jesus the Messiah is God's Son. As a result the reader enters the world of Mark's story with a knowledge that the characters within the narrative struggle to attain: Jesus is the Son of God.[3]

Following this opening verse, the next verses (1:2–8) further identify Jesus by introducing John the Baptist. The Old Testament quotation in vv. 2–3, a composite of Isaiah 40:3 and Malachi 3:1, identifies John as God's final messenger who prepares[4] the way for Jesus: ''Behold, I send my messenger before thy face, who shall *prepare* thy way; the voice of one crying in the wilderness: *Prepare* the way of the Lord, make his paths straight.'' Because of this quotation, the reader knows that John is an authentic messenger, and that what he says about Jesus is reliable. Therefore, the reader takes heed when, in v. 7, the Baptist identifies Jesus as the Mightier One (*ho ischuroteros*) whose sandals he is not worthy to stoop and untie. Whereas John baptizes with water, Jesus will baptize with the Holy Spirit.

The climax of this section occurs at the baptism of Jesus (1:9–11).

Jesus comes from Nazareth of Galilee, and John baptizes him. But as he rises from the waters, Jesus sees the heavens opened and the Spirit like a dove, or in a dove-like motion, descend upon him. At the same time, a voice from heaven declares that Jesus is God's beloved (*agapētos*) Son in whom he is well pleased.

The Father's declaration, "Thou art my beloved Son; with thee I am well pleased," recalls three Old Testament texts. The first refers to the Suffering Servant described in the latter half of the Book of Isaiah: "Behold my servant, whom I uphold, my chosen, in whom my soul delights" (Is 42:1). The second recalls Isaac,[5] Abraham's beloved (*agapētos*) son: "Take your son, your only son Isaac, whom you love, and go to the land of Moriah, and offer him there as a burnt offering upon one of the mountains of which I shall tell you" (Gen 22:2). The third text is the most important and gives a new meaning to all the others. It refers to Psalm 2, a psalm sung on the day of the Israelite king's coronation. On that day, Yahweh adopted the king, his anointed one (*christos*), as his son. "I [the newly crowned king] will tell of the decree of the Lord; He [Yahweh] said to me, 'You [the Israelite king] are my son, today [the day of coronation] I have begotten you [made you my adopted son]" (Ps 2:7). The sense of the Father's declaration is that Jesus is the royal Messiah in the line of the Davidic kings. But as God's royal Messiah, he is God's Son in a unique fashion. Empowered with the Spirit, he is God's beloved (*agapētos*) Son (as Isaac was Abraham's beloved son) who will demonstrate his kingship in humble service as does the Servant in the Book of Isaiah.

Since it is God himself who identifies Jesus, this knowledge of Jesus' identity is crucial in order to read Mark's narrative correctly. But the reader should note that this knowledge comes in a private revelation to Jesus of which only the reader is privy. Not even John the Baptist, according to Mark, sees or hears the theophany. The reader learns what no human character in the story knows: Jesus is God's royal Son.

In the final incident of this section (1:12–13)), the Spirit with which Jesus has been empowered throws him into the wilderness where Satan tests him for forty days. The fact that angels minister to Jesus during (or at the end of) this period suggests that Jesus remains loyal to his Father.[6] Once more, Mark makes the reader privy to inside information. As a result, before Jesus' public ministry begins, the reader understands that Jesus the Messiah, the Mightier One, God's royal Son, has conquered

Satan. Jesus will refer to this fact when, during the Beelzebul controversy (3:20–30), he says "But no one can enter a strong man's house
and plunder his goods, unless he first binds the strong man; then indeed
he may plunder his house" (3:27). Jesus is the strong man who enters
Satan's house and binds him.

B. Jesus' Galilean Ministry (1:14—8:26)

The second portion of Mark's Gospel describes Jesus' ministry in
and around Galilee. During this period, Jesus preaches the Gospel of
God, announcing the kingdom of God and calling people to repentance
(1:14–15). He summons his first disciples (1:16–20; 2:13–14) and he
chooses twelve to be with him, whom he can send out to preach and to
have power over demons (3:13–19). During this period Jesus exorcises
demons (1:21–28; 5:1–20), heals many sick people (1:29–31,40–44;
5:21–43; 7:24–37; 8:22–26), teaches in parables (4:1–34), and performs
mighty deeds such as calming a storm (4:35–41), walking upon the sea
(6:45–52), and providing food for the vast crowds (6:30–44; 8:1–10).
Despite controversies with, and opposition from, the religious leaders
(2:1—3:6; 7:1–23), his fame spreads. Mark summarizes the success of
Jesus' ministry in three important passages (1:32–39; 3:7–12; 6:53–56).

Although the reader knows that Jesus accomplishes this activity as
God's royal Son, the characters within the story do not. As a result, there
is questioning and confusion about Jesus' identity. Four episodes focus
upon this questioning. The first occurs after Jesus heals a man with an
unclean spirit in the synagogue of Capernaum (1:21–28). At the conclusion of the story, Mark writes that all were amazed, and questioned, saying, "What is this? A new teaching! With authority he commands even
the unclean spirits, and they obey him" (1:27). Although the remark
centers upon Jesus' teaching, it is intimately tied to his person. The
townspeople are amazed that Jesus teaches with authority because they
do not know the source of his authority. They do not realize, as the reader
does, that Jesus is the royal Son of God. If they did, they would not be
amazed (*ethambēthēsan*,), a reaction which, in Mark's Gospel, bespeaks
a lack of faith.[7]

In the second incident, Jesus forgives the sins of a paralytic and then
heals him (2:1–12). When Jesus forgives sins the scribes ask themselves,
"Why does this man speak thus? It is blasphemy! Who can forgive sins

but God alone?'' (2:7). Their thoughts concern what Jesus says but have implications for his identity. The scribes believe that Jesus has blasphemed since they only understand him as a man. Like the townspeople in the previous incident, they are ignorant of Jesus' true identity as the royal Son of God.

The third question concerning Jesus' identity is clearer still and comes from his own disciples. After Jesus stills a storm (4:35–41), the disciples, filled with awe, ask each other, ''Who then is this, that even wind and sea obey him?'' (4:41). The reader expects that at least Jesus' chosen disciples would recognize who he is. But the disciples are not privy to the Father's baptismal declaration. They do not know that Jesus is the royal Son of God.

The fourth incident occurs in Nazareth, Jesus' hometown, where his fellow citizens reject him (6:1–6). Hearing him preach, they are astonished (*exeplēssonto*), another reaction symptomatic of disbelief, and they say, ''Where did this man get all this? What is the wisdom given to him? What mighty works are wrought by his hands? Is not this the carpenter, the son of Mary and brother of James and Joses and Judas and Simon, and are not his sisters here with us?'' The reader, of course, wants to reply that Jesus is the Son of God. But the folk of Nazareth do not comprehend this because they are not privy to the baptismal declaration of Jesus' royal sonship.

In 6:14–16, Mark offers some of the current speculation about Jesus. Some people, like Herod, think that Jesus is John the Baptist raised from the dead. Others think that he is Elijah come back to life. And still others believe that he is one of the prophets of old. But the reader knows that all of this speculation is false. Jesus is not John since John is Jesus' forerunner. Jesus is not Elijah because, as the reader will learn, Elijah has already returned (9:13). Jesus is more than one of the prophets; he is God's royal Son.

Although the human characters of the story cannot pierce the mystery of Jesus' identity, the demons, because they are supernatural beings, know that Jesus is the Son of God. On three occasions, then, Mark notes that the demons call Jesus the Son of God. In the synagogue of Capernaum, the demon cries out, ''I know who you are, the Holy One of God'' (1:24). In a passage summarizing Jesus' activity Mark reports, ''And whenever the unclean spirits beheld him, they fell down before him and cried out, 'You are the Son of God' '' (3:11). And in the healing of the

Gerasene demoniac, the demon screeches, "What have you to do with me, Jesus, Son of the Most High God?" (5:7). In addition, in another summary passage, Mark writes, "and he would not permit the demons to speak, because they knew him" (1:34). But since these cries come from the demons, the people do not accept or understand them. They remain unaware that Jesus is the Son of God.

Jack D. Kingsbury points out that the cries of the demons and the questions of the human characters form a contrapuntal pattern[8] that runs like this: demonic cry (1:24), question (1:27), demonic cries (1:34), question (2:7), demonic cries (3:11), question (4:41), demonic cry (5:7), question (6:3). Kingsbury writes: "The effect of this pattern is that it exposes the reader, from the beginning of Jesus' public ministry, to a sustained sequence of utterances in which cries revealing the identity of Jesus alternate with questions about who he is."[9] By the end of the second part of Mark's narrative, the reader begins to wonder if the characters in the story will ever discover Jesus' true identity.

C. *Journey to Jerusalem and Jesus' Death (8:27–16:8)*

In the final section of Mark's Gospel, exorcisms and miracles all but disappear from the narrative (but see 9:14–27; 10:46–52). Instead, through a series of passion predictions (8:31; 9:12,31; 10:33–34), Jesus teaches that he, the Son of Man, must be rejected, suffer and die. In this section, as Kingsbury notes, Mark also discloses Jesus' true identity through three important incidents.[10]

The first occurs at Caesarea Philippi where Peter makes his confession (8:27–30). Jesus asks the disciples who people say that he is. He receives the same list of opinions found in 6:14–16: John the Baptist, Elijah, one of the prophets. Jesus then inquires what the disciples think, and Peter replies, "You are the Christ."[11] The response is correct since it corresponds to the beginning of the Gospel (1:1). But the disciples do not yet understand the full implications of Jesus' messiahship, and Jesus commands them that they not tell anyone about him.

That the disciples do not comprehend the full implication of Jesus' messiahship is evident from the next incident. Jesus teaches that the Son of Man must be rejected by the chief priests, the scribes, and the elders and be put to death (8:31). At this, Peter rebukes Jesus (8:32). Jesus then rebukes Peter (8:33) for aligning himself with the human evaluation of Messiahship rather than with the divine (8:33).

Six days later, Jesus takes Peter, James and John to a high mountain where he is transfigured before them (9:2–8). As Jesus talks with Moses and Elijah, God the Father declares that Jesus is his beloved (*agapētos*) Son (9:7), the same declaration he made at the baptism (1:11). This time, however, he adds "listen to him," thereby confirming what Jesus said earlier about his destiny of suffering and death. The disciples must learn that as the Messiah Jesus must follow the path of the suffering Son of Man.

As Jesus and the three disciples descend from the mountain, he instructs them not to tell anyone what they have seen until he has risen from the dead (9:9). That the disciples do not fully comprehend the transfiguration experience becomes evident in the next verse: "So they kept the matter to themselves, questioning what the rising from the dead meant" (9:10). The scene concludes with Jesus making yet another passion prediction and telling the disciples that Elijah has already come (9:11–13). The disciples, through Peter's confession, have begun to pierce the mystery of Jesus' person, but they do not grasp the full meaning of his messiahship.[12]

The second revelation of Jesus' identity occurs as he leaves Jericho and begins to approach Jerusalem (10:46–52). A blind beggar, Bartimaeus, twice calls Jesus the Son of David (10:47,48), an appellation which is a surrogate title for Messiah. Although the crowds rebuke the beggar, Jesus commends the man for his faith and heals him: "Go your way; your faith has made you well" (10:52). It is apparent that Jesus accepts the blind man's estimation of his person.[13]

Immediately following this episode, Jesus enters Jerusalem (11:1–10) as the crowds cry out, "Hosanna! Blessed is he who comes in the name of the Lord! Blessed is the kingdom of our father David that is coming! Hosanna in the highest!" (11:9b–10) Jesus enters Jerusalem as the Davidic king, and, once there, he takes possession of his temple (11:15–17).

Although Jesus is the Son of David, a brief incident, during the course of his Jerusalem ministry, discloses that the title is not sufficient to express the fullness of his identity. After a series of debates with the religious leaders (11:27–12:34), Jesus asks how can the scribes say that the Messiah is David's son (12:35). Employing a quotation from Psalm 110:1, Jesus argues that in the psalm the author of the psalm, David, calls the Messiah his Lord. How can the Messiah, therefore, be his son? I reproduce the quotation with appropriate interpretative remarks. "David himself, inspired by the Holy Spirit declared, 'The Lord [God] said to my [David's] Lord [the Messiah], Sit at my [God's] right hand, till I put thy [the Messiah's] enemies under thy [the Messiah's] feet' " (12:36). It is clear that the Messiah must be more than David's son because he is greater than David.

But whose son is the Messiah? Jesus does not answer the question for the crowds, but the reader of the story knows from the baptismal revelation that the Messiah is the royal Son of God. Jesus hints at this in allegorical form when he tells the parable of the vineyard and the wicked tenants (12:1–11).[14] By the parable Jesus identifies himself with the beloved (*agapētos*) son (12:6) whom the tenants of the vineyard kill in order to obtain the inheritance. As the beloved son, Jesus is the rejected stone which becomes the cornerstone of the building: "The very stone which the builders rejected[15] has become the head of the corner; this was the Lord's doing, and it is marvelous in our eyes" (12:10b–11). Like Messiah, Son of David is an authentic way to identify Jesus. But as commonly understood it does not express the full reality of his person. Bartimaeus and the crowds have not yet comprehended that as the Davidic Messiah,[16] Jesus is preeminently the Son of God. They cannot because they are not privy to the baptismal declaration. In addition, they do not understand that as Messiah, Jesus must trod the path of the suffering Son of Man.

The final revelation of Jesus' identity comes in the passion, more specifically with the centurion's confession (15:39). In the trial before the Sanhedrin, the high priest asks Jesus if he is the Christ, the Son of the Blessed (14:61), that is, the Messiah, the Son of God. Jesus responds, "I am" (14:62). But it is evident that the high priest does not believe Jesus since he immediately accuses him of blasphemy (14:64). The secret of Jesus' identity remains intact.

It is only *after* Jesus' death that a Roman centurion, a Gentile, makes the proper confession of Jesus' identity: "Truly this man was the Son of God!" (15:39). But how can this centurion who has not known or been instructed by Jesus make such a confession? To answer this, the reader must keep in mind that for Mark the centurion is more than an historical witness to Jesus' death. He is also a figure who represents all those who stand on the other side of the crucifixion and acknowledge that Jesus' messiahship involves suffering and death. The centurion confesses that Jesus is God's Son because he has seen what no other human character, to this point in the story, has seen: the death of Jesus.[17] Like his baptism, therefore, Jesus' death functions as a theophany. When he dies, the temple curtain is torn, revealing God's glory and making it possible for all who acknowledge the crucified Messiah to confess him as the Son of God.

But what is the relationship between the royal titles (King of the Jews/King of Israel) of chapter 15 and the centurion's confession? Earlier I noted that at Jesus' baptism, God the Father identifies him as his royal Son in the line of the Davidic kings. This was especially apparent from the allusion to Psalm 2:7. In chapter 15, Jesus' persecutors mock him as the King of the Jews and the King of Israel. They ridicule him as a pretender because, in their estimation, Jesus does not possess the necessary qualifications for kingship. He is neither a political nor a national figure. He has neither authority nor power. But the irony of chapter 15 is that Jesus is a King, though not in the sense his opponents would expect. He is a King who endures rejection and suffering. He is a King who refuses to save himself. He is a King who trusts in his Father. The centurion's confession expresses this because it corresponds to the Father's declaration at Jesus' baptism that Jesus is his royal Son. As the royal Son of the Father, Jesus exercises his kingship, not with human power and might, but by accepting the Father's will for his messiahship: suffering and death.

II. JESUS AND THE DISCIPLES

Throughout chapter 14, the disciples play a prominent role in the passion story. They celebrate the Passover supper with Jesus, and they are present at the moment of his arrest. But the portrait of the disciples, in this chapter, portrays them as failing and forsaking Jesus. Judas betrays him. Peter, James and John fail to watch in the garden of Gethsemane. The disciples, at the moment of Jesus' arrest, flee in utter confusion. Peter, despite his protestations, denies him. In chapter 15, at Jesus' crucifixion and death, none of the disciples is present. Only a few women, standing at a distance, watch. Finally, after Jesus' death, Joseph of Arimathea, not one of the twelve, buries the Lord.

Mark counterbalances this negative picture, however, with Jesus' prophecy in 14:27–28: ''You will all fall away, for it is written, 'I will strike the shepherd, and the sheep will be scattered.' But after I am raised up, I will go before you to Galilee.'' In the final episode of the Gospel (16:1–8), the young man at the empty tomb repeats this prophecy to the women, ''But go, tell his disciples and Peter that he is going before you to Galilee; there you will see him, as he told you'' (16:7). Because Jesus' prophecies find fulfillment, the reader can correctly suppose that the prophecy of 14:27–28 is fulfilled, even though Mark does not describe the meeting of the risen Lord with his disciples. Although the disciples abandon Jesus at the passion, their apostasy is not final.

This theme of discipleship, by which Mark presents Jesus' followers in both a positive and negative light, constitutes an important narrative line in his story.[18] Once more I make the point that the full meaning of the passion narrative only becomes apparent when read in the context of Mark's total story. Therefore, I review Mark's story of Jesus again, but this time from the point of view of discipleship.

A. The Privileged Role of the Disciples

There are several occasions when Mark makes it evident that the disciples enjoy a privileged role. The first act of Jesus, after beginning his Galilean ministry (1:14—8:26), is to call four disciples: Andrew, Peter, James and John (1:16–20). These men respond generously, leaving their livelihood in order to follow him. Jesus captures their imagination, and one of the first miracles he performs is on behalf of Peter's mother-in-law (1:29–31).

The disciples are loyal to their new teacher, and Jesus protects them. When the scribes complain to the disciples that Jesus eats with sinners (2:16), and when the Pharisees accuse the disciples of breaking the sabbath (2:24), Jesus comes to their defense (2:17,25–28). Jesus describes the disciples as wedding guests of the bridegroom (*hoi huioi tou numphōnos,* literally, ''sons of the bridegroom'') who cannot fast as long as he, the bridegroom, is with them (2:19).

Eventually, Jesus calls twelve men to himself whom he appoints "to be with him, and to be sent out to preach and have authority to cast out demons" (3:14–15). Immediately following this, his family comes to seize him because people were saying "He is beside himself" (3:21). But Jesus looks at those sitting around him, including his disciples, and says, "Here are my mother and my brothers! Whoever does the will of God is my brother, and sister, and mother" (3:34–35). The disciples form Jesus' true family.

In chapter 4, Jesus speaks to the crowds in parables. After withdrawing from the crowds, those around him with the twelve ask about the parables. Jesus responds, "To you has been given the secret of the kingdom of God, but for those outside everything is in parables" (4:11). Next, he explains the parable of the sower to these chosen few (4:14–20). Following this explanation, Jesus offers still more parables (4:21–32), and at the conclusion of the parable discourse, Mark comments, "With many such parables he spoke the word to them, as they were able to hear it; he did not speak to them without a parable, but privately to his own disciples he explained everything" (4:33–34). The disciples become recipients of special knowledge; Jesus teaches them the mysteries of the kingdom.

In chapter 6, Jesus sends the disciples out on mission to preach and cast out demons (6:7–13). The apostles return triumphant (6:30), and Jesus, solicitous for their well-being, takes them to a desert place for rest.

Some time later, Jesus enters into a debate with the Pharisees over the question of ritual purity (7:1–13). After explaining to the crowds that there is nothing outside a man which can defile him (7:15), Jesus withdraws to a house with his disciples. There, he explains to them the meaning of this saying (7:17–23). Once more, the disciples become recipients of privileged information.

As Jesus progresses toward Jerusalem (8:27–10:52), he teaches his disciples by three passion predictions (8:31; 9:31; 10:33–34) that he will suffer and die, and after three days, he will rise from the dead. In addition to these predictions, Jesus privately explains to the disciples the hard sayings about divorce (10:10–12) and riches (10:23–27). He also instructs them about the true meaning of discipleship (8:34–38; 9:35–50; 10:42–45). Although the disciples do not comprehend the full meaning of Jesus' teaching, they continue to manifest a generous spirit. Peter can say, "Lo, we have left everything and followed you" (10:28). And

James and John think that they can drink from the cup from which Jesus will drink and be baptized with his baptism (10:38–39). These three disciples, Peter, James and John, also witness Jesus' transfiguration (9:2–8) and hear yet another passion prediction (9:12).

During Jesus' Jerusalem ministry (11:1—13:36) the disciples are among those who welcome his arrival at Jerusalem as the inauguration of David's kingdom (11:7–10). While in Jerusalem, he explains to them the meaning of the withered fig tree (11:20–25) and the widow's offering (12:43–44). Finally, at the close of his Jerusalem ministry, Jesus delivers a discourse to Peter, James and John and Andrew on the coming of the Son of Man (13:3–37). There can be no doubt that the disciples enjoy a privileged place in Mark's Gospel. They are Jesus' constant companions. They manifest a generous spirit, and Jesus provides them with special instruction.

B. The Disciples' Lack of Understanding

Although the disciples are generous and receive special teaching, they manifest a misunderstanding about Jesus' mission and identity which culminates in their flight at the passion. For example, they do not understand the parable of the sower although Jesus implies that they should: "Do you not understand this parable? How then will you understand all the parables?" (4:13). After Jesus' teaching about ritual purity, the puzzled disciples ask him for further instruction. Although he grants it, he again implies that they should have understood: "Then are you also without understanding? Do you not see that whatever goes into a man from outside cannot defile him?" (7:18).

In the last part of the Gospel (8:27—16:8), the disciples manifest this misunderstanding by a number of actions. They are unable to exorcise a boy possessed by a demon (9:18) because they have not prayed (9:28–29). They try to forbid a strange exorcist from casting out demons in Jesus' name because he does not follow them, i.e., the disciples (10:38). And they foolishly try to prevent little children from "bothering" their master (10:13).

In addition to these incidents there are six major scenes which portray the disciples' lack of understanding. The first three occur in the second section of the Gospel (1:14—8:26). Each takes place in a boat. The first (4:35–41) comes after the day of parables (4:1–34). Jesus and his disciples cross the lake of Galilee. As Jesus sleeps, a great storm arises. The disciples awaken him and he calms the sea. But after the miracle, Jesus rebukes them. "Have you no faith?" The disciples then manifest their ignorance of Jesus' identity, saying, "Who then is this, that even wind and sea obey him?" (4:41).

The second boat scene (6:45–52) comes after Jesus has fed the five thousand (6:35–44). Jesus sends the disciples ahead, by boat, to Bethsaida. Once more a storm arises, but this time Jesus is not with them. Suddenly he appears walking on the sea. They call to him, and he replies, "Take heart, it is I; have no fear." Jesus then enters the boat and the wind ceases. At the end of the scene, Mark adds an editorial comment which highlights their misunderstanding: "And they were utterly astounded, for they did not understand about the loaves, but their hearts were hardened" (6:51–52). Mark suggests that the disciples, who witnessed the multiplication of the loaves, should know that Jesus would have protected them. But their hearts are hardened.

The last boat scene (8:14–21) is the most severe criticism of the disciples. It also occurs after a feeding story, the feeding of the four thousand (8:1–10). This time Jesus is in the boat with the disciples who have forgotten to bring bread. He says, "take heed, beware of the leaven [Greek reads bread] of the Pharisees and the leaven [bread] of Herod." The disciples think that Jesus is talking about ordinary bread, at which point he responds: "Do you not yet perceive or understand? Are your hearts hardened? Having eyes do you not see, and having ears do you not hear?" (cf. 4:12). Jesus then reminds the disciples about the two miracles of the loaves and concludes, "Do you not yet understand?" Having witnessed the feeding of the five thousand and the four thousand the disciples should understand something of Jesus' teaching, but they do not.

Corresponding to the three misunderstandings in 1:14–8:26 are three major failures by the disciples in the last part of the Gospel (8:27–16:8). Each centers around one of the three passion predictions. After the first prediction (8:31), Peter rebukes Jesus for saying that he must suffer and die as the Messiah (8:32). Although Peter has confessed Jesus to be the Christ, he has misunderstood the content of Jesus' messiahship. As a result, Jesus rebukes him (8:33) and then offers a teaching on the true meaning of discipleship (8:34–38).

As Jesus passes through Galilee, he makes a second passion prediction (9:31). Mark then notes, "But they did not understand the say-

ing, and they were afraid to ask him'' (9:32). As if to explain the nature
of this misunderstanding, Mark portrays the disciples discussing with
one another who is the greatest (9:34). The disciples have not grasped
the purpose of Jesus' mission or the nature of discipleship. Consequently, Jesus instructs them further on the meaning of discipleship
(9:35–37).

The last misunderstanding comes as Jesus approaches Jerusalem
and gives his third and most detailed passion prediction (10:33–34). On
the heels of this prediction, James and John ask for the seats of honor at
his right and left (10:35–37). Upon hearing this, the other disciples become indignant (10:41). They have not understood Jesus' mission or the
nature of discipleship. For a third time, Jesus must instruct them about
the meaning of discipleship (10:42–44). Jesus concludes with the ransom
saying which explains the purpose of his life: ''For the Son of Man also
came not to be served but to serve, and to give his life as a ransom for
many'' (10:45).

Mark has carefully crafted this section, and most scholars observe
the following pattern which is repeated three times.[19]

prediction	8:31; 9:31; 10:33–34
misunderstanding	8:32; 9:32; 10:35–41
teaching	8:34–38; 9:35–37; 10:42–45

In Mark's Gospel the disciples manifest a progressive misunderstanding
of Jesus' person, teaching, and mission. Because of the parable discourse, the two feeding miracles, and the three passion predictions they
should know who he is and the purpose of his mission. But they do not.
Why?

C. The Mystery of the Cross

The inability of the disciples to understand the nature of Jesus' messiahship and their own discipleship is not simply a moral failure. That
is, it does not derive from a weakness in their character. The reader
should not imagine that if the disciples were more courageous men, or
if they paid closer attention to Jesus' instruction, they would not have
betrayed him. The mystery of the passion is that it happens in accordance
with God's will for the Messiah.[20] Therefore, at the Last Supper Jesus

can predict that the disciples will abandon him *because* Scripture fore-tells it: "You will all fall away; for it is written, 'I will strike the shep-herd, and the sheep will be scattered' " (14:27). In a similar fashion there is a divine inevitability to Judas' betrayal (14:21) and the denial of Peter (14:30). Although these events involve human failure and even malice, they are greater than these.

The reader of the Gospel knows who Jesus is and realizes the pur-pose of his mission because Mark provides inside information about his identity of which the characters in the story are ignorant. In addition, Mark makes an important editorial aside which explains something of the disciples' blindness; "for they did not understand about the loaves, but their hearts were hardened" (6:52). In his story, Mark never provides any motive for the hardening of the disciples' hearts. To the contrary, he presents the disciples as generous followers of the Lord.

Why are the hearts of the disciples hardened, and why do they not understand? In a sense, I answered this question in the discussion of the centurion's cry. There, I noted that the centurion confesses Jesus as the Son of God, not because of any moral rectitude on his part, but because he stands on the other side of Jesus' death. The failure of the disciples is the reverse of this situation. During Jesus' public ministry the disciples *cannot* understand who he is or the purpose of his mission because he has not died[21] and they have not experienced the passion. But once Jesus dies, the disciples, like the centurion, are capable of understanding Je-sus' mission and identity. This is the reason that, after the passion, the risen Lord summons them to Galilee.[22] There, for the first time, they will see *and understand* that the risen One is none other than the crucified One, Jesus of Nazareth (16:6).

III.
JESUS AND THE TEMPLE

Mark refers to the temple three times during the passion narrative. At Jesus' trial before the Sanhedrin, false witnesses testify, "We heard him say, 'I will destroy this temple that is made with hands, and in three days I will build another, not made with hands' " (14:58). At Jesus' cru-cifixion, the passers-by deride him, "Aha! You who would destroy the temple and build it in three days, save yourself, and come down from the cross!" (15:29b–30). Finally, after Jesus' death, "the curtain of the temple was torn in two, from top to bottom'' (15:38). In discussing these references to the temple, I suggested that Mark sees a relationship between temple and Messiah.[23] The charge that Jesus threatened to destroy and rebuild the temple is, in effect, an accusation that he claims to be the Messiah. But the temple theme goes beyond the passion story. It is the conclusion to a theme which Mark begins in chapter 11.[24] From that point forward, the temple figures prominently in his Gospel. To appreciate its full meaning in the passion story it is important to appreciate how the temple theme functions in the rest of Mark's narrative.

A. The End of the Temple (11:1–25)

In 11:1–10, Mark describes Jesus' entry into Jerusalem. In comparison to the description of the other evangelists, Mark's portrayal of this event is measurably subdued.[25] There is no explicit reference to the text of Zechariah 9:9 (cf. Mt 21:5), and it appears that only Jesus' entourage, not the inhabitants of the city (cf. Mt 21:10–11), were involved. Moreover, when Jesus arrives, his destination is not so much the city as it is the temple: "And he entered Jerusalem, and went into the temple; and when he had looked round at everything, as it was already late, he went out to Bethany with the twelve'' (11:11).

The next day (11:12) Jesus returns to the city. On the way he curses a fig tree for not bearing fruit, even though it was not the time for figs (11:12–14). Once in the city, Jesus drives the money-changers from the temple precincts (11:15–19). When evening comes, he again withdraws from the city (11:19). On the next day, when Jesus returns to Jerusalem, Peter notices that the fig tree which Jesus cursed has withered and died (11:20–21).

Most scholars recognize that Mark intends a relationship between the cleansing of the temple and the cursing of the fig tree since the latter incident frames the cleansing of the temple.[26] The cursing of the fig tree is a symbolic action by which Jesus announces the fate of the temple. But why?

When Jesus enters Jerusalem for the first time, he goes to the temple and surveys the situation (11:11). The next day he returns in order to rectify the problem he has observed: the desecration of the temple. He expels the merchants and money-changers from the temple, and he forbids anyone to carry anything through it. In explaining his action, Jesus says, "Is it not written, 'My house shall be called a house of prayer for all the nations'? But you have made it a den of robbers'' (11:17). The Scripture passage to which Jesus refers comes from Isaiah 56:7. It is part of a prophetic oracle in which God promises that even foreigners will share in the blessings of Israel and, more specifically, in temple worship: "these I will bring to my holy mountain, and make them joyful in my house of prayer; their burnt offerings and their sacrifices will be accepted on my altar; for my house shall be called a house of prayer for all peoples." By his prophetic action, Jesus denounces the profanation of the temple and proclaims that he comes to fulfill Isaiah's prophecy: the Gentiles will also have access to Israel's God.

The latter part of Jesus' teaching ("But you have made it a den of robbers") alludes to Jeremiah 7:11: "Has this house, which is called by my name, become a den of robbers in your eyes?" This text is part of a devastating temple critique in Jeremiah 7:1–15 in which the prophet condemns the men of Judah for practicing all kinds of abominations and then retreating to the temple, saying, "We are delivered!" (7:10) At the end of the oracle, Jeremiah reminds the people how God destroyed the temple at Shiloh and predicts the same fate for Jerusalem's house of worship: "therefore I will do to the house which is called by my name, and in which you trust, and to the place which I gave to you and to your fathers, as I did to Shiloh" (7:14). By having Jesus allude to these words, Mark hints that the temple will be destroyed.

But to whom is Jesus addressing these remarks? The next verse points to the religious leaders: "And the chief priests and the scribes heard it and sought a way to destroy him; for they feared him, because all the multitude was astonished at his teaching" (11:18). In the following episodes, the chief priests, the scribes and the elders oppose Jesus (11:27–12:34) by challenging his authority to do such things (11:28). The narrative flow of Mark's story indicates that the religious leaders are the ones who, in Jesus' eyes, have turned the temple into a den of robbers. By allowing such commercial activity to take place in the outer court of the temple, the Court of the Gentiles, they have hindered the Gentiles from worshiping in the one place of the temple which the law allowed them. Jesus stops such commercial activity in order to restore this space, at least temporarily, for the Gentiles.

But the allusion to Jeremiah 7:11 and the cursing of the fig tree indicate that the ultimate fate of the temple has been sealed. Like the fig tree, the temple has not borne fruit; it has not found a place for the Gentiles. It has not become a house of prayer for all the nations. Therefore, like the fig tree, the temple will wither and die. That the temple cult is coming to an end may be indicated in Jesus' refusal to "allow any one to carry anything (*skeuos*) through the temple" (11:16). The Greek word *skeuos* can refer to the "vessels used in worship" as it does in Hebrews 9:21. If this is the case, by refusing to allow anyone to carry the instruments of worship through the temple, Jesus effectively calls a halt to the temple cult. With Jesus' death and the tearing of the temple curtain, the function of the temple, in Mark's view, comes to an end.

But by prophesying the end of the old temple, Jesus does not exclude a new temple which will be a house of prayer for all nations. It is at this point that the temple charge brought against Jesus at his trial (14:58) becomes important. Although Mark presents it as false, there is a sense in which it contains a truth that the false witnesses do not understand. Donald Juel has effectively argued that the new temple, not built with hands, is the Christian community to whom Mark addresses his Gospel.[27] This community, composed of Gentiles as well as Jews, is the new temple, the temple not made with hands ("and in three days I will build another, not made with hands"—14:58b).

In light of these remarks, Jesus' admonitions to faith, prayer, and forgiveness in 11:23–25, take on added meaning. Peter points to the withered fig tree, a symbol of the old temple. In response, Jesus speaks of the power that prayer possesses when rooted in faith and of the need to forgive others. Prayer, faith, and forgiveness will be three hallmarks of the new community that Jesus establishes, the temple not made with hands.

B. Controversies in Jerusalem (11:27–12:44)

After Jesus cleanses the temple, the religious leaders challenge his authority (11:27–28) and engage him in controversy (12:13–34). Jesus tells the parable of the vineyard (12:1–11), and the religious leaders realize that he directs it against them (12:12). At the conclusion of these controversies, Jesus asks the question about David's son (12:35–37) and denounces the scribes (12:38–40). The story of the widow's offering (12:41–44) follows. Throughout this section, the temple theme continues to play an important role.

The chief priests, the scribes and the elders (the three groups which compose the Sanhedrin) ask Jesus ''By what authority are you doing these things, or who gave you this authority to do them?'' (11:28). In the context of Mark's story, the question can only refer to the cleansing of the temple. Jesus refuses to answer because they will not tell him if the baptism of John was of human or divine origin. But following this challenge, he delivers the parable of the vineyard (12:1–11). In the parable, the beloved son (12:6) refers to Jesus, the owner of the vineyard to God, and the wicked tenants to the religious leaders (cf. 12:12). But to what does the vineyard correspond?

The imagery of the vineyard can be found in Isaiah's song of the vineyard (Is 5:1–7) where the prophet identifies the vineyard with the house of Israel (Is 5:7). It is also present in Psalm 80:8–9 where it refers to the people of Israel whom God redeemed from Egypt. The parable suggests that the people of Israel will be taken from the religious leaders because they have not returned to God the fruit of the vineyard: a people prepared for the coming of God's kingdom. In this regard, the parable is similar to the cursing of the fig tree and the cleansing of the temple. At the cleansing of the temple Jesus accused the religious leaders of excluding the Gentiles from the temple; in this parable he condemns them for not preparing the people for the coming of God's kingdom. By announcing that the owner of the vineyard will destroy the tenants and give the vineyard to others (12:9), Jesus threatens the authority which they exercise from the temple. Although this parable does not contain an explicit reference to the temple, the wider context suggests a further polemic against it.

After the parable, the religious leaders engage Jesus in three controversies (12:13–34). The third of these controversies, the scribe's question about the greatest commandment (12:28–34), has a direct bearing upon the temple theme. After Jesus' response, the scribe praises him: ''You are right, Teacher; you have truly said that he is one, and there is no other but he; and to love him with all the heart, and with all the understanding, and with all the strength, and to love one's neighbor as oneself, is much more than all whole burnt offerings and sacrifices'' (12:32–33). In turn, Jesus tells the scribe that he is not far from the kingdom of God. The incident reveals the true nature of worship in the temple not made with hands that Jesus will establish: love of God and love of neighbor.

Another controversy story provides an ethic for the new people Jesus is establishing. He refuses to withhold taxes from Caesar (12:13–17). Instead, his followers will live in the present social order, obeying Caesar but giving their ultimate allegiance to God. The final nature of this allegiance is clear from the controversy with the Sadducees (12:18–27). While the Sadducees, members of the temple establishment, argue against the resurrection of the dead, Jesus employs Scripture to establish the reality of life beyond this life. The leaders of the old temple misunderstand the Scriptures and the power of God (12:24), but the members of the new temple, the temple not made with hands, look forward to the resurrection of the dead.

At the conclusion of this section, Jesus asks a question which shows that the scribes have not grasped the true nature of the Messiah (12:35–37), and he denounces them for their external display (12:38–40). To such behavior, he juxtaposes the generosity of the widow (12:41–44) who contributes all that she has to the temple treasury. The scribes continue to think of the Messiah as a warrior king who will dispose of the Romans.[28] But Jesus comes as the beloved Son of God who, like the widow, gives all that he has, his very life.

By portraying Jesus in conflict with the religious establishment, Mark implicitly criticizes the temple which it controls. The temple leaders have not borne fruit nor have they returned fruit to the owner of the vineyard. Consequently, the old temple will come to an end and be replaced by the temple not made with hands.

C. The Destruction of the Temple (13:1–37)

At the trial before the Sanhedrin, the false witnesses accuse Jesus of having said that *he* will destroy the temple (14:58). In fact, according to Mark, Jesus made no such statement. But in 13:2, after leaving the temple for the last time, Jesus did predict its destruction: ''Do you see these great buildings? There will not be left here one stone upon another, that will not be thrown down.'' This prediction becomes the occasion for Jesus' apocalyptic discourse (13:5–37).

As Jesus is seated on the Mount of Olives, opposite the temple,[29] Peter, James, John and Andrew ask when this will occur and what will be the sign that these things are about to take place. The discourse which follows (13:5–37) answers these questions. It has been variously termed

Jesus' apocalyptic discourse, his eschatological discourse, and his fare-well discourse.[30] Here I am primarily interested in what refers to the destruction of the temple. In the next section I shall return to other aspects of the material.

The discourse may be outlined in the following manner. In vv. 5–8 Jesus speaks of *preliminary* signs (wars and natural disasters) which must occur before the end. In vv. 9–13 he describes the trials and persecutions that his followers endure. In vv. 14–23, he points to a great tribulation which will be a signal for those in Judea to flee. In vv. 24–27 he speaks of the *cosmic signs,* which nobody can mistake, that will herald his coming as the Son of man. In vv. 28–31 he draws a lesson from a fig tree. Finally, in vv. 32–37 he encourages his followers to watch because nobody knows the day or the hour.

On first reading, it may appear that Jesus ignores the disciples' original question. They inquire about the destruction of the temple, but he informs them about the persecution they will face and the signs of his return as the Son of Man. But in v. 14 he says, "But when you see the desolating sacrilege (*to bdelugma tēs erēmōseōs*) set up where it ought not to be (let the reader understand), then let those who are in Judea flee to the mountains."

Although this cryptic phrase was probably understandable to Mark's original audience, today it continues to puzzle students of Mark. But because the expression "desolating sacrilege" (*bdelugma tōn erē-mōseōn*) occurs in Daniel 9:27; 11:31; 12:11; 1 Mac 1:54 in reference to the "heathen altar which Antiochus Epiphanes built over the altar of burnt offering in 168 B.C.,"[31] I agree with those authors who explain that the text refers to the coming destruction of the temple. From a literary point of view, their argument receives further corroboration since there are no other verses which answer the question posed by the disciples in v. 4. Consequently, if this text does not have any relationship to the temple, the discourse does not respond to the disciples' question.

In v. 14, therefore, Jesus points to a sign that heralds the destruction of the temple. At that sign the Church in Judea must flee to the mountains because the destruction of Jerusalem[32] and its temple is at hand. But lest Mark's readers be overcome by apocalyptic fervor, Jesus indicates that the destruction of the temple is not the consummation of all things. It is part of the messianic woes; it is *one* of the signs preliminary to the end. But the end comes only with the cosmic signs listed in vv. 24–25 which announce the coming of the Son of Man: "the sun will be darkened, and the moon will not give its light, and the stars will be falling from heaven, and the powers in the heavens will be shaken."

It is with this final prediction that Jesus embarks upon the passion. When the false witnesses accuse him of threatening to destroy the temple and promising to build another, their witness is patently false. Jesus never said that he would destroy the temple. But by the cursing of the fig tree and his final discourse, he does announce its destruction. On a level that Jesus' persecutors cannot understand, there is truth in the temple charge. By his death, Jesus makes the old temple and its cultic worship obsolete. In its place, he establishes a new community of believers: Jews and Gentiles, a temple not made by human hands.

IV.
JESUS AND THE FUTURE

On several occasions during the passion narrative, Jesus looks to the future. Before the Last Supper, as a woman anoints his head, he says, "wherever the Gospel is preached in the whole world, what she has done will be told in memory of her" (14:9). During the supper, Jesus looks forward to the coming kingdom of God as he declares, "Truly, I say to you, I shall not drink again of the fruit of the vine until that day when I drink it new in the kingdom of God" (14:25). On the way to the Mount of Olives, he tells the disciples that they will abandon him, but he will gather them in Galilee "after I am raised up" (14:28). Finally, when the high priest asks Jesus if he is the Christ, the Son of the Blessed, he replies, "I am; and you will see the Son of Man seated at the right hand of Power, and coming with the clouds of heaven" (14:62).

The common element in these texts is Jesus' vision of the future. He believes that the Gospel will be proclaimed after his death. He trusts that beyond death he will share in God's kingdom. He is confident that the Father will raise him from the dead. And he even predicts that he will return as the triumphant Son of Man to judge his persecutors.

This trust concerning the future, so apparent in chapter 14, helps to explain Jesus' behavior throughout the passion, especially in chapter 15. Jesus does not respond to his persecutors or try to save himself because of his confidence that God will vindicate him. He trusts that God's kingdom will come in power and that he, in his capacity as the Son of Man, will return to inaugurate it. But this trust concerning the future is not peculiar to the passion narrative. It is a theme present throughout the Gospel. In what follows, I examine Jesus' vision of the coming kingdom, the coming Son of Man, and the coming persecution which his disciples must endure.

A. The Coming Kingdom

The kingdom of God is the content of Jesus' teaching. Immediately after Jesus' baptism and testing in the desert, Mark narrates that Jesus goes to Galilee and preaches "the Gospel of God" (1:14). What this Gospel of God is, Mark explains in the next verse. "The time is fulfilled, and the kingdom of God is at hand; repent and believe in the Gospel" (1:15). The Gospel of God is Jesus' announcement that the kingdom of God is at hand. The perfect tense of the Greek verb *ēggiken* ("is at hand") suggests that the kingdom has drawn so close that one can almost embrace it. Indeed, in one sense it is present. Therefore, there is need for repentance. But the full manifestation of the kingdom has not yet taken place. The kingdom remains hidden so that Jesus must announce its presence and coming manifestation.

There is a paradoxical aspect to the kingdom in Jesus' preaching best expressed in the phrase "already, but not yet." The kingdom has already drawn near, but its manifestation in power has not yet taken place. But because the kingdom has already drawn near, demons cry out at the approach of Jesus, "What have you to do with us, Jesus of Nazareth? Have you come to destroy us?" (1:24) Jesus' exorcisms demonstrate that God's kingdom is already being established. Satan's rule is coming to an end. In a controversy with the scribes occasioned by his exorcisms (3:22–27) Jesus implies that he has entered the strong man's house, the kingdom of Satan, and plundered it (3:27).

On several other occasions, Jesus emphasizes the nearness of the kingdom. After Peter's confession at Caesarea Philippi, immediately before the transfiguration, he gives an important instruction on the nature of discipleship (8:34–9:1). At the conclusion of that teaching he says, "Truly, I say to you, there are some standing here who will not taste death before they see the kingdom of God come with power" (9:1). Some commentators interpret this difficult text in terms of the transfiguration, but that event does not fully correspond to the coming of the kingdom *with power*. It seems more prudent to take the text literally. Jesus anticipates the imminent arrival of God's kingdom in power. There is some truth to the cries of the people, therefore, who hail Jesus' arrival in Jerusalem: "Blessed is the kingdom of our father David that is coming! Hosanna in the highest!" (11:10). The kingdom of God is about to arrive in power, but not in the manner they expect.

For Jesus the coming kingdom is so close that he can make extraordinary demands upon his followers. In a lesson on discipleship he requires them to receive the kingdom of God with the trust that characterizes children (10:15). In a teaching on scandal (9:42–50), he tells them, "And if your eye causes you to sin, pluck it out; it is better for you to enter the kingdom of God with one eye than with two eyes to be thrown into hell" (9:47). And in an encounter with a man seeking eternal life (10:17–22), Jesus requires him to sell everything, give his possessions to the poor, and follow him. In the discussion which follows (10:23–31), Jesus warns his disciples about the danger of riches.

Although the kingdom is present, it is hidden; it has not yet arrived in power. Jesus makes this point in his parable discourse (4:1–34). After the parable of the sower (4:3–9), he says to the disciples, "to you has been given the secret (*mystērion*, literally, "mystery") of the kingdom of God" (4:11). What this mystery of the kingdom is becomes clearer when Jesus explains the parable of the sower (4:14–20) and then offers further teaching and other parables (4:21–32). The beginnings of the kingdom are hidden and insignificant. The kingdom begins like seed scattered upon the ground. Suddenly and unexpectedly it produces a harvest (4:26–29). It begins as the smallest of seeds but becomes the greatest of shrubs (4:30–32). In the present time, the kingdom is hidden, but Jesus promises that one day it will come to light (4:21–22). In the present time, the task of Jesus is to sow the seed (4:14–20). Not all of the seed will bear fruit, but what does will produce a rich harvest.

Put another way, the mystery of the kingdom "consists in the fact that the divine plan of salvation is already at work in Jesus and the community. The kingdom is present, but it is still a hidden one, tending, with all its being, toward full revelation."[33] There is a correlation between the kingdom of God and the kingship of Jesus. In the present time, God's kingdom has drawn near. In the person of Jesus it is present. But the kingdom remains hidden from the view of the world until its final manifestation in power. The present concealment of the kingdom is like Jesus' kingship. Jesus is the King of the Jews and the King of Israel. But in the present time, and especially during the passion, that kingship is hidden from the world. The full manifestation of Jesus' kingship and God's kingdom will only occur when Jesus returns as the glorious Son of Man. Then the world will acknowledge his kingship and God's kingdom. In the meantime, the Church confesses this hidden kingdom and kingship as it confidently awaits their full manifestation.

B. The Coming Son of Man

During Jesus' ministry, and for a period after his death and resurrection, the kingdom, although present, remains hidden from the public view. But on three occasions (8:38; 13:26; 14:62), Jesus proclaims that he will return as the glorious Son of Man in order to inaugurate the public revelation of this kingdom. In addition to these sayings which speak of the coming Son of Man, Jesus refers to himself as the Son of Man when speaking of his death and resurrection (8:31; 9:9,12,31; 10:33; 14:21,41) and of his earthly activity (2:10,28; 10:45). Thus, Son of Man points to several aspects of Jesus' life.[34]

As the Son of Man, Jesus is a human being among other human beings. Therefore, the scribes ascribe blasphemy to him for claiming the power to forgive sins (2:7), and the Pharisees chide him for allowing his disciples to break the sabbath (2:24). In face of these objections, Jesus calls himself the Son of Man who, although he appears as a human among humans, has the power to forgive sins (2:10) and is Lord even of the sabbath (2:28). Similarly, when teaching his followers the meaning of discipleship, Jesus refers to himself as the Son of Man who came "not to be served but to serve, and to give his life as a ransom for many" (10:45). He is a human among humans, but his death has a ransoming effect. In each of these instances, there is something hidden about Jesus' identity that is not immediately apparent to those about him.

On other occasions, Jesus employs the title Son of Man in reference to his passion, death and resurrection. Son of Man indicates Jesus' destiny. As the Son of Man he will be rejected, put to death, and rise from the dead (8:31; 9:9,12,31; 10:33–34). All of this occurs according to God's plan (14:21). Once more there is something hidden about Jesus' identity. The one who betrays him and those who put him to death do not comprehend who he is. Here the earthly destiny of the Son of Man corresponds to the hidden aspect of the kingdom of God. Although Jesus publicly calls himself Son of Man, nobody understands his glorious destiny. Like the kingdom, his coming glory is hidden from public view.

But on three occasions Jesus proclaims that he will return as the glorious Son of Man. After describing the demands of discipleship he says, "For whoever is ashamed of me and of my words in this adulterous and sinful generation, of him will the Son of Man also be ashamed, when he comes in the glory of his Father with the holy angels" (8:38). The Son of Man who must suffer and be rejected is the same Son of Man who will return in the glory of his Father. In the present age, disciples may find it difficult to make this connection, and in the passion, Jesus' enemies do not recognize his kingship. But he assures his followers that there is a correspondence between the one who suffers and the one who will rule. Although his kingship is now hidden, it will be made manifest.

In chapter 13, Jesus makes his second reference to the coming Son of Man. After describing the signs which point to his coming, he says, "And then they will see the Son of Man coming in clouds with great power and glory" (13:26). The final act of history will occur after Jesus' death and resurrection. The suffering Son of Man (8:31; 9:12,31; 10:33) will return as the glorious Son of Man to "gather his elect from the four winds, from the ends of the earth to the ends of heaven" (13:27).

Both of these sayings (8:38; 13:26) help to interpret Jesus' final Son of Man saying spoken at the trial before the Sanhedrin. Much of the vocabulary found in these earlier sayings occurs in 14:62. The italicized words indicate this. "I am; and you will *see the Son of Man* seated at the right hand of *Power,* and *coming* with the *clouds* of heaven." Jesus affirms, before the entire Sanhedrin, that the suffering Son of Man whom they unjustly judge is none other than the glorious Son of Man who will return to gather the elect at the end of the ages.

The theme of the coming Son of Man ultimately coincides with that of the coming kingdom. During Jesus' earthly life, he proclaims a kingdom which is present but hidden from the view of the world. Likewise, as the earthly Son of Man who must suffer and die, his glorious identity is hidden from the world's view. But at the end of the ages, he will return as the glorious Son of Man, a royal figure,[35] to inaugurate the full disclosure of God's kingdom. At the public revelation of God's kingdom, all will recognize the glorious aspect of Jesus' kingship. But in the passion, that kingship, like the kingdom, remains hidden.

C. The Coming Persecution

Thus far I have examined Jesus' teaching about the coming kingdom and the coming Son of Man. But at different points in the Gospel, Jesus warns his followers that they will face persecution before the coming of the Son of Man and the arrival of the kingdom with power. This coming persecution which the disciples must endure will be their passion. Just as the Son of Man suffers before his return in glory, so the community of his disciples will face tribulation before the full revelation of the kingdom.

At several points in the Gospel, Jesus alludes to this coming persecution. At the beginning of the story, people ask him why his disciples do not fast as the disciples of John the Baptist and the Pharisees do (2:18). After explaining that they do not fast because he, the bridegroom, is with them (2:19), he says, "The days will come, when the bridegroom is taken away from them, and then they will fast in that day" (2:20). Jesus hints at his own death and the period of suffering which will follow.

In the parable discourse (4:1–34), Jesus interprets the parable of the sower for his disciples (4:14–20). His explanation applies the parable to the situation which the Church will face after his death. The various kinds of seed characterize the different types of people who will hear the Church's preaching. Some will abandon the message because Satan carries it away (4:15). Others will fall away because of riches (4:19). Still others will fail "when tribulation or persecution arises on account of the word" (4:17). This last verse is especially revealing since the words tribulation (*thlipsis*) and persecution (*diōgmos*) occur on two other occasions which clearly point to the coming persecution.

The first appears after Jesus explains the danger of riches (10:23–28). In response, Peter says, "Lo, we have left everything and followed you" (10:28). Jesus replies, "Truly, I say to you, there is no one who has left house or brother or sisters or mother or father or children or lands, for my sake and for the Gospel, who will not receive a hundredfold now in this time, houses and brothers and sisters and mothers and children and lands, with persecutions (*meta diōgmōn*), and in the age to come eternal life" (10:29–30).

The next occurrence is in chapter 13. Twice, Jesus speaks of the tribulation (*thlipsis*) that will precede the coming of the Son of Man

(13:19,24). The persecution and the tribulation mentioned in Jesus' explanation of the parable (4:17) point to the Church's future.

Jesus continues to prepare his disciples for this future when he commissions the twelve for mission (6:7–11), warning that some will not receive them (6:11). In a similar vein, he assures James and John that they will drink from his cup of suffering and be baptized with his baptism of persecution (10:39). But it is in chapter 13 that Jesus most explicitly points to the coming persecution.

I have already alluded to this chapter in my discussions of the temple theme and the coming Son of Man. In doing so, I noted that this discourse informs the disciples of two events: the destruction of the temple and the triumphal return of the Son of Man. In disclosing this information, Jesus discourages apocalyptic speculation: calculations when the end will come. In a parable at the conclusion of the discourse (13:32–37), he emphasizes that no one knows when these things will take place, not even the Son (13:32). What the disciples should understand, however, is that when certain signs take place, the end is not far away (13:28–31).

Jesus divides these signs into two groups. There will be cosmic signs in the heavens which no one will be able to mistake: "the sun will be darkened, and the moon will not give its light, and the stars will be falling from heaven, and the powers in the heavens will be shaken" (13:24–25). After these signs, the Son of Man will return (13:26). But preliminary to these signs, there will be other signs, a great tribulation (*thlipsis*) which Jesus describes in 13:6–23. This tribulation points to the end but should not be confused with the end. It is preliminary, and no one can calculate the time between it and the coming of the Son of Man.

This tribulation (13:24) includes the destruction of the temple and the events surrounding it (13:14–22). It also entails the persecution of Jesus' followers (13:9–13). The location of this discourse, immediately before the passion, is not haphazard. By placing it here, Mark draws a parallel between the passion of Jesus and the passion of his followers. What happens to Jesus will happen to them. He is delivered to the Jewish council. He stands before the Roman governor. He is betrayed by one of his chosen disciples. They will be delivered to councils and synagogues. They will stand before governors and kings. They will be betrayed by the members of their own families (13:9–12). But Jesus assures them that "he who endures to the end will be saved" (13:13).

CONCLUSION

In this chapter, I have examined four themes found in Mark's passion narrative: Jesus' royal sonship; Jesus and his disciples; Jesus and the temple; Jesus and the future. I have tried to demonstrate that each of these themes, so prominent in the passion story, is a part of Mark's larger narrative. The climactic cry of the centurion that Jesus was the Son of God is the final unveiling of the secret surrounding Jesus' identity. It shows that no one can proclaim Jesus as the Son of God until he recognizes him as the Messiah who must suffer and die. Judas' betrayal, Peter's denial and the flight of the disciples are the outcome of blindness and misunderstanding which characterize the disciples throughout the Gospel. During Jesus' public ministry they do not, and they cannot, comprehend the full meaning of his teaching because they do not understand that as Messiah he must suffer. The temple charge and the mockery that Jesus is a temple destroyer result from Jesus' temple cleansing. His death makes the old temple obsolete and opens the way for a new temple, not made with hands, of which even the Gentiles will be a part. Finally, Jesus endures suffering and humiliation confident that he will return as the glorious Son of Man to inaugurate the revelation of God's kingdom with power. Now that kingdom and Jesus' kingship are present in a hidden manner. But at the end time, both will be revealed to the world. In the interim the Church must endure its own passion just as Jesus did. But it does so with confidence knowing that the suffering Son of Man is also the coming Son of Man.

There is a correspondence between Mark's passion narrative and his Gospel theology. It would be a serious mistake to read his passion account in isolation from the rest of the Gospel. The framework of the Gospel gives breadth and depth to the passion story.

Chapter Four

THE PASSION ACCORDING TO
MATTHEW: OVERVIEW

Even the casual reader perceives that there is a striking similarity between the passion narratives of Mark and Matthew. Nils Dahl points out that "every episode in the Markan account is also found in Matthew, with the exception of two informative notes (Mark 14:51f; 15:21b) and some descriptive details."[1] The amount of non-Marcan material in Matthew amounts to approximately twenty-six verses.[2] Consequently one can legitimately ask if there is any need to submit Matthew's passion narrative to a detailed analysis. Is it not sufficient simply to examine the new material in Matthew's account? Although the proposal appears reasonable, it falters on two counts.

First, although Matthew's passion account reproduces nearly all of Mark, there are a number of significant differences which merit close attention. Although these do not alter the basic story, they do focus Matthew's account in a slightly different way. Second, the passion story has received a new context in Matthew's Gospel. The importance of this context should not be underestimated. Just as a diamond's appearance can be altered by a new setting, so the passion account receives a different emphasis because of its new setting in the Gospel of Matthew.

In Mark the passion account dominates the story. Mark begins his Gospel with John the Baptist and concludes it with the account of the women at the empty tomb. By contrast Matthew's Gospel opens with an infancy narrative (chapters 1–2) and ends with the appearance of the risen Lord to the eleven disciples on the mountain in Galilee (28:16–20). The infancy narrative explains Jesus' origins and identifies him as David's royal heir, the Messiah, the Son of God. Jesus is Emmanuel, God *with* us (1:23). The resurrection appearance proclaims that God has invested Jesus with full authority (28:18) and inaugurates the Gentile mission (28:19–20). Like the infancy narrative, it speaks of God's presence to his people through Jesus: "and lo, I am *with* you always, to the close of the age" (28:20).[3]

In addition to this beginning and conclusion, Matthew's Gospel contains a number of discourses and a series of Old Testament fulfillment quotations not found in Mark. The discourses constitute a major portion of Matthew's Gospel (5:1—7:29; 10:1—11:1; 13:1–53; 18:1–35; 24:1—25:46) and make it a more didactic document than Mark. The Old Testament fulfillment quotations (1:22–23; 2:5–6,15,17–18,23; 4:14–16; 8:17; 12:17–21; 13:14–15,35; 21:4–5; 27:9–10) demonstrate that Jesus is the realization of Israel's messianic hope.

Because of this new setting, Matthew's passion narrative has a slightly different emphasis. Mark's passion narrative is eminently Christological with an accent upon Jesus' weakness and suffering. The passion is the moment during which Jesus' identity is revealed; the centurion confesses that he was truly the Son of God. Matthew's passion narrative is also profoundly Christological stressing that Jesus is the Son of God even in the midst of suffering and humiliation. But the drama deriving from the secret of Jesus' identity no longer controls the account. The infancy narrative plainly identifies Jesus as the Messiah. The quotations from the Old Testament show that he is the fulfillment of Israel's messianic hope. The great discourses present him as the Teacher of the Church. And the great commission proclaims that he is the one to whom the Father entrusts all authority. As a result, during the passion narrative the reader is even more keenly aware that the one who suffers is the exalted Son of God, the Messiah of Israel.[4] The drama in Matthew is not the secret of Jesus' identity, as in Mark, but the rejection of the Messiah by Israel. The Gospel focuses the reader's attention upon this point.

I.
The Theological Character of Matthew's Narrative

Scholars note that Matthew's passion narrative has three focal points: Christology, ecclesiology, and moral exhortation.[5]

Martin Dibelius writes that Matthew's passion story "is distinguished by moments of the highest Christological significance which show Jesus even in suffering as the plenipotentiary Son of God who is master of His own fate."[6]

There is no doubt that in Matthew's narrative the one who suffers is the all-knowing and all-powerful Son of God. At the outset of the passion Jesus announces that he will be crucified: "You know that after two days the Passover is coming, and the Son of Man will be delivered up to be crucified" (26:2). When preparing for the Passover meal, he says that his time (*kairos*) has come (26:18). At the Last Supper Jesus not only discloses his betrayal, he identifies who the betrayer is (26:25). When he is about to be arrested, Jesus gives Judas permission to do his work: "Friend, do that for which you have come" (26:50).[7] When one of his disciples tries to defend him, Jesus responds, "Put your sword back into its place. . . . Do you think that I cannot appeal to my Father, and he will at once send me more than twelve legions of angels?" (26:52–53). At the trial witnesses come forward and testify, "This fellow said, 'I am able to destroy the temple of God, and to build it in three days' " (26:61). Although their testimony is false, what they say contains an ironic truth. Jesus possesses the power to destroy the temple. And, in fact, his death renders the temple cult obsolete. Finally, at the moment of Jesus' death a great earthquake occurs resulting in the resurrection of the dead (27:51b–53). The death of Jesus is no ordinary event; it is the death of God's own Son.

Although Matthew presents a more exalted Christological portrait of Jesus than is found in Mark, he does not do so at the expense of Jesus' suffering and humiliation. The Son of God does not use his power and authority to save himself but suffers as one forsaken by God.[8] Jesus shows that he is the Son of God, not by saving himself but by his obedient trust in the Father. Matthew achieves the paradox of presenting an exalted Christology without diminishing Mark's portrait of the God forsaken Son of God.

Nils Dahl contends that ecclesiology is the dominant concern of Matthew's passion narrative. He writes: "What one might call the theme of the passion narrative is stated in Matthew's conclusion to the parable of the vineyard: 'The kingdom of God will be taken away from you and given to a nation producing the fruits of it' (21:43)."[9]

Whether or not ecclesiology is the major motif of Matthew's passion story, there is no doubt that it is an important concern.[10] If the trial before the Sanhedrin was a high point in Mark's account, the trial before

Pilate becomes a climactic moment in Matthew.[11] The Gentiles, Pilate and his wife, defend the Jewish Messiah against the people of Israel. Pilate's wife says, "Have nothing to do with that righteous man" (27:19), and Pilate proclaims, "I am innocent of this man's blood" (27:24). By contrast "all the people" shout: "His blood be on us and on our children" (27:25). This dramatic scene culminates a narrative line in Matthew's Gospel in which the people of Israel reject their Messiah. Consequently, at the great commission the risen Lord instructs his disciples to "make disciples of all nations" (28:19).

One of the purposes of the Matthean passion narrative is to explain how the Church, composed of Jews and Gentiles, has come to inherit the promises made to Israel.[12] Matthew's passion narrative is the conclusion of a dramatic story that might be summarized as follows. Jesus was the fulfillment of God's messianic promises to Israel. Although he showed himself as Messiah, powerful in word and deed, Israel rejected him. Consequently, Israel has lost its exclusive claims to the messianic promises, and these have passed to the Church.

Finally, the Matthean passion narrative presents Jesus as the model of righteous behavior.[13] Righteousness is a major theme in Matthew's Gospel, and in the passion Jesus exemplifies what it means to practice righteousness. In the garden of Gethsemane he prays just as he taught his disciples (cf. 26:39,42 with 6:10b). When he is arrested, he does not resist his persecutors (cf. 26:52 with 5:39). Before the high priest, he refuses to be placed under oath, fulfilling his own injunction against oaths (cf. 26:64 with 5:33–37). Before Pilate, he remains silent, just as did the Servant of Isaiah 53. When mocked that he cannot save himself, he obediently trusts in the power of God to save him, knowing that "whoever would save his life will lose it" (cf.27:40,42 with 16:25). Because of Jesus' righteous behavior, Judas confesses that he has betrayed "innocent blood" (27:4). Pilate asks the Jews "what evil has he [Jesus] done?" (27:23), and his wife calls Jesus a "righteous man" (27:19). Her declaration is correct. Jesus is the righteous one who is "persecuted for righteousness' sake" (5:10).

Scholars disagree as to which of these three motifs is the major theme in the Matthean passion narrative.[14] But it appears that the Christological theme serves as the foundation for the others. Matthew's ecclesiology and his exhortation to righteous behavior are dependent upon his Christology. Nonetheless, perhaps the most distinctive aspects of

Matthew's passion are found in the heightened ecclesiological and par-
aenetic interests he brings to the story. These concerns are already found
in Mark's account,[15] but Matthew gives them greater prominence.

II.
THE QUESTION OF SOURCES

The question of the sources for Matthew's passion narrative is not
as greatly disputed as it is for Mark, Luke, and John.[16] The majority of
authors espouse the Two-Source Hypothesis.[17] This hypothesis proposes
that Mark was the first of our Gospels to be written, and that Matthew
and Luke are dependent upon it. In addition to Mark, Matthew and Luke
also had access to a collection of Jesus' sayings, usually referred to as
"Q" (from the German word *Quelle,* "source"). Moreover each evangelist may also have had access to other written or oral traditions.

In the case of the passion narrative, it is evident that Matthew's primary source is Mark since he reproduces nearly all of Mark's account.
But Matthew also contains non-Marcan material. Some of this appears
to come from the evangelist's editorial activity: the passion prediction
(26:1–2); the identification of Judas as the betrayer (26:25); placing the
reed as a mock scepter in Jesus' hand (27:29); the centurion's companions (27:54). But the rest of the material is more problematic: the saying
about the sword and the twelve legions of angels (26:52–54); the death
of Judas (27:3–10); Pilate's wife (27:19); Pilate's handwashing (27:24);
the people's cry (27:25); the earthquake and the resurrection of the dead
(27:51b–53); the guard at the tomb (27:62–66). Does this material also
derive from Matthew's editorial activity, or did he have access to other
traditions?[18]

I shall not address this question, but it seems to me that nearly all,
if not all, of the material can be accounted for by Matthew's editorial
activity. The vocabulary, style, and theological concern of the material
is Matthean. Hypotheses to the contrary will always be surrounded with
an unacceptable degree of conjecture. Fortunately, the interpretation of
the text is not dependent upon the outcome of these source questions.

The Two Source-Hypothesis is a valuable tool for interpreting Matthew's passion narrative. By observing how the evangelist edits Mark,
the interpreter gains many insights into Matthew's theological agenda.

Matthew is a meticulous writer, and when he adds, deletes or rearranges material, it is with a purpose in mind. Sometimes the changes are merely stylistic; he improves upon Mark's Greek. But at other times, the reason is theological. Matthew wishes to emphasize a point made by Mark or even alter it slightly.

It would be a mistake, however, simply to interpret Matthew in light of Mark. Although the Matthean passion narrative derives from Mark, it now stands in a new context: Matthew's Gospel. It is important to investigate Matthew's passion story on its own terms. That is, it must be read in the light of Matthew's total story. In what follows I present Matthew's passion with an eye both to Mark's account and to Matthew's wider Gospel narrative. While I am interested in the evangelist's editorial activity, especially if it has theological significance, my primary concern is the passion story in its new setting: Matthew's Gospel.

Chapter Five

THE PASSION ACCORDING TO
MATTHEW: COMMENTARY
Matthew 26:1–27:66

I.
PRELUDE TO THE PASSION, 26:1–16

Matthew begins his account of the passion with three incidents which serve as a prelude or introduction to the passion proper: the plot to kill Jesus, the anointing at Bethany, and Judas' agreement to betray Jesus. Although Mark narrates similar stories, Matthew edits Mark in order to highlight Jesus' prophetic knowledge. In doing this, he suggests that Jesus is in control of the events surrounding his humiliation and death. Jesus makes a passion prediction, *then,* as if by divine permission, the religious leaders plot to destroy him. Jesus explains why the woman anoints him at Bethany, *then,* as if by divine permission, Judas goes forth to betray him. Although the Matthean Jesus suffers the same abandonment as the Marcan Jesus, the first evangelist consistently emphasizes that the one who suffers is fully aware of the events which are about to transpire. They do not catch him by surprise.

A. The Plot (26:1–5)

The first two verses of this section are distinctively Matthean and relate the passion to the first part of Jesus' ministry.

> When Jesus had finished all these sayings, he said to his disciples, ''You know that after two days the Passover is coming, and the Son of Man will be delivered up to be crucified.''

The opening phrase "When Jesus had finished . . . " is a stock expression which Matthew employs to conclude each of Jesus' five great discourses: the Sermon on the Mount (5:1–7:29), the missionary discourse (10:1–11:1), the parable discourse (13:1–53), the discourse on Church life (18:1–19:1), and the apocalyptic discourse (24:1–25:46):

7:28	and when Jesus had finished these sayings
11:1	and when Jesus had finished instructing his twelve disciples
13:53	and when Jesus had finished these parables
19:1	now when Jesus had finished these sayings
26:1	when Jesus had finished *all* these sayings

The distinctive character of 26:1 is the addition of the word "all." On the one hand, in 26:1 Matthew refers to the apocalyptic discourse in which Jesus speaks of his return at the close of the ages (24:1–25:46), juxtaposing the glorious Son of Man portrayed in the apocalyptic discourse with the suffering Son of Man who will undergo the passion. But on the other hand, Matthew also refers to *all* of the discourses which Jesus has delivered thus far.[1] Having instructed his disciples by five great discourses, Jesus now teaches them the meaning of discipleship through his suffering and death. Thus Matthew draws an intimate connection between Jesus' teaching ministry and his passion.

Matthew relates Jesus' passion to his ministry by means of the passion prediction in 26:2. This is the last in a series of predictions which began at Caesarea Philippi (16:21; 17:12; 17:22–23; 20:17–19). According to them, the passion is the outcome of a deliberate decision on Jesus' part to accept the will of his Father. This final passion prediction, however, is distinctive inasmuch as Jesus now relates his death to the feast of Passover: "You know that after two days *the Passover is coming,* and the Son of Man will be delivered up to be crucified." The relationship between Jesus' death and the feast of Passover is not accidental; it is part of God's plan. Just as the events of Passover once brought salvation, so Jesus' death will effect a new and definitive redemption.

Immediately following Jesus' prediction, Matthew employs one of his favorite words, *tote* ("then"), to introduce the plot to destroy Jesus: "*Then* the chief priests and the elders of the people gathered . . . and took counsel together.'' The adverb ''then'' suggests that the plot only takes place because Jesus allows it. The leaders' decision not to arrest Jesus during the feast is of no avail since Jesus has predicted that he will die during the feast. The religious leaders can conspire, but God will determine the order of events.

Matthew identifies the religious leaders as the chief priests and the elders of the people. The latter represent the lay leadership within the Sanhedrin. Their introduction at this point may be Matthew's way of preparing for the guilt of the people which comes to a climax at the trial before Pilate (27:25).[2] The contrast between Jesus and the religious leaders could not be more striking. He deliberately and courageously faces his death. Filled with fear, they secretly plan to arrest him by stealth.

B. Anointed for Burial (26:6–13)

As in Mark's Gospel, the anointing at Bethany follows the plot to destroy Jesus. Matthew, however, abbreviates the story and highlights Jesus' divine foreknowledge. Whereas Mark says that ''some'' were indignant that the woman wasted the expensive ointment, Matthew identifies them as the disciples: ''But when the disciples saw it, they were indignant, saying, 'Why this waste?' '' On first appearance the disciples' behavior is confusing since Matthew usually presents them as those who understand.[3] But in this instance, the disciples' ignorance serves as a twofold foil. First, it indicates that only this anonymous woman comprehends that Jesus is about to die. Thus Jesus interprets her action as an anointing for burial. Her action is especially significant since the women will not come on Easter Sunday with the intention to anoint Jesus' body as they do in Mark's Gospel (cf. Mt 28:1 with Mk 16:1). Second, the incident highlights Jesus' majesty and clairvoyance.[4] Thus Matthew reports that Jesus was aware of their indignation even though the disciples only speak among themselves.

Jesus promises that because of her action, ''wherever this Gospel is preached in the whole world, what she has done will be told in memory of her.'' Matthew does not employ the noun ''Gospel'' as often as Mark does. But in the three occurrences previous to this, he associates the Gospel with the kingdom (4:23; 9:35; 24:14). ''The Gospel of the kingdom'' is another stock Matthean phrase. It is ''the news about the kingdom, which saves or condemns, that is revealed in and through Jesus Messiah, the Son of God, and is announced first to Israel and then to the Gentiles."[5] In this report, however, Matthew departs from that formula and refers to "this Gospel." The expression, of course, does not exclude the dimension of the kingdom, but it does place greater emphasis upon that aspect of the Jesus story which narrates the events of the passion.[6] The good news of the Gospel contains both the announcement of the kingdom and the saving events of Jesus' passion and death.

As in Mark's story, the phrase "for you always have the poor with you" (26:11) is not meant to discourage Christians from alleviating poverty.[7] In fact, no other Gospel is so concerned about doing good deeds. Rather, Matthew employs the phrase to emphasize the urgency of the moment. Such an extravagant manifestation of love is appropriate because Jesus will soon depart. The very structure of the saying shows this.

For *you always have the poor* with you,
but *you will not always have me.*

The point of the saying is to emphasize Jesus' imminent departure.

C. Judas' Betrayal (26:14–16)

Once more Matthew makes use of the adverb *tote* ("then"). Having described the anointing of Jesus at Bethany, he begins this section, "*Then* one of the twelve, who was called Judas Iscariot, went to the chief priests." The adverb effectively draws a relationship between the two incidents. Since Jesus' body has been anointed for burial, Judas now goes to betray his Lord.

The Matthean passion narrative gives more attention to the role of Judas than Mark's. At the Last Supper Judas asks if he is the betrayer (26:25) and Matthew describes his suicide (27:3–10) after Jesus' condemnation. In this incident the evangelist draws a double contrast between the behavior of Judas and that of the anonymous woman and Jesus. While the woman prepares Jesus' body for burial, Judas prepares to betray him. And while Jesus manifests a disregard for money, Judas sets a price for his treacherous activity: "What will you give me if I deliver him to you?"

Like all of the evangelists, Matthew sees the enormity of Judas' crime in light of his relationship to Jesus. Judas is one of the twelve. But Matthew compounds Judas' guilt by having the betrayer bargain with the chief priests. For Matthew and his readers the scene must have evoked bitter irony: the leaders of Israel barter for the betrayal of their Messiah.

The price agreed upon, thirty pieces of silver, alludes to Old Testament texts. In Zechariah 11:7–14, the prophet becomes the shepherd of his people who are doomed for destruction. At the end of his service, the wicked leaders pay him an insulting wage, the paltry sum of thirty pieces of silver. Thirty shekels of silver, according to Exodus 21:32, was the sum that the owner of an ox had to give to the master of a slave if the ox gored either a male or a female slave. So Matthew emphasizes that Judas betrays Jesus for an insignificant and mean sum. By mentioning the silver here, Matthew prepares for 27:3–10 when Judas returns the blood money to the leaders.

II.
THE PASSOVER SUPPER, 26:17–29

This section is composed of three scenes: preparations for the Passover meal, the prediction of Judas' betrayal, and the institution of the Eucharist. Although Matthew closely follows Mark, he makes slight editorial revisions in order to sharpen the portrait of Jesus. In the first scene, he emphasizes Jesus as the one who orders his disciples to prepare the meal. In the second, he stresses that Jesus knows his betrayer. And in the third, he transforms Mark's narration of the cup into a command of the Lord. In these and other ways, Matthew heightens Mark's Christological portrait of Jesus.

A. *Preparations for the Supper (26:17–19)*

Matthew abbreviates Mark by eliminating certain details such as the man with the water jar, the description of the upper room, and the remark that the disciples found everything as Jesus said (cf. Mk 14:13,15,16). By doing this, he achieves a more polished narrative which focuses upon *Jesus*[8] as the one who commands and the disciples as the ones who obey.

The narrative begins with the disciples asking Jesus, ''Where will you have us prepare *for you* to eat the passover?'' The emphasis (''for you'') clarifies that this is Jesus' Passover, and that it holds a unique significance for him.[9] In response to their question, he sends his disciples into the city with a message to an anonymous figure, ''My time is at hand; I will keep the passover at your house with my disciples.'' The time (*ho kairos*) refers ''to the critical moment of Jesus' passion.''[10] It is not just any hour, but the hour toward which his entire life has been directed. Thus the demons ask Jesus, during the first part of his ministry, ''What have you to do with us, O Son of God? Have you come here to torment us before the time?'' (8:29). And in the parable of the vineyard, an allegorical tale of Jesus' ministry, he says, ''When the time [RSV reads season] of fruit drew near, he sent his servants to the tenants, to get his fruit'' (21:34). The *kairos* is the time of Jesus' ministry which comes to its climax in the passion. There is a note of irony here. As Jesus tells his disciples that his time (*kairos*) is near, Judas looks for the opportune time (*eukairian*) to betray him (26:16).

At the end of this scene Matthew remarks, ''And the disciples did *as Jesus had directed them,* and they prepared the passover.'' The comment is a revision of Mark's statement, ''And the disciples set out and went to the city, and found it as he had told them; and they prepared the passover'' (Mk 14:16). Matthew emphasizes an important element in the relationship between Jesus and his disciples, a component of discipleship found throughout the Gospel. It is Jesus who summons, dispatches, commands, and teaches. It is the disciples who follow, go, obey, and heed.[11]

B. The Betrayer Foretold (26:20–25)

Matthew carefully follows his Marcan source in narrating the prediction of the betrayer. But in order to highlight Jesus' divine knowledge, he introduces a new incident. After all of the disciples have asked Jesus, ''Is it I, *Lord*?'' Judas says, ''Is it I, *Master*?'' to which Jesus replies, ''You have said so.'' It is the same answer that Jesus gives to the high priest who questions him about his messiahship (26:64) and to Pilate who interrogates him about his kingship (27:11). This ambiguous phrase places the burden upon the questioner.[12] He condemns himself by his own speech. The whole incident, of course, is calculated to manifest Jesus' foreknowledge. Not only does he predict his betrayal, he knows who will betray him and does nothing to stop him.

The different ways in which Judas and the other disciples address

Jesus is striking and has significance for Matthew's Christology. The disciples correctly address Jesus as Lord (*Kyrios*) because they recognize the divine power which resides in him as the Son of God and the Son of Man.[13] For example, at the stilling of the storm the disciples cry out, "Save, Lord; we are perishing" (8:25). After a sabbath controversy, Jesus declares to the Pharisees, "For the Son of Man is Lord of the sabbath" (12:8). Although the disciples do not completely understand Jesus, and although they will temporally abandon him, they acknowledge that divine authority resides in him.

Judas, by contrast, no longer addresses Jesus as Lord; he calls him Rabbi. In Matthew's Christology, Rabbi is synonymous with Teacher (*didaskalos*), the ordinary and polite form of address employed by a host of people, including Jesus' opponents (8:19; 22:16,24,36). In sum, Teacher and Rabbi are terms of human respect, but they do not include Jesus' authority as the heavenly *kyrios*. It is appropriate, therefore, that at the announcement of the betrayal, Judas employs Rabbi rather than Lord.[14]

C. The Eucharist (26:26–29)

One might expect the institution of the Eucharist to precede the announcement of the betrayer, thereby heightening the dramatic effect of the announcement. Luke has reversed the order of events (Lk 22:14–23), thereby achieving a more dramatic narrative logic. But Matthew preserves the Marcan order, perhaps because he is more interested in handing on the Eucharistic tradition than in achieving dramatic effect.

The accounts of Matthew and Mark represent one Eucharistic tradition while those of Luke (22:14–20) and Paul (1 Cor 11:23–26) preserve another.[15] In repeating Mark's account, Matthew only makes slight changes, and these result in an even more liturgical text which probably represents how Matthew's Church celebrated the sacrament.

In accordance with his Christological and ecclesiological interests, Matthew underlines the role of Jesus and the disciples. At the beginning of the account, he replaces Mark's pronoun "he" with the proper name "Jesus" ("Now as they were eating, Jesus took bread. . ."). And at the close of the story, he replaces Mark's "kingdom of God" with "in my Father's kingdom." For Matthew, Jesus is preeminently the Son of God.

And more often than Mark, the first evangelist has Jesus refer to God as his Father.[16]

Matthew emphasizes the role of the disciples because they represent the Church. In v. 26 he replaces Mark's pronoun "them" with the noun "disciples" ("Jesus took bread . . . and gave it to the disciples"). To Jesus' declaration that he will not drink wine again until he drinks it in the kingdom of his Father (26:29), Matthew inserts "with you" ("I tell you I shall not drink again of this fruit of the vine until that day when I drink it new *with you* in my Father's kingdom"). In this way the Lord promises that the disciples will share in his final victory. The promise establishes a relationship between the Eucharist which Matthew's Church celebrates and the messianic banquet that is reserved for the kingdom of God.

Matthew makes two other contributions to the Eucharistic narrative. First, whereas Mark narrates the drinking of the cup ("and they all drank of it"), Matthew transforms the narrative into a command ("*Drink of it,* all of you"). As a result, the text is more liturgical in character. Second, he explains the significance of Jesus' death by adding "for the forgiveness of sins" to the words over the cup.

This explanation of Jesus' death ("for the forgiveness of sins") is related to the whole of Jesus' destiny. At the birth of Jesus, the angel instructs Joseph to name him Jesus, "for he will save his people from their sins" (1:21). And Jesus, after his third passion prediction, explains that he comes as the Son of Man "not to be served but to serve, and to give his life as a ransom for many" (20:28). Most commentators note that whereas Mark describes the baptism of John as "a baptism of repentance *for the forgiveness of sins*" (Mk 1:4), Matthew simply says, "In those days came John the Baptist, preaching in the wilderness of Judea" (Mt 3:1). Matthew preserves the uniqueness of Jesus' ministry and death by reserving the forgiveness of sins to Jesus.

As in Mark, the "blood of the covenant" alludes to Exodus 24:8 and the covenant God established at Sinai with Israel. But the expression "for the forgiveness of sins" adds a new element by alluding to Jeremiah 31:31–34, a prophetic oracle in which God promises to establish a *new* covenant with Israel and forgive her sins ("for I will forgive their iniquity, and I will remember their sin no more"—Jer 31:34).[17] Matthew looks upon Jesus' death as a new covenant in which sins are forgiven.

III.
AT THE MOUNT OF OLIVES, 26:30–56

The setting changes to the Mount of Olives, and Matthew describes the events in three scenes: the prediction of Peter's betrayal, Jesus' prayer in the garden of Gethsemane, and the arrest. As in the earlier portion of the narrative, the evangelist focuses upon Jesus' person and his disciples. In the prediction of Peter's denial, Matthew concentrates upon the relationship between master and disciples. In the description of Jesus' prayer, he provides the Church with a model of prayer in time of trial and persecution. And in the account of Jesus' arrest, the evangelist demonstrates Jesus' sovereign freedom as he enters his passion.

A. Peter's Denial Predicted (26:30–35)

In this scene Matthew adheres closely to his Marcan source. But the minor alterations that he does introduce heighten the bond between Jesus and his disciples.

As in Mark, Matthew quotes from Zechariah 13:7 that the shepherd will be struck and the sheep will be scattered. But Matthew also inserts the phrase "of the flock," thereby emphasizing that the sheep, his disciples, belong to the flock, his Church ("I will strike the shepherd and the sheep *of the flock* will be scattered"). This seemingly minor addition is part of the larger Matthean fabric which, throughout the Gospel, stresses the bond between Jesus and his disciples.

When Matthew reports Jesus' prediction that all of the disciples will fall away, he adds the phrase "because of me," *en emoi* ("You will fall away *because of me*"—literally, be scandalized in me). And when he narrates Peter's reply to Jesus, he inserts a similar phrase "because of you," *en soi* ("Though they all fall away *because of you*"—literally, be scandalized in you). Although these appear to be minor editorial changes, they manifest major Matthean concerns: the relationship between Jesus and his disciples and the danger of falling away: being scandalized at Jesus' messiahship.

Matthew emphasizes the bond between Jesus and his disciples by the phrase "because of me" (*en emoi*) and warns of the danger involved in denying Jesus or being scandalized by him. In the missionary discourse (10:1–11:1), for example, Jesus says, "So every one who acknowledges me (*en emoi*) before men, I also will acknowledge before my Father who is in heaven; but whoever denies me before men, I also will deny before my Father who is in heaven'' (10:32–33). Likewise, after speaking to the messengers of John the Baptist, Jesus says, ''And blessed is he who takes no offense at me (*en emoi*)'' (11:6).

Disciples have a special relationship to Jesus because he has called them to ''follow me'' (8:22; 9:9; 16:24; 19:21). This relationship is so close that he identifies himself with disciples when others persecute them (25:45). Therefore Jesus can require a love which surpasses the affection for father, mother, son and daughter (10:37). He can even ask disciples to deny their very selves, take up their cross and follow him (16:24).

The great danger to discipleship, however, is to be scandalized at Jesus, that is, to stumble in face of his messiahship which is characterized by meekness, gentleness, suffering, and supreme freedom before the Mosaic law. So the Pharisees are scandalized (RSV reads ''were offended'') at Jesus' teaching about clean and unclean (15:12). The people of Nazareth are scandalized (RSV reads ''took offense'') at him (13:57). And Jesus says that many will be scandalized (RSV reads ''fall away'') at the moment of tribulation or persecution (13:21; 24:10).

When Jesus says to the disciples, ''You will all be scandalized (RSV reads ''fall away'') because of me,'' the reader needs to understand the theological background of the remark. Peter and the disciples will be scandalized at Jesus because they do not comprehend that as Messiah he must suffer. Instead of denying himself (see 16:24), Peter will deny Jesus.

B. Jesus in Gethsemane (26:36–46)

Although Matthew follows Mark's tripartite structure by which Jesus goes off to pray three times, some authors note a subtle shift of emphasis in Matthew's narrative. Whereas Mark stresses Jesus' triple return to the disciples only to find them asleep, Matthew seems more interested in the three occasions Jesus goes off to pray to his Father.[18] Thus three times Mark mentions that Jesus returns to his disciples (14:37,40,41) but only two times that he goes off to pray (14:35,39). By contrast, Matthew notes that Jesus goes off to pray three times (26:39,42,44). The result of this shift in emphasis is that Matthew's presentation of Jesus becomes a catechesis on prayer for the Church represented by the disciples.

With a view to this catechesis, Matthew again heightens the role of the disciples. He notes that Jesus comes *with them* to Gethsemane. There, he encourages them to watch *with him* (26:38,40). And when Jesus returns a second time, Matthew makes explicit, what Mark does not, that Jesus returns to the disciples (26:40). These seemingly minor changes are important for Matthew because he views Jesus' prayer as a model for the Church.

Because Jesus serves as a model for the Church, Matthew slightly alters Mark's presentation. The emphasis is not so much upon the agony of Jesus, although the struggle is still present, as it is upon his conformity to God's will. Mark portrays the struggle of Jesus by describing his distress (14:33), his falling on the ground and request that the hour might pass from him (14:35). But Matthew softens the agony by speaking of sorrow rather than distress (26:37), and by saying that Jesus fell on his face, the reverential Jewish posture of prostration,[19] rather than on the ground (26:39). Finally, as if to avoid any misunderstanding, Matthew eliminates Jesus' request that the hour might pass.

The prayer of Jesus is more developed in Matthew than in Mark. Jesus' first prayer is couched in language which is even more attentive to God's will than that found in Mark. "My Father, if it be possible, let this cup pass from me," instead of "Abba, Father, all things are possible to thee; *remove this cup* from me." At Jesus' second prayer, Mark says, "And again he went away and prayed, saying the same words" (Mk 14:39). But Matthew reports the prayer, "My Father, if this cannot pass unless I drink it, *thy will be done.*" The final phrase, of course, is an allusion to Jesus' own prayer which he taught the disciples (6:10). David Stanley notes that this second prayer "underlines the fact that Jesus has now reached total acceptance of the Father's design."[20]

Matthew's Gethsemane narrative should be read in light of his Gospel teaching on prayer.[21] Like Mark, he presents Jesus praying before the feeding of the five thousand (14:19) and the four thousand (15:36). Likewise Jesus prays after the first feeding story (14:23). But unlike Mark, Matthew reports Jesus' intimate prayer with the Father (11:25–26) and his extensive teaching on prayer in the Sermon on the Mount (6:5–15). Jesus' prayer in Gethsemane is the logical outcome of his intimate relationship with the Father and his teaching on prayer.

He prays at the hour of his passion because of the intimate relationship he enjoys with the Father: "All things have been delivered to me by my Father; and no one knows the Son except the Father, and no one knows the Father except the Son and any one to whom the Son chooses to reveal him'' (11:27). Jesus' prayer at Gethsemane is also the outcome of his teaching in the Sermon on the Mount. In that sermon Jesus calls his disciples to greater righteousness (5:20) and teaches them how to fulfill the three Jewish works of piety or righteousness: almsgiving, prayer, and fasting (6:1–18). Jesus' own prayer in Gethsemane testifies that he is the righteous one who accomplishes God's will. He does not pray in order to be seen (6:5–6). He does not pray by heaping up empty phrases (6:7–8). He prays just as he taught his disciples; he seeks God's kingdom and God's will (6:9–13).

C. Jesus' Arrest (26:47–56)

Donald Senior notes that with this scene Matthew brings the first major section of his passion narrative to a close.[22] Although Jesus could command the forces of twelve legions of angels, he freely and willingly submits to arrest in order to fulfill the Scriptures. The arrest scene is the last in which Jesus is with his disciples until after the resurrection. Scandalized by their Master's capture, the disciples flee.

Judas leads the arresting party, commissioned by the chief priests and elders of the people, the same group which originally devised the plot against Jesus (26:3). Matthew's description of the elders as the elders *of the people* is consistent with 26:3 and continues his preparation for the cry of responsibility which the people will make before Pilate (27:25). As at the Passover meal, Judas addresses Jesus as Rabbi, thereby showing that he no longer is Jesus' disciple. At the moment of arrest one of Jesus' disciples (Mark only identifies him as a bystander) tries to defend his Lord. Although Jesus' followers flee, they remain his disciples.

Matthew's most important contribution to the narrative is in terms of Christology. Through a series of additions and alterations he shows that Jesus maintains a sovereign composure even at the moment of arrest. The arrest occurs not only because of Judas' betrayal but because of Jesus' desire to fulfill the Scriptures.

Matthew portrays the encounter between Jesus and Judas in such a way as to focus upon the distance between the two characters and to show Jesus' control of the situation. At Judas' greeting, Jesus addresses him with the polite but decidedly cold response "friend" (*etaire*). It is the same address used by the master of the vineyard when speaking to the disgruntled worker (20:13), and by the king who encounters a guest at his banquet without the proper wedding garment (22:12). So Judas is cast as one who is not worthy of the kingdom of God.

The rest of Jesus' reply presents a difficulty of translation. The RSV renders the Greek phrase *eph ho parei* as a question: "why are you here?" But the text might also be interpreted "do what you are here to do" (New English Bible). The latter translation focuses upon Jesus' command of the situation. It implies that he grants Judas permission to hand him over. Immediately after these words, the arresting party seizes Jesus. Given Matthew's concern to present Jesus as being in control of the situation, it appears to be the better choice.[23]

When one of Jesus' own disciples tries to defend him with a sword, Jesus orders him to desist. Jesus' words to the disciple (26:52–54) are peculiar to Matthew and make three points. First, Jesus refuses to save himself by violence. The sword (*machaira*) symbolizes the power of the Roman state (Rom 13:4).[24] To resort to it at this moment would only invite violent reprisal. Instead, Jesus follows his own counsel for righteous behavior given at the Sermon on the Mount. "Do not resist one who is evil. But if anyone strikes you on the right cheek, turn to him the other also; and if any one would sue you and take your coat, let him have your cloak as well" (5:39–40).

The second point is related to the first. Jesus has no need to be defended by his disciples. If he wishes, his Father will send him twelve legions of angels. Did not the Father send angels to minister to him after Satan's temptations in the wilderness (4:11)? But just as Jesus refused to seek angelic help during those temptations (4:6–7), so he will not ask for angelic assistance at this moment.

The third point explains both the first and the second. Jesus does not resist, and he does not call for angelic aid because the Scriptures must be fulfilled. The fulfillment of Scripture is a major Matthean concern, and at the end of this section Matthew returns to it (26:56). Throughout the Gospel he introduces a number of Old Testament quotations to demonstrate that the events of Jesus' life correspond to the fulfillment of Old Testament prophecy. Such and such an event happened in order to fulfill what was spoken through the prophet (1:22–23; 2:5–6,15,17–18,23; 4:14–16; 8:17; 12:17–21; 13:14–15,35; 21:4–5; 27:9–10). While these quotations occur throughout the Gospel, the majority are found in the infancy narrative, and there is only one in the passion narrative. This is surprising, given Matthew's concern to show the correspondence between prophecy and fulfillment in Jesus' life. But John Meier is probably correct when he writes: "The reason for the omission of formula quotations in the passion seems to be that Mt conceives of the death-resurrection of Jesus as one great eschatological event which fulfills not this or that prophecy, but all prophecy."[25]

Having explained why he does not accept his disciples' defense, Jesus addresses the arresting party. He reminds them that he *sat* daily *in the temple,* and they did not try to arrest him. Only Matthew includes the detail of Jesus sitting in the temple. It corresponds with his Christological portrait of Jesus, the Teacher of his Church, The sitting position emphasizes Jesus' teaching authority (5:1; 13:1; 15:29).[26]

Jesus explains why the arresting party treats him as a robber. It is the fulfillment of Scripture. "But all this has taken place, that the Scriptures *of the prophets* might be fulfilled" (26:56). Once more Matthew shows his concern for scriptural fulfillment. But whereas Mark speaks of the fulfillment of the Scriptures, Matthew refers to the Scriptures of the prophets. The phrase recalls the several fulfillment quotations which punctuate Matthew's narrative and indicates that for Matthew all Scripture finds its fulfillment in Jesus.

Then, the disciples abandoned Jesus. Matthew's *tote* ("then") has the effect of relating the disciples' flight to Jesus' words. First, Jesus says that all of this had to take place in order to fulfill the Scriptures; *then* the disciples abandon him. The flight of the disciples is more than human failure; it is part of God's divine plan for his Messiah.

IV.
THE TRIAL BEFORE THE SANHEDRIN, 26:57–68

As in Mark, Jesus' arrest in Gethsemane leads to his trial before the Jewish high council, the Sanhedrin. The scene consists of three parts: the trial; the mockery of Jesus; Peter's denial. Once more the order of events is the same as that found in Mark. Matthew does not make major alterations, but the editorial changes he does initiate serve to strengthen his Christological portrait of Jesus. For example, at the trial Matthew emphasizes Jesus' power to destroy the temple, and in the mockery he introduces the title Messiah in order to highlight Jesus' person. In addition to these Christologically motivated alterations, Matthew portrays Jesus as the righteous one who observes his own admonitions for righteous behavior. Therefore, when the high priest tries to place Jesus under oath, Jesus refuses to answer directly. By contrast, Peter does place himself under oath and denies his Master.

A. The Jewish Trial (26:57–66)

The scene opens with the arresting party leading Jesus to the high priest whom Matthew, unlike Mark, identifies as Caiaphas. The scribes and elders assemble at the home of Caiaphas where it appears that the chief priests are already present. Jesus stands before the entire Jewish council: the chief priests, the scribes, and the elders.

Peter follows Jesus at a distance "to see the end" (26:58). The Greek work for end (*telos*) has a double meaning. On the one hand it refers to the death of the Lord. But on the other, it includes the broader notion of Jesus' destiny, the goal (*telos*) of his life. In witnessing Jesus' death, Peter witnesses the goal toward which Jesus' entire life has been directed.

From the outset, Matthew highlights the illegitimacy of the trial. Whereas Mark writes "the whole council sought testimony against Jesus to put him to death" (14:55), Matthew notes "the whole council sought *false* testimony against Jesus that they might put him to death" (26:59). Both Mark and Matthew agree that many false witnesses came forward. When the decisive witnesses testify that Jesus threatened to destroy the temple, however, the evangelists report the testimony differently. Mark states that their witness did not agree, thereby implying that it is false. But Matthew says, "At last two came forward and said, 'This fellow said, I am able to destroy the temple of God, and to build it in three days.' " The witness of two who agree implies that the testimony is true.[27] But Matthew understands the truth of their testimony in an ironic fashion. Jesus *is able* to destroy the temple and rebuild it, even though he will not physically destroy and build it as the witnesses suggest. The point is Christological. It agrees with another important statement in the Gospel, "I tell you, something greater than the temple is here" (12:6).[28]

On the basis of this testimony, the high priest places Jesus under oath, saying, "I adjure you by the *living God,* tell us if you are the *Christ, the Son of God*" (26:62). The high priest's question unwittingly takes up the language of Peter's confession at Caesarea Philippi: "You are the *Christ,* the *Son of the living God*" (16:16). But whereas Peter makes his declaration in faith, the high priest poses his question in utter disbelief.[29] Because of this, and because the high priest places him under oath, Jesus does not answer directly. Whereas Mark reports Jesus' response, "I am," Matthew has Jesus say, "You have said so," the same reply given to Judas (26:25). Jesus cannot answer Caiaphas directly since the high priest has a different understanding of messiahship (see 22:41–45). Furthermore, in the Sermon on the Mount, Jesus forbade his disciples to take oaths (5:33–37), and in his woes against the Pharisees he condemned their prescriptions for oath-taking (23:16–22). Jesus circumvents the high priest's oath, therefore, by his evasive answer.

Next Jesus utters his Son of Man prophecy: "*But I tell you, hereafter* you will see the Son of Man seated at the right hand of Power, and coming on the clouds of heaven." Except for the introduction, the prophecy is essentially the same as that found in Mark.[30] The introductory words, "But I tell you hereafter" (*plēn legō hymin ap' arti,*) imply that "the heavenly session is to start immediately."[31] Jesus' reign as the Son of Man will begin with his resurrection.[32]

As in Mark, the Son of Man plays an important role in Matthew's Gospel.[33] Son of Man is Jesus' way of identifying himself. It describes his activity as a human being (8:20; 11:19), his power to forgive sins (9:6), his authority over the sabbath (12:8), and his destiny of suffering and death (12:40; 17:9,12,22; 20:18,28; 26:2). But most importantly it describes Jesus' future activity as one who reigns in glory. Thus all of the Son of Man sayings which are peculiar to Matthew point to Jesus' activity between the resurrection and the parousia. The disciples will not have gone through all of the towns of Israel before the Son of Man returns (10:23). The Son of Man will send his angels to separate the good from the bad at the end of time (13:36–43). The Son of Man will sit upon a glorious throne and his disciples will judge the twelve tribes of Israel (19:28). Immediately before the parousia, the Son of Man will appear in the heavens (24:30). And at the close of the ages the Son of Man will judge the nations (25:31–46).[34]

Jesus' prophecy to the high priest implies that, as the Son of Man, he will judge those who judge him. The high priest understands this and declares, "He has uttered blasphemy." Matthew is more precise than Mark at this point, and makes it clear that Jesus' blasphemy consists in the Son of Man saying. The other members of the Sanhedrin concur, "He deserves death." But the final decision to put Jesus to death is not taken until the morning (27:1–2; cf. Mk 14:64).

B. The Ridiculed Messiah (26:67–68)

Because of Jesus' Son of Man prophecy, the members of the Sanhedrin mock him as a false prophet. In their mockery, they address him as "Christ," an element not found in Mark's account. Jesus has predicted that he will return as the Son of Man, but the members of the high council mock that he cannot even prophesy who has struck him.

The introduction of the title Messiah is in line with Matthew's wider Christology which accents Jesus' Davidic messiahship. Matthew begins his Gospel with a genealogy which traces Jesus' origin to Abraham through David and identifies him as the Messiah (1:1–17). At the arrival of the magi, Herod assembles the chief priests and scribes to discover where the Messiah is to be born (2:4). John the Baptist inquires if Jesus is the Messiah (11:2). And Peter confesses that Jesus is the Messiah, the Son of the living God (16:16). By employing the title at this point, Matthew informs the reader that the real issue at the trial is Jesus' messianic dignity.[35] The Romans will put Jesus to death as a political insurgent, but the Sanhedrin rejects his claim to be Israel's Messiah.

The scene is ironic since not only is Jesus the Messiah, but his prophecies will come true. He will return as the Son of Man to judge his judges, and at this very moment one of his prophecies (Peter's denial) is coming to completion.

C. Peter's Denial (26:69–79)

The account of Peter's denial is not significantly different from that found in Mark. The changes Matthew makes serve to accent the story's dramatic effect. The accusations of the maids and bystanders identify Peter as one who was *with* Jesus. The preposition "with" underlines Peter's chosen role as one of Jesus' disciples. Peter's replies grow in forcefulness. First he says, "I do not know what you mean." Next he denies *with an oath,* "I do not know the man," Finally, he invokes a curse and *swears,* "I do not know the man." Peter's use of an oath contravenes Jesus' injunction given in the Sermon on the Mount (5:33–37) and contrasts with Jesus' behavior when the high priest tries to place him under oath.

To appreciate the full force of Peter's denial it is important to review his role in Matthew's story where he is, after Jesus, the major character and the chief spokesman for the disciples. Peter, along with Andrew, James and John, is among the first disciples called by Jesus (4:18–22). He is one of the twelve apostles (10:2), and during Jesus' great cycle of miracles (8:1—9:38), Jesus heals his mother-in-law (8:14–15). When Jesus walks on the water, it is Peter who goes to Jesus (14:28–33). At Caesarea Philippi he confesses that Jesus is the Messiah, the Son of the living God (16:16), after which Jesus promises him the keys of the kingdom and the power to bind and loose (16:17–19). On several occasions Peter acts as spokesman for the disciples (15:15; 18:21; 19:27), and he enjoys a special relationship with Jesus which makes him one of the three witnesses to the transfiguration (17:1–8) and the one to pay the temple tax on behalf of his Master (17:24–27). But the same Peter who is so favored is not without fault. While walking on the water he loses faith (14:30–31), and after Jesus' first passion prediction he rebukes his Lord (16:22).

Matthew introduces a cycle of Peter stories not found in Mark (14:28–33; 16:17–19; 17:24–27; 18:21–22) which secure Peter's position as the chief apostle and spokesman of the twelve. Precisely because of this, Peter's denial takes on greater meaning in Matthew's Gospel. It is the same story as that found in Mark, but now it is the rock foundation of the Church, the one who walked on water, who denies his master. Just as a new setting alters the appearance of an old diamond, so a different literary context gives new meaning to an old story.

V.
THE TRIAL BEFORE PILATE, 27:1–26

The trial before Pilate constitutes a major part of Matthew's passion narrative and reveals some of his most significant editorial work. It reports the fate of Judas, the intervention of Pilate's wife, Pilate's hand washing, and the people's cry. Throughout the section the word "blood" ties the various incidents together. Judas admits that he has betrayed innocent blood; the chief priests refer to the thirty pieces of silver as blood money and purchase a field called the Field of Blood; Pilate declares that he is innocent of Jesus' blood; the people call down Jesus' blood upon themselves and their children. In addition to this theme, Matthew pursues his Christological interests by replacing some of Mark's references to Jesus as the King of the Jews with the title Messiah, and by making a more explicit comparison between Jesus and Barabbas. The material may be divided into three scenes: Jesus is delivered to Pilate; Judas despairs; Jesus stands before Pilate.

A. Jesus Delivered to Pilate (27:1–2)

The formal conclusion to the Jewish trial does not occur until these verses. They do not necessarily imply a second trial held in the morning. Rather, they suggest that the night trial continued until early morning, at which time the chief priests and elders of the people formed a plot (*symboulion elabon*) to put Jesus to death. The Greek expression is the same employed in 12:14 and 22:15 when the Pharisees plot against Jesus. It is used again in 27:7 when the priests decide what to do with Judas' thirty pieces of silver. Matthew gives the impression that after a period of consultation, the religious leaders devise a scheme whereby they can present Jesus to Pilate and be assured of his death. Their decision serves as the formal conclusion to Matthew's version of the Jewish trial.

Having formed their plan, the chief priests and elders lead (*apēgagon*) Jesus to Pilate. The Greek word for lead is the same as that in 26:57 and 27:31. So Matthew describes a movement whereby the arresting party *leads* Jesus to Caiaphas (26:57). The religious leaders *lead* Jesus to Pilate (27:2), and the soldiers *lead* Jesus to crucifixion (27:31). The entire process fulfills Jesus' third passion prediction: "the Son of Man will be delivered to the chief priests and scribes, and they will condemn him to death, and deliver him to the Gentiles to be mocked and scourged and crucified. . ." (20:18–19).

In this scene, and throughout the rest of the narrative, Matthew refers to Pilate as the governor (27:2,11,14,15,21,27; 28:14), thereby emphasizing his military and political power. The title recalls Jesus' earlier warning to his disciples, "you will be dragged before *governors* and kings for my sake, to bear testimony before them and the Gentiles" (10:18). Jesus' passion indicates what will happen to his followers.

B. Judas' Death (27:3–10)

Matthew's is the only passion narrative to give an account of Judas' fate. In the Acts of the Apostles, Luke reports a version of Judas' death in which the betrayer, after having bought a field, falls headlong so that "his bowels gushed out" (Acts 1:18–19). The common element between the two accounts is the reference to a field which became known as Field of Blood. It may well be that both Matthew and Luke were aware of a tradition which related a certain field to Judas' fate and, because of that fact, was given the name Field of Blood. The two stories are significantly different, however, and it is unlikely that one is dependent upon the other. It is more probable, as Donald Senior maintains, that the Matthean version is Matthew's own composition.[36]

The story has two parts. In the first (27:3–5), Judas returns the thirty silver pieces to the chief priests and then hangs himself, as did Ahithophel, the counselor who betrayed King David (2 Sam 17:23). In the second (27:6–10), the chief priests use the money to purchase a burial field for strangers and unwittingly fulfill a prophecy from Scripture.

The story opens with a double entendre: "When Judas, his betrayer, saw that *he was condemned,* he repented." "He was condemned" refers to Jesus, but it could also include Judas. Judas sees that *he* is condemned! Although the English translation says that he repented, the Greek does not employ the standard word for repent (*metanoein*). Instead, Matthew uses another word (*metamelomai*) which also has the sense of feeling regret or changing one's mind. It is unlikely that Matthew envisions a deep religious conversion on Judas' part. Nonetheless, Judas recognizes that he has betrayed innocent blood and becomes a witness to Jesus' innocence. He returns the thirty pieces of silver to the chief priests and elders, the two groups whom Matthew consistently portrays as Jesus' enemies in the passion narrative.

The priests take the money but do not put it into the temple treasury since even they admit that it is blood money, thereby acknowledging Jesus' innocence. After consultation, they decide to buy a field in which to bury strangers. They designate the unclean money for a burial place to accommodate unclean persons. Thus Matthew explains the name of the field as Field of Blood. He then notes that the purchase of the field fulfills another scriptural prophecy, thereby proving Jesus' messiahship.

> Then was fulfilled what had been spoken by the prophet Jer-
> emiah, saying, "And they took the thirty pieces of silver, the
> price of him on whom a price had been set by some of the sons
> of Israel, and they gave them for the potter's field, as the Lord
> directed me."

The scriptural text is notoriously difficult to identify since it does not
correspond exactly to any Old Testament text. The bulk of the text comes
from Zechariah 11:13 rather than any known text of Jeremiah: "So I took
the thirty shekels of silver and cast them into the treasury in the house
of the Lord." Since the text of Matthew speaks of a potter's field rather
than the temple treasury, most scholars look for references to a potter
and to a field in Jeremiah. Such references are found in Jeremiah 18:2–
4, 19:1–11, and 32:7–8. Although the exact process remains a puzzle,
it appears that Matthew combined the text of Zechariah 11:13 with elements from different texts of Jeremiah, especially Jeremiah 19:1–11.

> Thus said the Lord, "Go, buy a potter's earthen flask, and take
> some of the elders of the people and some of the senior priests,
> and go out to the valley of the son of Hinnom at the entry of
> the Potsherd Gate and proclaim the words that I tell you. . . .
> Because the people have forsaken me . . .
> and because they have filled this place with the blood of
>   innocents . . .
> therefore, behold, the days are coming, says the Lord,
> when this place shall no more be called Topheth,
> or the valley of the son of Hinnom,
> but the valley of Slaughter. . . .
> And I will make this city a horror,
> a thing to be hissed at. . . .
> Then you shall break the flask in the sight of the men who go
> with you, and shall say to them, "Thus says the Lord of hosts:
> So will I break this people and this city, as one breaks a potter's
> vessel, so that it can never be mended. Men shall bury in To-
> pheth because there will be no place else to bury."

Douglas Moo notes that in this last text Jeremiah prophesies that a lo-
cality associated with potters is renamed by a phrase connoting violence

and used as a burial place. It becomes a token of God's judgment upon Jerusalem.[37] The Field of Blood, purchased with Judas' blood money, serves as a reminder that Jerusalem crucified her Messiah.

But why does Matthew ascribe the text to Jeremiah? There may be a clue in the infancy narrative, the only other place where he attributes a quotation to this prophet. After the slaying of the innocents, Matthew writes, "then was fulfilled what was spoken by the prophet Jeremiah: 'A voice was heard in Ramah, wailing and loud lamentation, Rachel weeping for her children; she refused to be consoled, because they were no more' " (2:17–18). This text, like the first, points to the violence and hostility which the Messiah encounters.[38] Herod slaughters innocent blood in order to destroy the Infant King of the Jews. The religious leaders take blood money, earned by the Messiah's betrayal, and buy a potter's field. Perhaps Matthew ascribes the text of 27:9–10 to Jeremiah because he views this prophet as the one who foretells the violence and opposition the Messiah must encounter. Such a suggestion is probable since Jeremiah was, like Jesus, a persecuted prophet.

C. Jesus Before Pilate (27:11–26)

Although Matthew follows Mark's basic structure, he has significantly edited this scene in order to focus upon the guilt of the people and their rejection of the Messiah. At two important points he inserts new material (27:19,24–25), and at two others he replaces the title King of the Jews with Messiah (27:17,22). Finally, the entire scene is constructed in such a manner as to emphasize that the people must choose between Jesus, the Messiah, and Barabbas, a notorious prisoner. The scene progresses in five movements.

In the first (27:11–14), Pilate asks Jesus if he is the King of the Jews. Once more Jesus gives the guarded response, "You have said so," thereby dissociating himself from the form of Pilate's expression without denying its truth.[39] Jesus is the King of the Jews, but not in the sense Pilate understands the words, i.e., a political insurgent. Therefore, he cannot give the governor an unqualified, affirmative response. This is the third and final time Jesus has employed the expression, and in every case he uses it with people more or less hostile to him: Judas, the high priest, Pilate.[40] Although the chief priests and elders bring further accusations against him, Jesus does not respond to a single charge. So Matthew, like Mark, portrays Jesus as the servant of Isaiah 53:7 who "opened not his mouth."[41]

In the second movement (27:15–18) Pilate takes the initiative and asks the crowd whom they want him to release, Barabbas or Jesus called the Christ. Matthew rewrites Mark so that there is a clear choice between Barabbas, whose name means "Son of the Father," and Jesus the Messiah.[42] Where Mark says, "Do you want me to release for you the King of the Jews?" (Mk 15:9), Matthew writes, "Whom do you want me to release for you, [Jesus] Barabbas or Jesus who is called Christ?" The change allows Matthew to prepare for the climactic statement of 27:25 in which the people accept the responsibility for Jesus' death.

Matthew delays the choice between Jesus and Barabbas by inserting a brief incident in which Pilate's wife pleads for Jesus: "Have nothing to do with that righteous man, for I have suffered much over him today in a dream." The scene ironically portrays Pilate's wife, a Gentile, pleading for the Jewish Messiah while the chief priests persuade the Jewish people to ask for the criminal Barabbas (27:20). This benevolent portrayal of a Gentile is part of Matthew's wider theology which proclaims that Jesus, the Jewish Messiah, is destined for all nations. In the infancy narrative, wise men from the east, Gentiles, pay homage to the Infant King of the Jews (2:1–12). At the end of the Gospel, the risen Lord commands the eleven to "make disciples of all nations" (28:19).

Pilate's wife's dream also recalls the infancy narrative. On several occasions, characters within that story receive heavenly dreams instructing them what to do in regard to the Messiah (1:20; 2:12,13,19,22). Because Joseph and the magi heed those dreams, Herod cannot destroy the Infant King of the Jews. Now Pilate has an opportunity to save the adult King of the Jews if he obeys his wife's heavenly dream. He does not.

After this incident, Matthew returns to the question of Jesus and Barabbas (27:20–23). Again Matthew highlights the choice the people face. Mark writes that "the chief priests stirred up the crowd to have him release for them Barabbas instead" (Mk 15:11), but Matthew says "the chief priests and the elders persuaded the people to ask for Barabbas *and destroy Jesus.*" Next Matthew adds a phrase which underlines the choice: "Which *of the two* do you want me to release for you?" Then, in order to accent the religious nature of the decision, Matthew replaces Mark's King of the Jews with Messiah: "Then what shall I do with Jesus who is called *Christ*?" Matthew leaves no doubt that this is a religious, not a political matter. Finally, in order to highlight Jesus' innocence, Pilate asks what evil Jesus has done. The people can give him no answer except, "Let him be crucified."

The last movement (27:24–26) is the most dramatic and represents Matthew's own contribution. Taking up the word blood, the evangelist has Pilate wash his hands and declare, "I am innocent of this man's *blood;* see to it yourselves." The people answer, "His *blood* be on us and on our children!" Pilate's action is based upon an Old Testament practice recorded in Deuteronomy 21:1–9. When the corpse of a slain man was found between two cities, the elders of the city nearest the body were required to wash their hands over a heifer whose neck was broken and declare, "Our hands did not shed this blood, neither did our eyes see it shed" (Dt 21:7). By having Pilate appropriate this Jewish practice, Matthew exonerates him of guilt and places the burden upon the people.

The cry of the people also has a background in the Old Testament. David says, "Your blood be upon your head" to the Amalekite who slew Saul (2 Sam 1:16). When Joab kills Abner, David says "I and my kingdom are for ever guiltless before the Lord for the blood of Abner the son of Ner. May it fall upon the head of Joab" (2 Sam 3:28–29). Finally, Jeremiah prophesies, " 'The violence done to me and to my kinsmen be upon Babylon,' let the inhabitant of Zion say, 'My blood be upon the inhabitants of Chaldea' " (Jer 51:35). The expression 'blood be upon the head of' implies guilt. In these Old Testament passages, David and Jeremiah apply the guilt to others, but in the passion the people take the guilt upon themselves.

This passage, so often the excuse for anti-Semitism, must be read in the light of Matthew's total theology. When he affirms that "all the people" (*pas ho laos*) made the cry, he intends the covenant people of Israel (see 1:21; 2:4,6). Until this point in the narrative, Matthew has only spoken of the crowd (*ochlos,* 27:15,20). The use of *laos* ("people") clearly indicates a change of perspective.

The cry of the people brings to a climax the words Jesus spoke in the parable of the vineyard, "Therefore I tell you, the kingdom of God will be taken away from you and given to a nation producing the fruits of it" (21:43).[43] In Matthew's theology, this new nation is the Church composed of Jews and Gentiles.

The people's cry fulfills what Jesus said at the conclusion of his woes upon the scribes and Pharisees: "Therefore I send you prophets and

wise men and scribes, some of whom you will kill and crucify, and some
you will scourge in your synagogues and persecute from town to town,
that upon you may come all the *righteous blood* shed on earth, from the
blood of innocent Abel to the blood of Zechariah the son of Barachiah''
(23:34–35). The shedding of Jesus' blood, in Matthew's view, is the culmination of a long history during which the religious leaders of the people rejected God's righteous prophets.

An exegesis of this text should acknowledge the following points.
First, Matthew places the responsibility for Jesus' death upon the people.
Second, the result of this is the transference of the kingdom of God to a
new nation (21:43). Third, the incident is primarily a theological recon-
struction on Matthew's part and does not necessarily correspond to the
historical facts. Note that there is no such cry in Mark's account, Matthew's primary source of information for the passion. It would be irre-
sponsible for Christians to employ this text in any manner which
suggests anti-Semitic sentiments such as that the Jews are God-killers,
or that the Jews are cursed. To the contrary, Matthew envisions the pos-
sibility that the great reversal which the historical Israel experienced can
also happen to those who believe that they are chosen (22:11–14).

VI.
THE CRUCIFIXION, 27:27–44

After the people's great cry, Pilate releases Barabbas and has Jesus
scourged (27:26). In the Gospel of John the scourging of Jesus occurs at
the midpoint of the Roman trial (Jn 19:1).[44] There it serves as a ploy on
Pilate's part to evoke pity for Jesus in order to insure his release.[45] But
in Mark and Matthew the scourging comes after the trial and serves as a
cruel preparation for crucifixion.

Matthew follows Mark's order, making minor editorial changes in
order to give greater coherence to his account. The evangelist's major
contribution is Christological. As in Mark, a royal motif controls this
section: Jesus is mocked as the King of the Jews and the King of Israel,
and the charge upon the cross proclaims that he is the King of the Jews.
But at two points, Matthew introduces his Son of God Christology,
thereby preparing for the confession of 27:54. I divide the material into
three scenes: Jesus is mocked as the King of the Jews; Jesus is crucified

as the King of the Jews; Jesus is mocked as the Son of God and the King of Israel. According to this arrangement, two mockeries surround the crucifixion.

A. The First Mockery (27:27–31)

Having scourged Jesus, the Roman soldiers mock him as the King of the Jews. The minor alterations Matthew makes to Mark's account give the material a more logical arrangement and serve to heighten the royal motif. The soldiers place (1) a scarlet robe upon Jesus, (2) a plaited crown of thorns upon his head, (3) and a reed in his right hand. Then they kneel before him in mock homage. The scarlet cloak replaces the purple cloak described in Mark and represents the ordinary tunic worn by the Roman soldiers. The crown of thorns is not an instrument of torture but is meant to imitate the rays of light radiating from the head of a royal divinity.[46] The use of the reed as a royal scepter is a new element introduced by Matthew and further emphasizes the royal motif.

The mockery, of course, unwittingly proclaims the truth since Jesus is a King. Matthew begins his Gospel with a genealogy which traces Jesus' origin to his royal ancestor David (1:1–17). At Jesus' birth, wise men from the east come in search of the King of the Jews (2:2). When Jesus enters Jerusalem, Matthew provides a quotation from the prophet Zechariah which identifies Jesus as the servant King: ''Tell the daughter of Zion, Behold, your king is coming to you, humble, and mounted on an ass, and on a colt, the foal of an ass'' (Mt 21:5). Finally, in his eschatological discourse, Jesus identifies himself as the kingly Son of Man who will come at the close of the ages to judge the nations: ''When the Son of Man comes in his glory, and all the angels with him, then he will sit on his glorious throne. . . . Then the King [i.e., the Son of Man] will say to those at his right hand . . .'' (25:31,34). The irony of the scene is that some of the Gentile soldiers who now offer Jesus mock homage will soon confess him as the royal Son of God (27:54).[47]

B. The Crucifixion (27:32–38)

Like all of the evangelists, Matthew narrates the events of the crucifixion with stark simplicity. The first Christians were well acquainted with this most feared of all punishments and there was no need to recount gory details.[48] The evangelists are more interested in the significance of the events they recount than in historical details whose sole purpose is to evoke horror.

These events are few: Simon of Cyrene helps Jesus to carry the cross; Jesus is offered wine mingled with gall; he is crucified; the soldiers divide his garments; a charge is placed over his head; two robbers are crucified on either side of him. Matthew eliminates the names of Simon's sons, Alexander and Rufus (see Mk 15:21), probably because they were not personally known to his community as they were to Mark's. He describes the wine as mingled with gall, rather than with myrrh as in Mark, thereby making a clearer allusion to Psalm 69:21: "They gave me poison [gall] for food, and for my thirst they gave me vinegar to drink." Jesus tastes it, but refuses to drink, realizing their cruel hoax.

After the crucifixion the soldiers divide Jesus' garments and unknowingly fulfill the prophecy of Psalm 22:18, a psalm which plays a prominent role in Matthew's passion narrative.[49] Next Matthew adds, "they sat down and kept watch over him there." The evangelist picks up this reference in 27:54 ("When the centurion and those who were with him, *keeping watch* over Jesus, saw the earthquake . . ."). The soldiers keep watch over Jesus to insure that no one steals the body; they guarantee that Jesus truly died. Their watch also serves as a vigil which ends at the great earthquake and their own confession that Jesus was truly the Son of God.

The climax of the section is the charge, "This is Jesus the King of the Jews." It only differs slightly from Mark's version, "The King of the Jews." But the addition of Jesus' name is in keeping with Matthew's editorial policy throughout the passion story. On numerous occasions the evangelist replaces Mark's pronouns (he, him) with the Lord's name, Jesus. Whereas Mark employs the name Jesus seventeen times in chapters 14–15, Matthew uses it thirty-eight times in chapters 26–27. This is a remarkable statistic since Matthew closely follows Mark's passion narrative. It takes on added meaning when one recalls that Matthew has the angel interpret Jesus' name for Joseph: "and you shall call his name Jesus, for he will save his people from their sins" (1:21). The irony is apparent. This Jesus, derided and crucified between two robbers as the King of the Jews, is the Savior of the people who reject him.

C. The Second Mockery (27:39–44)

The form of the second mockery is substantially the same as that found in Mark: a triple derision. First, a number of passers-by blaspheme Jesus as a temple destroyer. Next, the chief priests, the scribes, and the elders (the three groups which compose the Sanhedrin) ridicule him as the King of Israel who cannot save himself. Finally, the two robbers revile Jesus, but Matthew does not report their words.

Matthew's contribution to the narrative is twofold. First, he introduces the taunt, "If you are the Son of God . . ." into the first mockery. Second, he expands the second mockery by adding, "He trusts in God; let God deliver him now, if he desires him; for he said, 'I am the Son of God.' " This last addition is a composite of two scriptural quotations. The first part comes from Psalm 22:8 ("He committed his cause to the Lord; let him deliver him, let him rescue him, for he delights in him!"). The second part ("for he said 'I am the Son of God' ") comes from Wisdom 2:12–20. In this text the wicked persecute the just man because "He professes to have knowledge of God, and *calls himself a child of the Lord*" (Wis 2:13). They complain, he "boasts that God is his father" (Wis 2:16), and assert, "if the righteous man is God's son, he will help him" (Wis 2:18).

This portrayal of Jesus as the Son of God complements Matthew's royal Christology and is part of his wider theology. In the infancy narrative, Matthew employs a fulfillment quotation which points to Jesus' sonship: "Out of Egypt have I called my son" (2:15). At Jesus' baptism (3:17) and at the transfiguration (17:5), the Father declares that Jesus is his beloved Son, echoing the strains of Psalm 2, the royal psalm applied to the king on the day of his coronation. The disciples (14:33) and Peter (16:16) confess that Jesus is the Son of God, and even the demons acknowledge the same (8:29). Finally, Jesus prays to the Father with an intimacy reserved only for the the Son (11:25–26).

The text of this passage has a special affinity with Jesus' temptations in the wilderness (4:1–11). There Satan twice tempts Jesus with the same phrase the passers-by employ, "If you are the Son of God" (4:3,6). The mockery becomes a further temptation. Will Jesus exercise his divine power to save himself, or will he trust in the Father's power to deliver him? Jesus' mission is to save his people (1:21). On several occasions he does save others (8:25–26; 9:21–22; 14:30). But Jesus has taught that the one who tries to save his life will lose it (16:25) and only those who persevere until the end will be saved (10:22; 24:13). He refuses, to save himself. He proves that he is the Son of God precisely in his obedience to and trust in the Father. This King of Israel will not trust in his own might, but in God.

VII.

THE DEATH AND BURIAL OF JESUS, 27:45–66

The final portion of Matthew's passion narrative makes a number of significant departures from Mark's account. Matthew expands the list of miraculous events which accompany Jesus' death. He increases the number of people who confess that Jesus was truly the Son of God. He abbreviates the story of Joseph of Arimathea and identifies him as a disciple. Finally, he introduces an incident in which the chief priests and Pharisees make provisions to guard Jesus' tomb. The general thrust of the narrative remains the same as that found in Mark. Matthew underscores that Jesus dies as the Son of God whom the Father vindicates at the moment of death. But Matthew's rewriting of Mark points to the resurrection. Already the dead begin to rise, and despite the plottings of mortals, God's plan is not thwarted.

Several authors maintain that the notice of the women standing at a distance (27:55–56) serves as the conclusion to Matthew's passion narrative.[50] I do not dispute this opinion, but for the sake of completeness, I include all of the incidents prior to the story of the empty tomb. The material may be divided into three scenes: Jesus dies upon the cross; Joseph buries Jesus; the Jews guard the tomb.

A. Jesus' Death and the New Age (27:45–56)

Although he makes significant editorial alterations, Matthew faithfully follows Mark's order of events: (1) darkness covers the land for three hours; (2) Jesus utters a loud cry; (3) the bystanders misunderstand the cry as a call for Elijah; (4) Jesus utters a second cry and dies; (5) a series of dramatic signs follows Jesus' death; (6) the centurion confesses that Jesus was the Son of God; (7) women witness the events from afar.

In editing Mark, Matthew clarifies a number of Marcan ambiguities and adds new material which develops the theological significance of Jesus' death.

Like Mark, Matthew notes that darkness covered the land from the sixth (noon) to the ninth hour (3:00 P.M.). The darkness certainly alludes to the apocalyptic darkness mentioned in Amos 8:9, but Matthew's remark that it covered *all* the land may be an allusion to the ninth plague recounted in the Book of Exodus, the thick darkness which overspread the land of Egypt: ''So Moses stretched out his hand toward heaven, and there was thick darkness in *all the land* of Egypt three days'' (Ex 10:22). If Matthew intends this allusion, he places the people of Israel under the same judgment which God once inflicted upon Egypt, their arch-enemy!

At the conclusion of the darkness, Jesus utters the opening words of Psalm 22, ''My God, my God, why hast thou forsaken me?'' But whereas Mark begins the quotation in Aramaic (''Eloi, Eloi''), Matthew employs the Hebrew, ''Eli, Eli.''[51] This alteration offers a better explanation of the confusion which follows Jesus' cry. The bystanders hear Jesus cry ''Eli, Eli'' and suppose that he is calling for *Eli*jah. Thus, when one of the bystanders runs to give Jesus sour wine (an allusion to Psalm 69:21), others say, ''Wait, let us see whether Elijah will come to save him.''

Although the bystanders misunderstand Jesus, Matthew's introduction of the word ''save'' suggests that they do not truly believe Elijah will come. Whereas Mark says, ''Wait, let us see whether Elijah will come to take him down'' (15:36), Matthew reads, ''Let us see whether Elijah will come to *save* him,'' thereby recalling the earlier taunts, ''save yourself . . . he cannot save himself'' (27:40,42). Jesus, of course, has no need to call for Elijah because he knows, as he told his disciples, that Elijah has *already* come in the person of John the Baptist (17:12). He cries to Eli, that is, to God.

At the conclusion of this mockery, Matthew notes, ''And Jesus cried *again* with a loud voice.'' The addition of the word again establishes this as a second cry while the use of the verb cry (*kraxas*) suggests that this cry, like the first, is a prayer. The psalms frequently employ the word *krazein* (''to cry out'') to indicate a deep and heartfelt prayer to God (Ps 22:2,5,24). The Matthean Jesus does not die with a loud inarticulate cry, but with a prayer.

Two miraculous events occur at the moment of Jesus' death: the tearing of the temple curtain[52] and the resurrection of the dead. The resurrection of the dead is Matthew's special contribution and is preceded by an earthquake which leads to the splitting of rocks and the opening of tombs.[53]

In the Old Testament, the quaking of the earth can signal a theophany (Jgs 5:4; 2 Sam 22:8; Pss 68:8; 77:16–20), or the Day of the Lord (Hag 2:6–9,20–23).[54] In the Gospel of Matthew such shaking occurs on three other occasions in addition to Jesus' death. The storm on the sea which Jesus stills is described as a *seismos,* literally a ''shaking'' (8:24), the same word used for earthquake. When Jesus makes his triumphal entry into Jerusalem, Matthew says that the city was stirred, *eseisthē,* that is, shaken (21:10). And just before the angel rolls back the stone at the tomb, Matthew reports, ''And behold there was a great earthquake'' (28:2). In each instance the shaking accompanies a manifestion of God's power in Jesus: the stilling of the sea, the triumphal entry of the Messiah, the rolling back of the stone at Easter. The earthquake functions in the same fashion here. At Jesus' death, God manifests his power by the resurrection of the dead.[55]

If the tearing of the temple curtain signals the end of the old age, the resurrection of the dead marks the beginning of the new. This resurrection alludes to the prophecy of Ezekiel: ''Behold, I will open your graves, and raise you from your graves, O my people; and I will bring you home into the land of Israel'' (37:12). There is even a similarity between Ezekiel 37:12–13 and Matthew 27:52–54.

Behold, I will *open* your graves (*mnēmata*),	the tombs (*mnēmeia*) were *opened*
and *raise* you from your graves, O *my people*;	and many bodies of the *saints* who had fallen asleep were *raised,*
and I will bring you *home into the land of Israel*.	and coming out of the tombs after his resurrection they went *into the holy city* and appeared to many

And you shall know that *I am the Lord,* when I open your graves, and raise you from your graves, O my people.	When the centurion and those who were with him. . . *Truly, this was the Son of God!*

According to the text from Ezekiel, God promises to free his people from exile and return them to the land of Israel. By this mighty deed, they will discover that he alone is God. At Jesus' death, God raises many bodies of the saints, and by this action the centurion and those with him learn that Jesus was the Son of God.

The saints represent the pious ones of the Old Testament. After Jesus' resurrection, they go into the "holy" city of Jerusalem. As Maria Riebl explains,[56] for Matthew's readers this is more than the earthly city of Jerusalem. The adjective "holy" suggests the cultic and religious dimensions of Jerusalem. The saints of the Old Testament go into the city of God's promise, the center of salvation, the eschatological Jerusalem.

At Jesus' death, God fulfills his ancient promise made through Ezekiel to the covenant people. Furthermore, he fulfills a promise made at the beginning of the Gospel, "you shall call his name Jesus, for *he will save his people from their sins.*" Although the death of Jesus calls a new people into being, God does not forsake the saints of his covenant nation.

Anticipating the resurrection, Matthew says that these holy ones appeared to many *after* Jesus' resurrection. This order of events, first the resurrection of Jesus and then the resurrection of the Old Testament saints, corresponds with the schema Paul gives in 1 Corinthians 15:22–23: "For as in Adam all die, so also in Christ shall all be made alive. But each in his own order: Christ the first fruits, then at his coming those who belong to Christ." For Matthew, Jesus' death is the beginning of the new age.

As a result of the earthquake and the accompanying events, the centurion and those with him confess that Jesus was the Son of God. The centurion's confession functions differently in Matthew's Gospel than in Mark's. In Mark the soldier's confession is the revelation of Jesus' identity. It is the first time that a human character within Mark's story confesses that Jesus is God's Son. But in Matthew's Gospel, human beings confess that Jesus is the Son of God even before the passion (14:33; 16:16). The confession of the centurion and his companions is no longer related to Jesus' hidden identity. Instead, they represent the first fruits of the Gentiles. As a result of Jesus' death, the Gospel moves to the Gentiles.

As in Mark, a number of women stand from afar and witness the events of the crucifixion. They become the Church's witnesses to the Lord's death, burial, and resurrection since the disciples have fled. Although he does refer to them in the Gospel, Matthew says that they followed Jesus from Galilee and ministered to his needs: Mary Magdalene, Mary the mother of James and Joseph, and the mother of the sons of Zebedee. The last is the one who asked Jesus to grant her sons seats of honor in his kingdom (20:20–21). Although her sons have abandoned him, she remains faithful.

B. Jesus' Burial (27:57–61)

Matthew abbreviates Mark's account. He also eliminates Mark's reference to Joseph as a respected member of the council lest there be any suspicion that Joseph was associated with Jesus' death. Instead of describing him as one "who was also himself looking for the kingdom of God" (Mk 15:43), Matthew depicts Joseph as a rich man and a disciple of Jesus. The identification of Joseph as rich may be an allusion to Isaiah 53:9, "And they made his grave with the wicked *and with a rich man* in his death, although he had done no violence, and there was no deceit in his mouth." The portrayal of Joseph as a disciple shows that although the twelve deserted Jesus, there were disciples who did not.

The fate of Jesus' body must have been a concern for the early Church. Was he simply buried in a common, unclean grave? Did anybody know where he was buried? Matthew answers these questions. Like Mark, he avers that Jesus received a proper burial by Joseph of Arimathea and that certain women witnessed this. He goes one step further, moreover, affirming that Jesus' body was wrapped in a *clean* linen shroud and buried in a *new* tomb which belonged to Joseph. The evangelist guarantees not only the place of Jesus' burial but its dignity. Jesus, accused by the Pharisees of breaking the Jewish purity laws (15:1–20), receives a proper burial. Two women sit opposite the sepulchre, witnesses to Jesus' burial as they were to his crucifixion.

C. The Guard at the Tomb (27:62–66)

This incident is peculiar to Matthew for whom it serves an apologetic purpose. The apocryphal Gospel of Peter[57] contains a similar story dependent upon this one. But there the incident is greatly enhanced. The Gospel of Peter names Petronius as the centurion who guards the tomb and says that the elders and scribes also kept watch. Rolling a great stone over the tomb, they put seven seals on it. Although less detailed, Matthew's account is no less apologetic. He wishes to assure his readers that Jesus' body was not stolen since the Jews themselves set the guard for the tomb.

In Matthew's account, the priests and Pharisees request Pilate to post a guard lest the disciples steal Jesus' body. Matthew does not mention the Pharisees anywhere else in his passion story. But they and the priests are the two groups who recognized that Jesus told the parable of the vineyard against them (21:45). Now they depict Jesus as an impostor (*planos*), a description not otherwise applied to him in the Gospel. In his apocalyptic discourse (24:4,5,11,24), Jesus warns the disciples to beware of false messiahs and prophets who will lead others astray (*planao*). In the Gospel of John those who do not believe in Jesus accuse him of leading the people astray (7:12). And in the Babylonian Talmud (*Sanhedrin* 43a), Jesus is portrayed as a deceiver or beguiler of the people.[58]

The religious leaders recall Jesus' prophecies that he would be raised up after three days (16:21; 17:23; 20:19). Their request, "order the sepulchre to be made secure until the third day, lest his disciples go and steal him away, and tell the people, '*He has risen from the dead*,' " contains what must have been one of the first Christian confessions, "He has risen!" (see 1 Cor 15:20). Having been forced to cooperate with Jesus' death, Pilate refuses any further assistance. His reply, "You have a guard of soldiers; go, make it as secure as you can," is filled with irony. No matter how secure the Jews make their guard, they will not prevent Jesus' resurrection. God will vindicate his Christ.

CONCLUSION

Although Matthew's passion narrative is heavily dependent upon Mark's, Matthew has rewritten Mark's story in such a way as to highlight his own theological concerns. First, as regards Christology, Matthew stresses Jesus' divine dignity in several ways. He points to Jesus' knowledge of events which are about to take place. He introduces the titles Messiah and Son of God on several occasions. And where Mark is content to employ the pronouns he and him, Matthew prefers to focus upon Jesus' person by the use of the proper name "Jesus." Building upon Mark's Christology, Matthew heightens the reader's awareness that the one who suffers is none other than God's Son, the royal Davidic Messiah, the one who will return as the Son of Man.

Second, as regards Jesus' behavior, Matthew focuses upon his righteous conduct. In the garden of Gethsemane, Jesus provides a model for prayer and refuses to resist arrest. In the trial before the Sanhedrin he does not allow the high priest to place him under oath. Standing before the governor, Pilate, he silently trusts in his Father. And hanging from the cross, he refuses to save himself.

Finally, as regards ecclesiology, Matthew portrays the passion as the decisive moment when the kingdom passes from the people of Israel to the Gentiles. The people of Israel make their fateful cry before Pilate that Jesus' blood is upon their heads. As a result, at Jesus' death a new age begins and Israel's inheritance passes to the nations. The next chapter examines these themes in greater detail, showing how the theology of Matthew's passion narrative is rooted in his Gospel theology.

Chapter Six

MATTHEW'S GOSPEL THEOLOGY

I.

JESUS MESSIAH THE SON OF GOD

Although Matthew's passion narrative follows Mark's account, the first evangelist makes a number of changes in order to heighten his Christological portrait of Jesus. At the beginning of the passion (26:1–16), for example, Matthew shows that nothing surprises Jesus. He undertakes his suffering with full prophetic knowledge. He announces his passion, *then* the religious leaders plot against him. He interprets the woman's action as an anointing for burial, *then* Judas betrays him. Furthermore, Jesus willingly accepts his suffering. In Gethsemane he says, "My Father, if it be possible, let this cup pass from me; nevertheless, not as I will, but as thou wilt" (26:39). In addition to emphasizing Jesus' foreknowledge and willingness to accept the passion, Matthew calls attention to Jesus' exalted status as Messiah and Son of God by employing these titles on occasions that Mark does not. In the mockery before the Sanhedrin (26:67–68), Jesus is ridiculed as Messiah. At the Roman trial Pilate taunts the Jews, "Whom do you want me to release for you, Barabbas or Jesus who is called the Christ?" (27:17). Finally, the passers-by and the religious leaders deride Jesus, saying, "If you are the Son of God come down from the cross" (27:40), and, "He trusts in God; let God deliver him now, if he desires him; for he said, 'I am the Son of God' " (27:43). The result of Matthew's editorial activity is a more exalted Christology than that found in Mark. The reader is made aware that the one who suffers is the Messiah, the Son of God. As Hans-Ruedi Weber observes, "The significant point here is that the Son of God, with all his power and authority, does not use his power but becomes god-forsaken." [1]

Matthew's heightened Christology is not limited to the passion narrative. Throughout the Gospel he expands upon Mark's Christological portrait of Jesus. This section reviews Matthew's story in light of his Christology. It will show the convergence of Matthew's passion narrative and his Gospel theology.

Matthew's story is not as dramatic as Mark's. The Gospel of Mark reaches its climax when the centurion confesses that Jesus is the Son of God (Mk 15:39), thereby breaking the secrecy which surrounds Jesus' identity. Matthew, however, has begun to dismantle Mark's messianic secret.[2] Already, at two significant moments before Jesus' death, his disciples confess that he is the Son of God (14:33; 16:16). The drama in Matthew's Gospel is no longer grounded in the disclosure of Jesus' identity at the moment of his death. Instead, as Lloyd Gaston has put it, ". . . Matthew's Gospel is a theological tragedy, the story of the advent and rejection of the Messiah of Israel."[3] It is precisely by his heightened Christological portrait that Matthew achieves this end. Israel's rejection of her Messiah is a tragedy because, in Matthew's view, Jesus' messianic credentials are so impeccable.

A. *The Origin and Identity of Jesus (1:1–4:16)*

Matthew begins his story with an infancy narrative (1:1–2:23), the primary purpose of which is to establish Jesus' identity.[4] A genealogy (1:1–17) traces Jesus' lineage to David and Abraham and demonstrates that he is "the Son of David, the Son of Abraham" (1:1). As the Son of David, Jesus can claim the pedigree required of the Messiah. As the Son of Abraham, the father of all believers (Rom 4:1), he shares an ancestry that makes him accessible to the Gentiles.

But how can Jesus be a descendant of David if he was conceived through the Holy Spirit? (1:18). Matthew solves this problem in an annunciation story (1:18–25) which explains that Joseph, a descendant of David, takes Jesus as his own and makes him part of David's royal line. From the outset of the Gospel, therefore, Matthew establishes Jesus' messianic pedigree.

But the evangelist is not content simply to call Jesus the Messiah, the Son of David. In the annunciation to Joseph, the angel explains that Mary has conceived by the Holy Spirit, and he instructs Joseph to name the child Jesus (Savior) because "he will save his people from their sins"

(1:21). Matthew points to the significance of this event by one of his formula quotations: "All this took place to fulfill what the Lord had spoken by the prophet: 'Behold a virgin shall conceive and bear a son, and his name shall be called Emmanuel' (which means, God with us)" (1:22–23). Within the first chapter of his story, Matthew identifies Jesus as son of Abraham, Son of David, Messiah, the one conceived by the Holy Spirit, Jesus (Savior), Emmanuel (God with us).

Having explained Jesus' Davidic lineage, Matthew devotes the second chapter of his infancy narrative to a slightly different question. How is it that this Davidic Messiah comes from Nazareth of Galilee?[5] Is not the Messiah to be born in Bethlehem? To respond to this question, Matthew explains that Jesus was born in Bethlehem in accordance with the ancient prophecy: "And you, O Bethlehem, in the land of Judah, are by no means least among the rulers of Judah; for from you shall come a ruler who will govern my people Israel" (2:6). Because of Herod's jealousy, however, the infant Messiah must flee to Egypt (2:13–14). But the flight into Egypt leads to another prophecy: "Out of Egypt have I called my son" (2:15). Because Herod's successor, his son Archelaus, rules over Judea, Jesus' parents settle in Nazareth rather than Bethlehem. So Matthew explains that Jesus the Galilean was indeed born in Bethlehem, but was reared in Nazareth, thereby fulfilling the prophecy: "He shall be called a Nazarene" (2:23).

Despite the poor reception the Messiah receives in Jerusalem, wise men from the east, Gentiles, acknowledge him as the King of the Jews (2:2), that is, the Messiah. Furthermore, when "they saw the child with Mary his mother" (2:11), they fell down and worshiped him. Professor Kingsbury has pointed out that the expression "the child and his mother" (2:11,13,14,20,21) is Matthew's way of reminding the reader that the son of Mary is the Son of God,[6] since the omission of Joseph's name suggests Jesus' marvelous conception by the Holy Spirit. By the end of chapter two, the reader discovers that Jesus the Galilean was born in Bethlehem, the city of David, in accordance with the ancient prophecies. Although the inhabitants of Jerusalem did not recognize him, Gentiles hailed him as the King of the Jews: the Messiah.

Although the infancy narrative concludes with chapter two, the preparatory section of Matthew's Gospel continues through chapter three and into chapter four.[7] In chapter three John the Baptist makes his appearance, announcing the Mightier One who will baptize with the Holy

Spirit and fire (3:11). When Jesus presents himself for John's baptism, the Baptist tries to prevent it (3:14). But Jesus explains that he has come to fulfill all righteousness (3:15): that is, to "carry out the total will of God."[8] As a result of the baptism, the Father proclaims, "This is my beloved Son, with whom I am well pleased" (3:17). The distinctive nature of Jesus' messiahship is rooted in his divine sonship.

Immediately following the baptism, Satan tests the Messiah by three temptations (4:1–11). In the first two he challenges Jesus, "If you are the Son of God . . ." (4:3,6). The address is similar to the taunts of the passers-by at Jesus' crucifixion, "If you are the Son of God, come down from the cross" (27:40). Israel of old faced similar temptations in the wilderness and failed. But Jesus shows that he is worthy of the Father's baptismal declaration. As the messianic Son of God he places his trust in the Father.

Having overcome Satan's temptations, Jesus retires to Galilee, thereby fulfilling yet another Old Testament prophecy: "The land of Zebulun and the land of Naphtali, toward the sea, across the Jordan, Galilee of the Gentiles—the people who sat in darkness have seen a great light, and for those who sat in the region and shadow of death light has dawned" (4:15–16). As Jesus embarks upon his ministry, it is clear from 1:1–4:16 that he is the Messiah, the Son of David, the ruler of Israel, the King of the Jews. But inasmuch as he has been conceived by the Holy Spirit, he is Emmanuel (God with us), the Savior (Jesus), capable of saving his people from their sins. He is none other than the Son of God.

B. A Ministry of Teaching and Healing (4:17–11:1)

After establishing Jesus' messianic credentials, Matthew concentrates upon his teaching and healing activity. From this point forward, the reader knows who Jesus is; he is the Messiah the Son of God. In what follows, therefore, the reader must keep in mind that Jesus carries out his ministry in his capacity as the messianic Son of God. The first part of Jesus' ministry consists of the Sermon on the Mount (5–7), a series of ten mighty works (8–9), and a missionary discourse to the disciples (10:1–11:1).

The Sermon presents Jesus as the authoritative Teacher who brings the Mosaic law to its fulfillment (5:17). Jesus insists that he has not come to abolish the law but to fulfill it. It is in fulfilling the law, moreover, that he manifests a sovereign authority which belongs to the messianic Son of God. On six occasions Jesus Messiah draws a contrast between himself and Moses by the formula, "You have heard that it was said. . . . But I say to you" (5:21–22,27–28,31–32,33–34,38–39,43–44). As a result of his authoritative teaching, "the crowds were astonished . . . for he taught them as one who had authority, and not as their scribes" (7:28–29).

Ten mighty works or miracles (8:1–9:34) follow Jesus' teaching ministry:[9] (1) the cleansing of a leper (8:1–4); (2) the healing of a centurion's servant (8:5–13); (3) the healing of Peter's mother-in-law and many people (8:14–17); (4) the calming of a storm (8:23–27); (5) the healing of two demoniacs (8:28–34); (6) the cure of a paralytic (9:1–8); (7) the cure of a ruler's daughter (9:18–19,23–26); (8) the healing of a woman with a hemorrhage (9:20–22); (9) the healing of two blind men (9:27–31); (10) the healing of a dumb man (9:32–34). After the first three of these, Matthew produces another of his fulfillment quotations: "This was to fulfill what was spoken by the prophet Isaiah, 'He took our infirmities and bore our diseases' " (8:17). The verse comes from Isaiah 53:4 and casts Jesus, the messianic Son of God, in the role of servant. Although powerful in word and deed so that people address him as Lord (8:2,6,8,21,25), Jesus comes to serve the needs of his people.

Toward the conclusion of these mighty works, two blind men cry out to Jesus, "Have mercy on us, Son of David" (9:27). Although they play no significant role in Israel's society, they recognize that Jesus is the Messiah.[10] Then, after Jesus' last miracle, the crowds marvel, "Never was anything like this seen in Israel," while the Pharisees complain, "He casts out demons by the prince of demons" (9:33). Jesus' mighty works, like his teaching, make a great impression upon the crowd, but there are ominous warnings that not everyone will accept him.

Having shown himself mighty in word and deed, Jesus calls twelve disciples and sends them on mission to the lost sheep of the house of Israel (10:1–11:1). For the moment, Jesus confines his disciples' mission to Israel (10:5–6), thereby confirming that he is Israel's Messiah. In the course of this discourse, he identifies himself as the Son of Man who will return quickly: "When they persecute you in one town, flee to the next; for truly, I say to you, you will not have gone through all the towns of Israel, before the Son of Man comes" (10:23). He assures his followers that whoever acknowledges him before men, he will acknowledge before his Father in heaven (10:32).

The result of this section, 4:17–11:1, is a picture of Jesus Messiah, the Son of God, powerful in word and deed who comes to reestablish Israel. Acknowledged as Lord and Son of David, he is cast in the role of servant. But at the end of the ages he will return as the exalted Son of Man.

C. Rejection and Confession of the Messiah, 11:2–16:20

Beginning with chapter eleven, a crisis occurs in Jesus' ministry. John the Baptist, hearing about his deeds, sends messengers to inquire if Jesus is the long-expected one (11:2–3). Jesus points to the mighty works he has performed and his Sermon on the Mount as authentic signs that he is the Coming One (11:4–5), and he warns those who would be scandalized at such a Messiah (11:6). Jesus is the Messiah but in a most unexpected way.

Questions about Jesus' identity persist and reach a climax when the Pharisees accuse him of casting out demons by Beelzebul the prince of demons (12:24). In the face of rejection, Jesus presents himself as the "gentle and lowly" Son of God (11:25–30). As the Son, he possesses an intimate knowledge of the Father who has delivered all things to him (11:27; cf. 28:18). Echoing the invitation of divine Wisdom (Sir 24:19; 51:23,26), Jesus invites the weary to find refreshment in him. "Come to me, all who labor and are heavy laden, and I will give you rest" (11:28).

Next, in a controversy with the Pharisees over the sabbath (12:1–8), Jesus identifies himself as the one who is greater than the temple: "I tell you, something greater than the temple is here." As God's Son, he is the Son of Man who is Lord of the sabbath (12:8), the Messiah who does what David did, but is greater still. In yet another controversy, the demand for a sign (12:38–42), Jesus presents himself as the one who is greater than Jonah and Solomon.

In the midst of these controversies, Matthew provides an extended fulfillment quotation in which he portrays Jesus as the servant described by Isaiah (12:17–21). "Behold, my servant whom I have chosen, my beloved with whom my soul is well pleased. . . ." Again Matthew casts Jesus as the Servant Messiah. Jesus does not come as the warrior King but as the Servant who heals the ills of his people and proclaims "justice to the Gentiles" (12:18).

Although all segments of Israel reject him in 11:2–13:58, Jesus' disciples believe in him, and twice they proclaim that he is the Son of God.[11] After feeding the five thousand, Jesus orders the disciples to cross the lake without him. When a storm arises, they suddenly see Jesus walking on the sea (14:25–27). Peter calls to him and asks, "bid me come to you on the water" (14:28). When he begins to sink, Peter cries out, "Lord, save me" (14:30). Jesus saves not only Peter but all of the disciples, and they worship him, saying, "Truly you are the Son of God" (14:33). Shortly after this a Canaanite woman, a Gentile, addresses Jesus as the Son of David and asks him to heal her daughter (15:22–28). Although Israel does not recognize her Messiah, a foreigner does.

The climax of this section, however, comes with Peter's confession at Caesarea Philippi (16:13–20). Jesus asks his disciples, "who do men say that the Son of Man is?" They respond, "Some say John the Baptist, others say Elijah, and others Jeremiah or one of the prophets" (16:14). The conjectures are incorrect, and next Jesus inquires what the disciples think. Peter confesses, "You are the Christ, the Son of the living God" (16:16).

In this third section (11:2–16:20), Matthew presents Jesus the Messiah, the Son of God, rejected by Israel but recognized as the Son of David by a foreign woman and confessed as the Son of God by his disciples. He enhances the picture of Jesus' messiahship. He is the one who is greater than the temple (12:6), greater than Jonah and Solomon (12:41–42). He is the humble and gentle Messiah (11:25–30), the Servant who heals the ills of his people (12:15–21). He is the Son to whom the Father has entrusted all things (11:27).

D. On the Way to Jerusalem (16:21–20:34)

Although the disciples confess that Jesus is the Son of God, they do not understand the full implications of what it means to call him God's Son. Beginning with 16:21, therefore, Jesus teaches his disciples that he must go to Jerusalem and suffer. As in Mark's Gospel, Peter resists the notion of a suffering Messiah (16:22). But Jesus rebukes him (16:23) and explains that only the way of the cross will allow the disciples to share the victory he will enjoy as the glorious Son of Man (16:24–28).

On the Mount of Transfiguration, the Father confirms that Jesus is his beloved Son and commands Peter, James and John to listen to him (17:5). Descending from the mountain, Jesus avers once more that the Son of Man must suffer (17:12).

On two other occasions (17:22–23; 20:18–19), Jesus makes the same prediction. The Son of Man, that is, Jesus the Messiah, will be delivered up and condemned to death. Nonetheless, Jesus is conscious that he will be vindicated and promises Peter and the other disciples, ''in the new world, when the Son of Man shall sit on his glorious throne, you who have followed me will also sit on twelve thrones judging the twelve tribes of Israel'' (19:28).

At the conclusion of Jesus' Jerusalem journey, two blind men hail him as the Son of David, that is, the Messiah (20:29–34). Like the blind men (9:27–31) and the Canaanite woman (15:21–28), they are no-accounts, people on the fringe of society. But they recognize what Israel does not: Jesus is the Messiah.

By the close of this section, it is clear that Jesus Messiah, the Son of David, God's Son, must suffer and die in Jerusalem before he can return as the glorious Son of Man.

E. Jesus in Jerusalem (21:1–28:15)

Matthew describes Jesus' entry into Jerusalem in such a way that there is no doubt that he is the Messiah, the royal Son of David. At his entry the crowds cry, ''Hosanna to the Son of David!'' (21:9). Matthew interprets the entry with another formula quotation: ''This took place to fulfill what was spoken by the prophet, saying, 'Tell the daughter of Zion, Behold, your king is coming to you, humble, and mounted on an ass, and on a colt, the foal of an ass' '' (21:4–5). Drawing from the prophet Zechariah (9:9), Matthew portrays Jesus as the meek and humble messianic King.

After cleansing the temple (21:12–13), Jesus Messiah does what has been distinctive throughout his ministry: he heals the blind and the lame (21:14). Once more it is only the no-accounts, this time the children, who recognize him and cry out, ''Hosanna to the Son of David'' (21:15).

Although Jesus is undisputedly the Son of David inasmuch as he is the Messiah, Matthew knows that Jesus is more than the traditional Messiah. Toward the conclusion of Jesus' Jerusalem ministry, therefore, Jesus poses a question about the Messiah's identity: "If David thus calls him Lord, how is he his son?" (22:45). The answer, of course, is that the Messiah is not merely David's Son. He is preeminently the Son of God.

Before beginning the passion, Jesus delivers a final series of discourses (23–25). In the first, he denounces the scribes and Pharisees for their hypocritical behavior (23:1–36). The discourse, with its series of woes, almost serves as an antithesis to the Sermon on the Mount. At the beginning of it, Jesus reminds his disciples that they only have one Teacher and Master, the Messiah (23:8–10). As in the Sermon on the Mount, Jesus the Messiah is the preeminent Teacher of his people.

In Jesus' final discourse (24–25), he prepares his followers for the destruction of the temple and his return as the glorious Son of Man. False messiahs will appear (24:5,23,24), but the signs announcing his return will be unmistakable (24:29). When Jesus comes, it will be as the kingly Son of Man who separates the sheep from the goats (25:31–46). In the meantime, the community of his disciples must live in vigilance (25:1–13), producing fruit worthy of the kingdom (25:14–30).

By the time the passion begins Matthew has provided the reader with a detailed explanation of Jesus' identity which surpasses the Christological portrait found in Mark. Jesus the Messiah, the King of the Jews, is the royal descendant of David. He ministers to the blind, the lame, the no-accounts of Israel. Although he is the exalted Lord, he is a Servant Messiah who heals the ills of his people. But Jesus is more than the traditional Davidic Messiah. He is the Savior (Jesus), the one who can deliver his people from their sins. He is Emmanuel, God present to his people. He is preeminently the Son of God, the one to whom the Father has handed over all things. At the close of the ages, Jesus Messiah, the Son of God, will return in his royal capacity as the exalted Son of Man. It is not surprising, therefore, that Matthew concludes his Gospel with the risen Lord, endowed with all authority, commanding the eleven to make disciples of all nations (28:16–20). Matthew has enhanced the Christological portrait of Jesus not only in the passion narrative but throughout the Gospel.

II.

THE REJECTION OF JESUS THE MESSIAH

In terms of Christology, the Matthean passion narrative does not provide the kind of drama found in Mark. No longer is the disclosure of Jesus' identity Matthew's primary concern. Nonetheless, Matthew's narrative does contain a dramatic element which comes to a climax at the Roman trial. There, the people of Israel cry out, "His blood be on us and on our children" (27:25). The drama of Matthew's Gospel consists in this refusal by Israel to accept Jesus as the Messiah.

In the last chapter, I noted how Matthew carefully edited the scene before Pilate, in order to heighten the responsibility of the Jews. Pilate's wife declares that Jesus is a righteous man (27:19). Pilate, the Gentile, washes his hands before the people, thereby implying Jesus' innocence (27:24). And Matthew arranges the scene so that the people of Israel must choose between Barabbas the criminal and Jesus the Messiah. By these changes, Matthew places the burden of guilt upon the religious leaders and the people. In his view, they have rejected their Messiah.

The theme of rejection is not peculiar to the passion narrative. As in the case of Matthew's exalted Christological portrait of Jesus, it is developed earlier in the narrative and comes to a climax in the passion story. Israel's rejection of Jesus the Messiah *is* the dramatic element in the Gospel. Matthew's Gospel is the tragic story of why and how Israel rejected her Messiah.

Although there are elements of the rejection theme throughout Matthew's Gospel, there are three areas where the theme is especially prominent: the infancy narrative (1–2), the crisis in Jesus' Galilean ministry (11–13), and Jesus' conflict with the religious leaders during his Jerusalem ministry (21–23).

A. The Rejection of the Infant Messiah (1:1–2:23)

Matthew's infancy narrative does not merely identify Jesus as the Messiah of David's lineage. It points to his destiny by foreshadowing the passion narrative.

Matthew explains that even as a child Jesus Messiah encounters rejection. When wise men from the east come to Jerusalem seeking the Infant King of the Jews, they go to Herod expecting that, as the king of the Jews, he knows where to find the Messiah. Herod is ignorant of the Messiah's birth, but he inquires of the religious leaders who inform him that according to the prophet the Messiah will be born in Bethlehem (2:5). Although the religious leaders know the prophecies concerning the Messiah's birth, they do not go to Bethlehem and welcome him. Instead, Gentiles receive the Jewish Messiah. At his birth, therefore, Jesus the Messiah is ignored by Herod, the king of the Jews, and by the religious leaders.

Herod's ignorance of the Messiah turns to jealousy and persecution. He instructs the wise men to find the child and bring him word so that he can also worship. But through a series of dreams, not unlike the dream experienced by Pilate's wife (27:19), God protects the infant Messiah. First, the wise men are warned in a dream not to return to Herod (2:12). Then in three dreams, an angel directs Joseph. He must flee to the land of Egypt (2:13). He is told when it is safe to return (2:19–20). Finally, he is instructed to withdraw to Galilee to escape Herod's ruthless son, Archelaus (2:22). There is a relationship between the dreams in the infancy narrative and the dream of Pilate's wife. At Jesus' birth, Herod seeks to destroy the Messiah because he perceives the Infant King of the Jews as a threat to his rule. But Joseph and the wise men heed the instructions given them in dreams so that neither Herod nor his son Archelaus can harm the child. In the passion, the religious leaders will accuse Jesus of pretending to be the King of the Jews, and Pilate will ask Jesus about the charge. But at the crucial moment, Pilate will not heed his wife's dream. As a result, Jesus is rejected and crucified as the King of the Jews.

B. The Rejection of the Messiah's Galilean Ministry (11:2–13:58)

The turning point in Matthew's Gospel occurs in chapters 11–13 when Jesus experiences rejection on all sides from Israel.[12] Until this point in the narrative, Jesus encounters minimal opposition. He delivers the Sermon on the Mount, and Matthew notes, ''the crowds were astonished at his teaching, for he taught them as one who had authority, and not as their scribes'' (7:28–29). Then he performs ten mighty works, and after the tenth the people proclaim, ''Never was anything like this seen in Israel'' (9:33). But in chapter 11 the first major notes of opposition are sounded, and they come to a climax at the close of chapter 13 when Jesus is rejected at Nazareth (13:53–58).

The questioning of Jesus' messianic credentials begins with John the Baptist (11:2–6). Earlier in the narrative, he announced a powerful Messiah who would carry out judgment: "His winnowing fork is in his hand, and he will clear his threshing floor and gather his wheat into the granary, but the chaff he will burn with unquenchable fire" (3:12). But the works of Jesus to this point have not fulfilled John's expectations. Therefore, he sends disciples to ask, "Are you he who is to come, or shall we look for another?" (11:3) Even John wonders about this Messiah. Jesus assures John's disciples that he is the Coming One by pointing to the mighty words and deeds he has just performed, and he adds, "And blessed is he who takes no offense (*skandalisthē*) at me" (11:6). Jesus' praise of John in the following section (11:7–15) implies that although the Baptist questions Jesus' messianic credentials, he is not scandalized by him. But by the end of this section, the folk of Jesus' home town, Nazareth, take offense (*eskandalizonto*) at him (13:57).

Following his praise of John, Jesus accuses "this generation" of being fickle (11:16–19) because it does not accept either John the Baptist or himself, even though they are different from each other. The reference to the present generation occurs several times in Matthew, usually in a negative context (12:39,41,42,45; 16:4; 17:17; 23:36).

In the next section, (11:20–24), Jesus rebukes the Galilean cities of Chorazin, Bethsaida, and Capernaum for not repenting even though they witnessed his mighty works. Although Matthew does not mention anything about the opposition of these cities in the Gospel, it becomes clear that Jesus' Galilean ministry was not entirely successful. Despite his mighty works, he cannot bring about the repentance he required when he announced the arrival of the kingdom: "Repent, for the kingdom of heaven is at hand" (4:17). Despite this opposition, Jesus issues an invitation to those "who labor and are heavy laden" to come to him (11:28–30).

In chapter 12 the opposition to Jesus comes primarily from the religious leaders. In two incidents, the Pharisees accuse Jesus and his disciples of violating the sabbath (12:1–14). At the conclusion of the second incident, a healing on the sabbath, the Pharisees "went out and took counsel (*symboulion elabon*) against him, how to destroy him" (12:14). This conspiracy becomes the first announcement of the plot to kill Jesus.

Matthew will use the same language in 22:15 and 27:1 when the religious leaders again plot against Jesus. But the passion cannot take place before the appointed hour; therefore Jesus, aware of the plot, withdraws from their midst (12:15). At this point, as if to emphasize Jesus' willingness to suffer, Matthew introduces the text on the Servant from Isaiah (12:17–21).

Jesus' next encounter with the Pharisees occurs when he heals a blind and dumb demoniac. The crowd wonders if Jesus might be the Son of David (12:22–23), but the Pharisees accuse him of casting out demons by Beelzebul, the prince of demons (12:24–32). In face of this opposition, Jesus likens the Pharisees to trees which bear rotten fruit (12:33–37). They stand condemned by their own words. They have spoken the unforgivable sin against the Holy Spirit (12:32). They attribute the works God performs through Jesus to Satan.

The opposition mounts when the Pharisees ask Jesus for a sign (12:38–42). He responds that their request comes from "an evil and adulterous generation" (12:39). Indeed, this generation is so wicked that the city of Nineveh, legendary for its sinfulness, will judge it. Jesus then likens the present generation to a possessed man who has been cured and then repossessed by a demon seven times more powerful than the first (12:43–45). The man's final situation is worse than it was, even though he was cured for a time. At the conclusion of chapter 12, Jesus designates his disciples as his true family because they do the will of his Father in heaven (12:46–50). Jesus' Galilean ministry has not succeeded with the vast majority of Israel: it has failed especially among Israel's leaders.

In chapter 13 Jesus speaks to the crowds in parables. The parables, however, are not meant to be understood by the crowds because, in Jesus' view, Israel has hardened its heart, fulfilling the prophecy of Isaiah: "You shall indeed hear but never understand, and you shall indeed see but never perceive. For this people's heart has grown dull, and their ears are heavy of hearing, and their eyes they have closed, lest they should perceive with their eyes, and hear with their ears, and understand with their heart, and turn for me to heal them" (13:14–15).

But to his disciples, Jesus reveals the mysteries of the kingdom, and in the middle of the parable discourse (13:36), he withdraws from the crowd. Entering a house, he explains everything to his disciples. If the old Israel refuses to hear and understand the Messiah, the Messiah will gather a new people about him.[13]

At the end of the parable discourse, Jesus asks his disciples if they have understood all that he has taught; they answer affirmatively. Next, Matthew has Jesus return to Nazareth where the townspeople take offense at him (13:57), thereby creating a contrast between the disciples' understanding and the people's refusal to believe. Such scandal, of course, is precisely what Jesus warned about at the beginning of chapter 11 when John's messengers arrived (11:6).[14] Thus Matthew brackets this entire section with two references to taking offense at Jesus (11:6; 13:57). In the material between these verses, Israel and her leaders reject the Messiah.

C. The Rejection of the Messiah's Jerusalem Ministry (21:1–23:39)

To be sure, the ultimate rejection of Jesus' Jerusalem ministry is the passion. But even before the passion, Jerusalem rejects her Messiah. Having entered the city as the Messiah (21:1–11), Jesus cleanses the temple and heals the blind and lame in its precincts (21:12–14). The children of the city acclaim him as the Son of David, but the chief priests and the scribes, seeing "the wonderful things that he did, and the children crying out" (21:15), become indignant. As in Mark's Gospel, they proceed to question Jesus' authority (21:23–27). But whereas Mark has Jesus reply with a single parable, the parable of the vineyard (Mk 12:1–12), in Matthew Jesus responds with three parables: the parable of the two sons (21:28–32), the parable of the vineyard (21:33–46), and the parable of the marriage feast (22:1–14).

From one point of view, each of the parables might be interpreted as the Messiah's rejection of Israel. In the first, Jesus tells the religious leaders that the tax collectors and harlots are entering the kingdom of God before them (21:31). In the second, he informs them that the kingdom of God will be taken away from them and given to a nation that will produce the fruits of it (21:43). And in the third, he proclaims that those who were invited to God's messianic banquet are no longer worthy (22:8).

But from another perspective, the same parables point to Israel's rejection of the Messiah. According to the first, the religious leaders refuse to repent at the coming of John the Baptist even though he preaches a way of righteousness (21:32). According to the second parable, when the Messiah makes his appearance, these same leaders refuse to accept him. Indeed they kill him (21:38). But the rejection of the Messiah, according to the second and third parables, is not an isolated event. It is part of a long history in which Israel continually destroyed God's messengers (21:35–36; 22:3–6).

Following these parables, the religious leaders engage Jesus in a series of controversies concerning the payment of taxes to Caesar (22:15–22), the problem of resurrection (22:23–33), and the question of the greatest commandment (22:34–40). All of this is similar to material found in Mark. But unlike Mark's Gospel, Matthew concludes these controversies with a vehement denunciation of the scribes and Pharisees (23:1–36). Employing a series of seven woes (23:13,15,16,23,25, 27,29), Jesus condemns the religious leaders "for they preach, but do not practice" (23:3).

The seventh and the final woe is the most devastating. Jesus accuses the Pharisees of continuing in the tradition of those who murdered the prophets: "Therefore I send you prophets and wise men and scribes, some of whom you will kill and crucify, and some you will scourge in your synagogues and persecute from town to town" (23:34). On one level, Jesus' words are a prophecy of what will happen to the members of his Church during the time of their mission to Israel. But on another level, the woe is the most damning of Jesus' accusations against the religious leaders. They belong to a history of murderers who have rejected God's messengers. In the past, their fathers killed the prophets. Now they are about to reject the Messiah.

Having been rejected in Galilee (11–13) and now in Jerusalem (21–23), Jesus pronounces a final lament over the city: "O Jerusalem, Jerusalem, killing the prophets and stoning those who are sent to you! . . . Behold, your house is forsaken and desolate" (23:37–38).

Israel's rejection of the Messiah in the passion narrative, especially at the trial before Pilate, is part of Matthew's wider theology. The rejection theme begins at the infancy narrative (1–2). During Jesus' Galilean ministry (11–13), Israel's hardness of heart grows to critical proportions. Finally, in Jerusalem (21–23), the religious leaders repudiate Jesus' messianic credentials and enter into a series of fierce controversies with him. The repudiation of the Messiah during the passion is the outcome of a theme that runs throughout Matthew's Gospel.

III.
GOD'S NEW NATION, THE CHURCH

Israel's dramatic rejection of the Messiah results in the transferral of the kingdom of God to another people: the Church. In the passion narrative, this occurs at the moment of Jesus' death. The apocalyptic events which surround that death, the tearing of the temple curtain and the resurrection of the dead, indicate the beginning of a new age[15] and they lead the Roman centurion, and those with him, to proclaim that Jesus was truly the Son of God (27:51–54).

In my commentary on this passage, I noted that the centurion's confession functions differently in Matthew than in Mark. In this Gospel, the confession does not reveal the messianic secret. Instead, it counterbalances the mockery of the passers-by and the religious leaders (27:39–44). While Israel mocks Jesus as the Son of God, the King of Israel, the Gentiles confess that he truly was God's Son. "The confession of the centurion and his men that the crucified Jesus is the Son of God foreshadows the conversion of the Gentiles to Christ."[16]

After the passion, the risen Lord summons his disciples to Galilee (28:10). There, at the mountain, Jesus commissions them, "Go therefore and make disciples of all nations, baptizing them in the name of the Father and of the Son and of the Holy Spirit, teaching them to observe all that I have commanded you; and lo, I am with you always, to the close of the age" (28:19–20). Jesus directs his followers to preach the Gospel, originally intended for Israel, to all the nations, i.e., the Gentiles.

The commission to preach the Gospel to the nations is striking because earlier in the narrative, on two occasions, Jesus says that his mission is only to the lost sheep of Israel. The first of these occurs in chapter 10 when he delivers his missionary discourse. Immediately after choosing the twelve, he instructs them, "Go nowhere among the Gentiles, and enter no town of the Samaritans, but go rather to the lost sheep of the house of Israel" (10:5b–6).

The second incident comes in chapter 15 after Jesus' dispute with the Pharisees over the ritual laws of purity: laws intended to separate Israel from the nations. A Canaanite woman, a Gentile, acclaims Jesus as the Son of David and begs him to heal her daughter. Jesus responds, "I was sent only to the lost sheep of the house of Israel" (15:24). Thus

Jesus proclaims that as the Messiah, the Son of David, his mission is to Israel.

Matthew makes a mighty leap between these two stories and the great commission of chapter 28. I have explained why this happened: Jesus came as the Messiah, the Son of God, but Israel rejected him. In this section I shall explain the result of that rejection: the establishment of the Church. The confession of the Gentiles at the cross and the great commission of 28:16–20 are the climax of a theme Matthew nurtures throughout his narrative. The kingdom of God passes to a new nation which Matthew calls the Church.[17]

A. Intimations of a New People

There are several hints within Matthew's story that the Gospel will eventually reach the Gentiles. The infancy narrative is a prime example. Matthew's genealogy of Jesus identifies him as the "Son of David, the Son of Abraham" (1:1). The first title assures the reader that Jesus is the Jewish Messiah from David's lineage. To that extent Jesus' messiahship seems to exclude non-Jews. But the title Son of Abraham establishes Jesus' identity in such a way that it has relevance for the Gentiles since God promised Abraham, "by you all the families of the earth shall bless themselves" (Gen 12:3b). Matthew takes up this theme when he writes, "I tell you, many will come from east and west and sit at table *with Abraham,* Isaac, and Jacob in the kingdom of heaven" (8:11).[18]

In addition to Abraham, Matthew mentions four non-Israelite women in his genealogy as ancestors of Jesus: Tamar, Rahab, Ruth, and the wife of Uriah.[19] From the genealogy it is clear that this Jewish Messiah of David's lineage will have great significance for the Gentiles. This is immediately confirmed when wise men from the east come to offer homage to the infant king. They, and not the Jews, bring him gifts of gold, frankincense and myrrh (2:11). If the Messiah's own people will not recognize him, another nation will.

John the Baptist makes a similar point as he calls for repentance. When the Pharisees and Sadducees present themselves for baptism, he perceives their hypocrisy and says, "Bear fruit that befits repentance, and do not presume to say to yourselves, 'We have Abraham as our father'; for I tell you, God is able from these stones to raise up children to Abraham" (3:8–9). For the Baptist, the test of incorporation into God's people is bearing good fruit (3:10). Once more Matthew hints that God will raise up a new nation. Like the Messiah, this nation will be the true sons of Abraham, even if it cannot claim physical descent from him.

Before Jesus begins his ministry to Israel, he dwells in Capernaum by the sea (4:13). The choice of such an insignificant city in heathen Galilee seems to contradict what is expected of the Davidic King. Should not David's descendant settle in Jerusalem, the nation's capital and David's royal city? Matthew explains the anomaly by a fulfillment quotation. "The land of Zebulun and the land of Naphtali, toward the sea, across the Jordan, Galilee of the *Gentiles*—the people who sat in darkness have seen a great light, and for those who sat in the region and shadow of death light has dawned" (4:15–16). By the quotation, Matthew shows that the Messiah's residence in Galilee is the fulfillment of a messianic prophecy. The choice of Galilee of the Gentiles, as Jesus' base of operations, points to the future movement of the Gospel to the nations.

After this fulfillment quotation, Jesus begins his ministry of preaching, teaching, and healing (4:23–25; 9:35; 11:1). Although Jesus directs his mission to the lost sheep of the house of Israel, Matthew intimates that someday the mission will include the Gentiles as well. In a summary statement of Jesus' activity, the evangelist notes, "So his fame spread throughout all Syria, and they brought him all the sick, those afflicted with various diseases and pains, demoniacs, epileptics, and paralytics, and he healed them" (4:24).

Later a centurion, presumably a Gentile, asks Jesus to heal his servant. When he agrees, the petitioner responds, "Lord, I am not worthy to have you come under my roof; but only say the word, and my servant will be healed" (8:8). Impressed by the man's trust, Jesus declares that he has never found such faith in Israel and prophesies, "many will come from east and west and sit at table with Abraham, Isaac, and Jacob in the kingdom of heaven, while the sons of the kingdom will be thrown into the outer darkness" (8:11–12). Abraham's children are children of faith as Paul makes clear in Galatians (3:23–29) and Romans (4:1–24).

In chapters 11–12, Jesus is rejected by all segments of Israel. In the midst of that rejection, Matthew applies yet another fulfillment quotation to Jesus (12:17–21). The first part of the quotation (12:18–20) comes from Isaiah 42:1–4. It describes Jesus' healing ministry to Israel in terms of Isaiah's servant. But the conclusion of the quotation, "and in his name will the Gentiles hope," comes from another section of Isaiah (Is 11:10,

Greek version). Matthew has joined the two texts to emphasize that the Servant of Israel, Jesus Messiah, is also the hope of the nations.

At the conclusion of this section which describes Jesus' rejection by Israel (11:2–12:50), Jesus acknowledges his true family: "For whoever does the will of my Father in heaven is my brother, and sister, and mother" (12:50). Becoming a member of Jesus' household is more than a matter of physical descent. The Messiah's family consists of those who do the Father's will. In Matthean parlance, the phrase means doing righteousness as explained by Jesus in the Sermon on the Mount (5:1–7:29).

Because the scribes and Pharisees do not do such righteousness (5:20), Jesus prophesies that they will be excluded from the kingdom. When the Pharisees are offended by his teaching concerning the purity laws (15:3–11), Jesus says, "Every plant which my heavenly Father has not planted will be rooted up" (15:13). The warning is clear. Physical descent does not guarantee membership in God's people. Jesus' Father did not engender all of the members of the present Israel.

It is in a series of parables, however, that Matthew makes his most explicit statements that there will be a future for the Gentiles. At the conclusion of the parable of the workers hired to go into the vineyard (20:1–16), Jesus proclaims, "so the last will be first, and the first last." The last are the Gentiles who have not "borne the burden of the day and the scorching heat" (20:12) but whom God has placed on a footing equal to Israel. In a series of parables (21:28–22:14), Matthew points to the future prepared for the Gentiles. The kingdom will be taken away from Israel's leaders and "given to a nation producing the fruits of it" (21:43). Because the invited are no longer worthy, the messianic banquet hall will be filled with as many as can be found (22:8–10). The many are the Gentiles, and the nation producing the fruit of the kingdom is the Church.

B. The Messiah Turns to His Disciples

What is this nation called the Church which Jesus' death effects? Although the Church does not come into existence until Jesus' death and resurrection, Matthew gives several descriptions of it during Jesus' ministry. Among the most important is that presented in the parable discourse of chapter 13.

This chapter signals an important turning point in Jesus' ministry.[20]

Israel rejects the teaching and healing ministry of Jesus the Messiah in chapters 11–12. As a result, in chapter 13, Jesus addresses Israel in parables, a form of speech which the people cannot understand. When the disciples inquire why Jesus speaks to Israel in parables, he answers: ''because seeing they do not see, and hearing they do not hear, nor do they understand'' (13:13). Chapter 13 serves as the Messiah's response to Israel. If Israel will not listen to his word, he will speak in a language she cannot understand.

Although Jesus turns from Israel in chapter 13, he explains the meaning of the parables to his disciples: ''To you it has been given to know the secrets of the kingdom of heaven, but to them it has not been given'' (13:11). Midway through the chapter, Jesus leaves the crowds and withdraws into the house with his disciples (13:36) where he explains to them the parable of the weeds in the field and delivers still other parables (13:37–50). At the conclusion of this discourse, Jesus asks his disciples, ''Have you understood all this?'' (13:51), and they reply affirmatively.

The movement of this chapter is of supreme importance for grasping Matthew's ecclesiology. When Jesus turns from Israel to instruct his disciples, he is teaching those who will be the nucleus of his Church. The disciples form the core, drawn from Israel, which accepts Jesus as the Messiah and understands his teaching. Throughout this chapter, therefore, Matthew employs the word ''understand'' to define the quality which distinguishes the disciples from Israel. Israel does not understand Jesus' teaching (13:13,14,15,19), but the disciples, the nucleus of the Church, do (13:23,51).

The seven parables of this chapter deal with the nature of the kingdom of heaven. The Church is not identical with the kingdom. But inasmuch as members of the Church are ''sons of the kingdom'' (13:38) to whom God has given the kingdom (21:43), Matthew associates the Church with the kingdom.[21]

In chapter 13 Jesus teaches about the Church in which the ''sons of the kingdom'' anticipate the coming of the kingdom. In the parable of the sower, for example, the reader learns that although many respond to the word, the kingdom is beset by persecution and worldly cares (13:18–23). In the parables of the weeds and of the dragnet, Jesus explains that at the present time the kingdom is a mixed body of good and bad, but at the end of the ages there will be a final separation (13:36–43,47–50). In the meantime, the "sons of the kingdom" must endure this uncomfortable situation. The parables of the mustard seed and the leaven teach that despite the kingdom's insignificant beginnings, it will embrace a multitude of people. Parables such as these imply that the Church, as the community which awaits the Kingdom, will embrace a vast variety of people.

C. The Messiah and His Church

The reality of the Church becomes more explicit in chapters 16 and 18, the only places in the Gospels where the word Church occurs. After Peter's confession at Caesarea Philippi, Jesus pronounces a beatitude upon Peter and makes him the rock foundation of the Church. "Blessed are you, Simon Bar-Jona! For flesh and blood has not revealed this to you, but my Father who is in heaven. And I tell you, you are Peter [rock], and on this rock I will build my Church, and the powers of death shall not prevail against it" (16:17–18). Jesus then gives Peter the authority to bind and loose (16:19). In Matthew's view, he makes Peter the supreme rabbi of the Church, the authorized interpreter of his teaching.[22]

In chapter 18, after his second passion prediction, Jesus delivers his fourth discourse: the Discourse on Church Life. From the point of view of Matthew's story, the Church has not yet come into existence. Nonetheless, Jesus instructs his disciples on the proper relationships which should characterize the new community. The chapter has four distinctive units.[23]

In the first (18:1–5), Jesus defines for his disciples the meaning of true greatness in the kingdom of heaven. It belongs to the one who humbles himself like a child. Jesus says, "Whoever receives one such child in my name receives me" (18:5). Child in this verse does not simply refer to an infant or youngster. As the next section (18:6–14) makes clear, it signifies a member of the Church.

In the second unit (18:6–14), Jesus teaches the disciples the necessity of caring for the "little ones who believe in me" (18:6). The last phrase, "who believe in me," indicates that Jesus is referring to disciples. Thus Matthew coordinates this unit with the first (18:1–5). The members of Jesus' Church are "the little ones" because they have made themselves like children for the sake of the kingdom of heaven. The care of these little ones is so important that scandal within the Church must be avoided at all cost (18:6–9). And if one of these little ones should go astray, it is justifiable to leave the entire congregation in order to retrieve him (18:10–14).

In the third unit (18:15–20), Jesus instructs the disciples how to deal with sinners within the community. The local community of the Church possesses the authority to bind and loose in disciplinary matters (18:18) just as Peter enjoys it in teaching matters.[24] But lest this unit appear overly harsh, Matthew adds a fourth section (18:21–35) which stresses the need for forgiveness. When Peter asks Jesus how often he should forgive his brother, the Lord replies, ''I do not say to you seven times, but seventy times seven'' (18:22). Jesus then delivers the parable of the unforgiving servant (18:23–35) in which he explains the nature of forgiveness. Like the Parable Discourse of chapter 13, the Discourse on Church Life points to the Church that will be established after Jesus' death and resurrection.

In the passion narrative, Israel's disclaimer that Jesus is her Messiah and the confession of the Gentiles indicate that the kingdom is being given to a new nation. At the great commission, the risen Lord instructs his disciples to make disciples of all the nations. Israel is not excluded,[25] but she has lost her exclusive rights. A new nation composed of *all* the nations is born. Matthew has carefully prepared for its arrival. Once more there is a convergence between passion narrative and Gospel theology.

IV.
JESUS THE MODEL OF RIGHTEOUSNESS

Although the main theme of the Matthean passion narrative is Israel's rejection of her Messiah, a number of subsidiary themes play important roles. Chief among them is the picture Matthew presents of Jesus the model of righteousness. It is true, of course, that no disciple can imitate the unique suffering of Jesus whose death effects the forgiveness of sins (26:28). But Jesus' behavior in the face of persecution offers disciples an example to follow when they are faced with the trials that will surely beset them.

In editing the Gethsemane story (26:36–46), Matthew emphasizes Jesus' perseverance in prayer. In the story of Jesus' arrest, he adds special material to show Jesus' complete acceptance of his Father's will (26:52–54). At the trial before the Sanhedrin, Jesus refuses to be put under oath (26:64). In the scene before Pilate, Matthew presents Jesus standing silently before the governor while the chief priests and elders accuse him (27:11–14). In that same scene, Pilate's wife refers to Jesus as "that righteous man" (27:19), and Pilate washes his hands before the crowd, saying, "I am innocent of this man's blood" (27:24). Even Judas confesses that he has betrayed "innocent blood" (27:4). Finally, when Jesus is mocked as the Son of God and the King of Israel (27:39–44), he refuses to save himself or to return insult for insult. Trusting in his Father, he dies as a righteous sufferer.

In his passion story, Matthew presents Jesus as fulfilling his own teaching, especially the instruction given in the Sermon on the Mount (5:1–7:29). The key to this interpretation is the manner in which Matthew begins his passion story, "When Jesus had finished *all* of these sayings, he said to his disciples, 'You know that after two days the Passover is coming, and the Son of Man will be delivered up to be crucified' " (26:1–2). The reference to "all of these sayings" points to the Sermon on the Mount and the other great discourses of Matthew's Gospel (10:1–42; 13:1–52; 18:1–35; 24:1–25:46). Having taught his disciples in word, Jesus teaches them through his passion so that they will be able to go and make disciples of all nations (28:19). The passion becomes Jesus' final teaching, the lesson without which the disciples cannot fully understand his identity.

In fulfilling his own teaching, Jesus becomes a model of righteousness, that is, he does the will of God. The theme of doing God's will, righteousness, is an important motif for the first evangelist.[26] In this section, I examine that theme in order to show how Matthew's picture of Jesus' behavior during the passion is related to his Gospel theology.

A. *Jesus Comes To Fulfill All Righteousness (3:15)*

Matthew's first presentation of the adult Christ comes in chapter 3, the baptism of Jesus (3:13–17). Matthew and Mark describe the scene in the same general fashion. Jesus arrives at the Jordan to be baptized. John baptizes him and a heavenly voice declares that Jesus is God's beloved Son. But Matthew differs from Mark in one significant way. Be-

fore Jesus' baptism, there is a conversation between Jesus and John. The
Baptist tries to prevent Jesus' baptism, saying, "I need to be baptized
by you, and do you come to me?" (3:14), at which Jesus responds, "Let
it be so now; for thus it is fitting for us to fulfill all righteousness (*dikaiosynē*)" (3:15). In his first presentation of the adult Christ, Matthew
describes him as fulfilling all righteousness.

The concept of righteousness in Matthew should not be confused
with the idea of righteousness in the letters of Paul.[27] There righteousness indicates the salvation which God effects on behalf of humankind
in the Christ event. The primary focus of the Pauline notion is what God
has done for humanity. To emphasize this, Paul contrasts the righteousness which comes through Christ with the righteousness that derives
from doing the works of the Mosaic law (Gal 2:15–21).

In Matthew, the concept of righteousness receives an added emphasis. Like the Pauline notion, righteousness in Matthew still connotes
the element of gift, the new relationship established between God and
the individual (5:6; 6:33). But in addition, righteousness for Matthew
includes the demand for proper conduct in keeping with God's will
(3:15; 5:10,20; 6:1; 21:32).[28] Righteousness is God's demand upon his
creatures, and therefore it refers to proper conduct before him.[29] It de-
notes "the God-demanded behavior which is characteristic of those who
are to enter the kingdom of heaven."[30] The Pauline and Matthean no-
tions are not contradictory inasmuch as they speak of what *God* wills for
humanity (Matthew) and of what *God* has done for humanity (Paul). But
"where Paul speaks of righteousness as God's gift and of faith as the
human response, Matthew sees the kingdom as the gift and righteousness
as the response."[31] Conzelmann puts it well when he writes that "the
parallel is between righteousness in Paul and the kingdom of God in Matthew."[32]

To explain this, I refer to an incident which occurs during Jesus'
Jerusalem ministry: the question of Jesus' authority. When the religious
leaders ask by what authority he carries out his Jerusalem ministry, Jesus
questions them about John's baptism (21:25). After they refuse to answer, he tells the parable of the two sons, the parable of the wicked tenants, and the parable of the marriage feast (21:28–22:14). In the first of
these, he condemns the Pharisees for not repenting at John's baptism.
"For John came to you *in the way of righteousness,* and you did not

believe him, but the tax collectors and harlots believed him; and even when you saw it, you did not afterward repent and believe him'' (21:32). From this it is clear that righteousness refers to correct, moral behavior.[33] John preached a way of righteousness, that is, a way in conformity to God's will. Because the religious leaders refused to repent at his preaching, they stand condemned.

In light of the above, the conversation between John and Jesus takes on deeper meaning. Matthew presents Jesus as the one who comes to fulfill all righteousness: to do God's will. John tries to prevent this baptism because he knows that the Messiah will baptize ''with the Holy Spirit and with fire'' (3:11). The baptism of Jesus, therefore, seems superfluous, a humiliation of the Messiah. But Jesus insists because his messiahship surpasses ordinary expectations. He comes to do the will of the Father (26:42). The acceptance of John's baptism is the first step to the passion. The doing of God's will is the hallmark of Jesus' life.

B. Jesus' Disciples and the Greater Righteousness (5:17–20).

Jesus' primary teaching concerning righteousness comes in his first great discourse, the Sermon on the Mount (5:1–7:29). This sermon explains the radical demands of God's will. It provides a program of behavior for Jesus' disciples, and during the passion narrative Jesus exemplifies what he preaches in this discourse.

The sermon begins with eight beautitudes (5:3–10), but its programmatic statement[34] is found in 5:17–20:

Think not that I have come to abolish the law and the prophets; I have come not to abolish them but to fulfill them. For truly, I say to you, till heaven and earth pass away, not an iota, not a dot, will pass from the law until all is accomplished. Whoever then relaxes one of the least of these commandments and teaches men so, shall be called least in the kingdom of heaven; but he who does them and teaches them shall be called great in the kingdom of heaven. For I tell you, unless your righteousness exceeds that of the scribes and Pharisees, you will never enter the kingdom of heaven.

According to Matthew, despite what Jesus' detractors say, Jesus has not come to destroy the Mosaic law. In this regard, Matthew is one of the more conservative writers of the New Testament. Like James, in the Acts of the Apostles (Acts 21:20), Matthew's vision of Christianity includes being zealous for the law. Thus Jesus says, "Think not that I have come to abolish the law and the prophets." But at the same time, Matthew and his community practice the Mosaic law *as interpreted* by Jesus Messiah. So Jesus says, "I have come not to abolish them [the law and the prophets] but to fulfill them."

The word fulfill has a double sense. On the one hand, it can simply mean to do. But on the other, it can also mean to complete, to bring to fruition. In light of Matthew's concern to present Jesus as the fulfillment of Old Testament prophecy, the second interpretation must not be neglected. Jesus comes not only to do the law, but to fulfill it by bringing it into accord with God's original will.

The Pharisees practice the law, but since they do not practice it as Jesus the Messiah interprets it, they do not fulfill God's will. Therefore Jesus says, "unless your righteousness exceeds that of the scribes and Pharisees, you will never enter the kingdom of heaven." It is not enough, now that the messianic age has begun, to practice the law. One must practice the law as Jesus the Messiah interprets it. One must practice the greater righteousness, that is, accomplish God's will as Jesus teaches it.

Jesus calls his disciples to the demands of this righteousness several times in the Sermon on the Mount. In the fourth beatitude he says, "Blessed are those who hunger and thirst for righteousness, for they shall be satisfied" (5:6). That is, God will answer the request of those who seek to know and do his will. At the close of a long section on care and anxiety (6:25–34), Jesus promises, "But seek first his kingdom and his righteousness, and all these things shall be yours as well" (6:33) That is, God will provide for those who seek to do his will by submitting to his kingly rule.

Finally, Matthew shows the concrete nature of righteousness when he explains it in terms of almsgiving, prayer, and fasting (6:1–18). At the beginning of this section, Jesus says, "Beware of practicing your piety [*dikaiosynē*, righteousness] before men in order to be seen by them; for then you will have no reward from your Father who is in heaven" (6:1). Next, in 6:2–18, Jesus describes righteousness in terms of almsgiving, prayer, and fasting. Righteousness as interpreted by Jesus involves "doing."

The clearest expression of doing the law as interpreted by Jesus comes in the six antitheses (5:21–48) which follow the programmatic statement of 5:17–20. As if to explain that statement, Matthew has Jesus give six explicit examples: teaching about anger (5:21–26); teaching about adultery (5:27–30); teaching about divorce (5:31–32); teaching about oaths (5:33–37); teaching about retaliation (5:38–42); teaching about love for enemies (5:43–48). In all of these antitheses the pattern is the same. Jesus begins, "You have heard that it was said to the men of old . . ." Then he continues "But I say to you . . ." thereby contrasting his authority with that of Moses.

In the first, second, and sixth antitheses (anger, adultery, love for enemies), Jesus intensifies the law by increasing its demands. In the second, third, and fourth (divorce, oaths, retaliation) he abrogates the law and replaces it with more stringent requirements. There should be no oaths, no divorce, no retaliation since on these issues the law contravenes God's original purpose. So Jesus calls his disciples to practice the greater righteousness, that is, God's original will as Jesus teaches it.

The Sermon on the Mount presents Jesus' programmatic statement for discipleship. It pronounces a blessing upon those who strive to do God's will. But in addition, it provides a key to understanding Jesus' behavior during the passion. He refuses to be placed under oath by the high priest (26:64) because such oaths violate God's will. He refuses to retaliate when mocked (26:67–68; 27:27–31,39–44) because retaliation does not accord with God's will. He prays to the Father in the same words that he teaches his disciples (26:39,42) because he seeks to do God's will. Jesus is the ultimately happy man because he fulfills the demands of righteousness by doing God's will. For Matthew, the passion exemplifies the deepest meaning of the Sermon on the Mount.

C. Persecuted for the Sake of Righteousness (5:10–11)

Why was Jesus put to death? Matthew provides many answers, but his most profound response has to do with righteousness: the performance of God's will.

The Pharisees and scribes accuse Jesus of violating the sabbath (12:1–14) and transgressing the tradition of the elders (15:1–2). During his Jerusalem ministry, the confrontation comes to a head when Jesus cleanses the temple and heals the blind and lame within its precincts. As a result, the children acclaim him as the Son of David (21:12–17). But in the trial before the Sanhedrin the religious leaders condemn Jesus to death on the grounds of blasphemy (26:65–66). Because Jesus does not deny that he is the Messiah, the Son of God, and because he prophesies that he will return as the Son of Man, they deliver him to Pilate.

The Sanhedrin condemns Jesus to death for blasphemy, but the readers of Matthew's Gospel know that he is the Messiah, the Son of God, who will return at the end of the ages as the Son of Man. Jesus has not blasphemed. The charge of blasphemy is only the *apparent* reason for his condemnation. The real cause is righteousness. Jesus dies because he insists upon doing his Father's will; he fulfills all righteousness (3:15).

According to Matthew, righteous behavior results in persecution. In the eighth beatitude Jesus promises, ''Blessed are those who are persecuted for righteousness' sake, for theirs is the kingdom of heaven'' (5:10). That is, blessed are those who are persecuted for doing God's will. Jesus is the primary example of the righteous man persecuted for performing God's will.[35]

In several texts, Jesus points to the suffering which his disciples will face because of their association with him. Immediately after the eighth beatitude, he pronounces a ninth, longer and different in form from the others: ''Blessed are you when men revile you and persecute you and utter all kinds of evil against you falsely *on my account*'' (5:11). In his missionary discourse to the disciples (10:1–42), Jesus warns them, ''and you will be dragged before governors and kings *for my sake,* to bear testimony before them and the Gentiles'' (10:18). Jesus establishes a relationship between himself and the disciples. Just as he was persecuted for doing his Father's will, they will be persecuted for their performance of God's will by confessing and preaching that he is the Messiah. Righteousness, doing God's will, ultimately leads to persecution.

In the passion, Matthew presents Jesus as the model of righteous behavior. The real cause for Jesus' death is that he fulfilled all righteousness by doing God's appointed will. The passion of Jesus is the fulfillment of his teaching, especially his Sermon on the Mount. Disciples who follow Jesus in the way of the greater righteousness can expect that their association with him will lead to similar persecution.

CONCLUSION

This chapter has examined four themes suggested by Matthew's passion narrative and endeavored to show their growth and development in the rest of the Gospel. The first theme was Christological in nature, the advent of Jesus Messiah, the Son of God. The heightened Christology of Matthew's passion narrative is part of the wider fabric of his Gospel story. Matthew adopts Mark's basic Christology and then elaborates upon it. To accomplish this, he begins his story with an extended introduction concerning the origin and identity of Jesus (1:1–4:16). He increases the Christological titles applied to Jesus, gives new emphasis to Jesus as Son of David, and expands upon Jesus' relationship to his heavenly Father.

The second and third themes of this chapter were more ecclesiological in nature. Israel's rejection of her Messiah, so evident in the trial before Pilate, is the major dramatic movement of this Gospel. Matthew's story explains how the Gospel moves from Israel to the Church. This transferral does not necessarily exclude Israel, but it does limit her exclusive rights. With Israel's rejection of the Gospel, the kingdom of God is given "to a nation producing the fruits of it" (21:43). For Matthew, this refers to the Church which Jesus Messiah begins to gather even during his ministry. Because Israel rejects Jesus during his Galilean ministry (11:1–12:50), he turns from Israel (13:36) and instructs his disciples. These disciples become the nucleus of the nation producing the fruits of the kingdom. At the end of the Gospel, the risen Lord commissions them to make disciples of all nations (28:19).

The final section returned to the theme of Christology. Jesus Messiah is a model of righteousness for his Church inasmuch as he performs God's will. Jesus is persecuted because he insists upon fulfilling all righteousness. In doing righteousness, he offers an example of his own teaching, especially as presented in the Sermon on the Mount.

As in the Gospel of Mark, there is a convergence between Matthew's passion narrative and his Gospel theology. Important emphases in the passion narrative are the outcome of Matthew's Gospel theology.

Chapter Seven

THE PASSION ACCORDING TO LUKE: OVERVIEW

At the beginning of this century, Martin Dibelius, a form critic and pioneer in researching the passion narratives, wrote:

> For Luke, the suffering Saviour is the Man of God who is attacked by evil powers and who, with His patience and forgiveness, is a model of innocent suffering. Luke regards these events in the place where he consequently puts them not as the completion of salvation, but as the story of a saintly man closely united with God. The literary consequence of this view is that Luke presents the Passion as a martyrdom.[1]

Dibelius' verdict has held sway in New Testament studies for more than fifty years. The reasons why seem obvious. In several places, Luke does portray Jesus' suffering in terms of martyrdom. For example, in the Roman trial, Pilate declares Jesus innocent three times (23:4,14,22), giving the impression that this is the ordeal of an innocent sufferer. As Jesus is led out to be crucified, a group of women follow him and lament his plight (23:27), thereby making a similar point. During his crucifixion, Jesus prays for his persecutors (23:34a)[2] and by the example of his innocent suffering manages to convert a criminal crucified with him (23:40–43). Finally, at the moment of his death, Jesus dies peacefully (23:46). As a result, a centurion declares him innocent (*dikaios,* 23:47), and the multitudes return home beating their breasts (23:48). On first reading, it appears that Dibelius' verdict is sound: Luke presents the passion as a martyrdom.

I.

The Theological Character of Luke's Narrative

Although there are several elements common to the genre of martyrdom in Luke's passion, it would be misleading to categorize the narrative as such. First, a closer reading of Luke's account discloses that the evangelist presents Jesus as more than a martyr. According to Luke, Jesus undertakes his passion because it is God's will for him; it is his destiny. There is an important difference between the death of Jesus and the death of a martyr.[3] The martyr endures unjust persecution and suffering as a righteous sufferer, but Jesus undergoes the passion because it is his *destiny* as Messiah to suffer (''Was it not necessary that the Christ should suffer these things and enter into his glory?''—24:26).

Second, it is true that Luke presents Jesus' death as a model of innocent suffering, thereby making him an example for future martyrs such as Stephen (Acts 7). However, he also portrays the whole of Jesus' life, especially his journey to Jerusalem, as a model for would-be disciples. When the centurion declares that Jesus was innocent he pronounces more than a juridical verdict. In terms of Luke's story, the centurion makes a statement which evaluates the *whole* of Jesus' life. Consequently, the preferred translation for *dikaios* in 23:47 is ''righteous.'' The centurion acknowledges that the whole of Jesus' life demonstrates that he, not his enemies, stood in the correct relationship to God.[4] Jesus, not his enemies, was righteous.

Finally, although Luke highlights Jesus' innocent suffering, he views him as more than a martyr. On several occasions he reminds the reader that the one who suffers is God's Son (22:29,42,70; 23:34,46). This Son of God is also a Prophet (22:63–65; 23:29–31), a Savior (23:35), a King (23:2,37, 38), and the Messiah (22:67; 23:2,35,39). In other words, while it is true that Jesus suffers innocently, as many martyrs before him did, he endures his passion in his capacity as Prophet, Savior, King, Messiah, Son of God.

Dibelius' category of martyrdom has been readily accepted because many commentators have not read Luke's passion narrative in light of his Gospel theology. In what follows, I interpret Luke's account against this wider background. Reading the passion, it is evident that certain themes arise again and again: the passion as Jesus' destiny; the passion as a model for discipleship; the passion as the rejection of Jesus the Prophet; the passion as the death of God's royal Son. In light of these themes, I shall review Luke's Gospel theology and show how the evangelist develops each theme throughout his narrative.

II.
THE QUESTION OF SOURCES

When examining the passion according to Matthew, I indicated that Mark is Matthew's primary source. It was important to make a detailed comparison between Mark and Matthew inasmuch as changes on the part of Matthew often reveal important aspects of his theology. The passion according to Luke presents special problems. Even a casual reading discloses that Luke differs from Mark in several ways. For example, his narrative (1) does not contain all of the incidents found in Mark, (2) offers new material not present in Mark, and (3) has a different arrangement of several important events.

How can these differences be explained? What is their significance? These questions have vexed scholars for more than a generation. It is not my intention to offer a new solution, but since it is helpful for the reader of Luke's passion narrative to be acquainted with the question of sources, I shall review the possibilities.

The data is as follows.[5] First, in his passion story Luke does not relate all of the incidents found in Mark. Among these the most important are: the anointing of Jesus at Bethany (Mk 14:3–9); Jesus' intense grief in Gethsemane (Mk 14:33–34); the fact that Jesus returned to prayer, while in Gethsemane, a second and third time (Mk 14:38b–42); the flight of the disciples (Mk 14:50–52); the false witnesses at Jesus' trial and the leadership role played by the high priest (Mk 14:55–61a); the silence of Jesus before the Sanhedrin (Mk 14:61) and Pilate (Mk 15:4–5); the mockeries by the Roman soldiers (Mk 15:16–20a) and the passers-by (Mk 15:29–30); Jesus' great cry and the reference to Elijah (Mk 15:34–35); the amazement of Pilate at Jesus' quick death (Mk 15:44–45).

Second, the Lucan passion narrative contains material not found in Mark: the intense desire of Jesus to eat the Passover meal with his disciples (Lk 22:15–16); the dispute among the disciples and Jesus' admonitions about discipleship (Lk 22:24–30); Jesus' words to Peter concerning the denial (Lk 22:31–34); the saying about the two swords (Lk 22:35–38); the appearance of the angel during Jesus' agony (Lk 22:43–44); the mockery by Herod's soldiers (Lk 23:6–12); Pilate's defense of Jesus' innocence (Lk 23:13–16); the women of Jerusalem (Lk 23:27–31); the incident of the two criminals (Lk 23:39–43).

Finally, the Lucan narrative presents several events in an order different from that found in Mark. In Luke the disclosure of the betrayer occurs after the meal (22:21–23); in Mark it comes before. In Luke the announcement of Peter's betrayal happens while the disciples are still at supper (22:33–34); in Mark it occurs in Gethsemane. In Luke Peter's denial of Jesus (22:54–62) and the mockery of Jesus (22:63–65) precede the trial before the Jewish authorities (22:66–71); in Mark the trial takes place prior to both events.

Scholars interpret these data differently. Several authors are struck by both the amount and the distinctiveness of the non-Marcan material in Luke's passion account. On the basis of this non-Marcan material, they argue that Luke had access to another passion account in addition to Mark's. They claim that in composing his version of the passion, Luke followed this other narrative. At various points Luke would have inserted sections of the Marcan passion or expanded this passion narrative in light of Mark's.[6] The general approach of this theory is to explain the additions, omissions, and rearrangement of Luke's story in light of another narrative. One of the most compelling arguments on behalf of the theory is that whenever Luke employs Mark as a source in the rest of the Gospel, he seems to follow Mark's order of events. That there is rearrangement in the passion story suggests that Luke followed another narrative in addition to Mark, one with a slightly different order of events.

A second group of scholars offers another interpretation of the data. They contend that Luke's only source is Mark and that all of the additions, omissions and rearrangements in Luke can be explained in terms of Luke's editorial activity. These scholars see Luke as a creative writer and theologian who is the master of his material. Changes in Luke's story do not necessarily point to another source. They result from his style or theological agenda.[7]

The objection that Luke usually follows his sources without changing the order of events is not as damaging as it appears. A closer examination of the text reveals that Luke's order in the passion narrative is substantially the same as that found in Mark. Joseph Fitzmyer writes:

> The Marcan passion narrative is the shortest of the four canonical accounts and is devoid of any peculiar traditions of its own, save that of the flight of the naked young disciple (14:51–52). If one counts that story of flight separately from the account of Jesus' arrest (14:43–50), the Marcan narrative consists of eighteen episodes. The twenty episodes of the Lucan passion narrative, as I have subdivided it (see pp. 141–142), correspond to fourteen of the Marcan episodes *in almost the same order*. The continuous thread of his account is based on Mark. The significant correspondence argues strongly for Lucan dependence on the Marcan narrative in this part of the Gospel.[8]

In addition, Marion Soards points out that there are other places in the Gospel, besides the passion narrative, where Luke differs substantially from Mark (e.g., the transfiguration) and where it is not necessary to posit a source other than Mark.[9] He writes, "That Luke often follows Mark closely should not create a maxim that he always must do so, as if Luke wrote in a rigidly uniform manner."[10] In fact, Luke's second volume, the Acts of the Apostles, reveals that he can be a creative writer. That he has freely edited his primary source (Mark) for the passion narrative should come as no surprise.

The importance of these theories is twofold. First, if either could be proved, it would teach us something about the manner in which the passion narrative was transmitted. This, in turn, would increase our knowledge of early Christianity. Second, each hypothesis says something about the kind of author that Luke is. The first envisions him as a conservative editor, one who hesitates to alter his sources. The second interprets him as a more creative writer. He is the master of the traditions he received, and he edits them in light of his theological vision.

Although neither solution has met with unanimous approval, I am in agreement with those authors who view Luke as a more creative writer. This is not to say that he created events where there were none. By calling Luke creative I mean that he edits and arranges his traditions in a manner which expresses his theological convictions.

What traditions were available to Luke? Only Mark's narrative? Mark's narrative plus some scattered traditions? Mark's narrative plus another continuous passion narrative which we no longer possess? The answer may never be known. But I suspect that nearly all of the differences between Luke and Mark can be accounted for by Luke's editorial activity and the availability to him of special traditions not employed by or known to Mark.

Chapter Eight

THE PASSION ACCORDING TO LUKE: COMMENTARY
Luke 22:1–23:56

I.

THE PLOT TO DESTROY JESUS, 22:1–6

The Lucan passion narrative, like those of Matthew and Mark, begins with a plot to destroy Jesus. The plotting occurs just before the Feast of Unleavened Bread, which Luke identifies as the Passover. The principal actors are the chief priests, the scribes, Judas, and Satan. The reason for the conspiracy is that the religious leaders have begun to fear the influence which Jesus enjoys among the people.[1]

Like the other passion stories, Luke's recalls and emphasizes that the death of Jesus took place during Passover. The Feast of Unleavened Bread, called Mazzoth, followed Passover and continued for seven days, the fifteenth to the twenty-first of the month of Nisan (March/April). During this period the people ate only unleavened bread in order to recall how their ancestors ate similar bread at the time of the exodus (Ex 23:15; 34:18). Although the two festivals were distinct, at the time of Jesus popular usage merged the two and treated them as a unity, as does Luke.[2] What is important for Luke, and for all of the evangelists, is that Jesus died during this cherished feast of national liberation. The implications are not difficult to decipher. At the first Passover, God delivered his people from the slavery of Egypt. On the Passover of Jesus' death, God performed a similar miracle of salvation. Thus in the account of the transfiguration (9:28–36), Luke foreshadows this exodus motif when he writes, "And behold, two men talked with him, Moses and Elijah, who appeared in glory and spoke of his departure [the Greek is *exodon*, literally, 'exodus'], which he was to accomplish at Jerusalem'' (9:30–31).

The chief priests, the scribes and Judas conspire against Jesus. All of them appeared earlier in the narrative. Judas is one of the twelve who was destined to receive a share in the kingdom (12:32). But as early as the selection of the twelve, Luke indicates Judas' destiny: "and Judas Iscariot who became a traitor" (6:16).

The chief priests formed a sort of consistory or advisory council with the high priest. With him they were responsible for running the daily affairs of the temple. They make their appearance in the last portion of Luke's Gospel during the time of Jesus' Jerusalem ministry (19:45–21:38). The scribes were the theologians of the day and could belong to either the party of the Pharisees or that of the Sadducees. They appear much earlier in Luke's account. During the period of Jesus' Galilean ministry (4:14–9:50), they oppose Jesus' activity (5:21,30; 6:7; also see 11:53; 15:2). Their opposition now does not catch Jesus by surprise. They plot in secret, but Jesus has long been aware of his fate and the role they will play as the first passion prediction shows: "The Son of Man must suffer many things, and be rejected by the elders and chief priests and scribes, and be killed, and on the third day be raised" (9:22).

Upon his arrival in Jerusalem, Jesus cleansed the temple (19:45–46). Instead of being scandalized at this behavior, the people hang upon Jesus' words (19:48). The chief priests and scribes, by contrast, decided to destroy Jesus. When they demand to know by what authority he does such things (20:2), he asks them if the baptism of John was from heaven or from men (20:4). They refuse to answer because they realize that if they do not acknowledge John as a prophet, the people will stone them (20:5–7). As a result of this encounter, Jesus tells the parable of the vineyard (20:9–18) which he directs at the religious leaders. They, in turn, seek to arrest him, but because "they feared the people," they do not (20:19).

The religious leaders continue their attempts to trap Jesus (20:20–40), none of which succeed. At the end of chapter 20, Jesus warns the people to beware of the scribes (20:45–47). It is during the course of Jesus' Jerusalem ministry, especially as narrated in chapter 20, that Luke explains the reasons for the plot against Jesus. He has dared to challenge the temple establishment. He has aroused the hopes of the people, so that "early in the morning all the people came to him in the temple to hear him" (21:38). In effect, Jesus Messiah has taken possession of his Father's house, an event foreshadowed in the infancy narrative (2:41–51). He teaches Israel in the temple, the place of authority which properly belongs to the religious leaders. His teaching authority has replaced theirs, and for this he must die.

But how can the religious leaders bring about this destruction? Because they fear the people, they seem powerless to act. It is at this point that Judas *and Satan* intervene.

Matthew and Mark highlight the role of Judas, but only Luke speaks of Satan. In this regard, he is similar to John who notes, at the beginning of the Last Supper, that the devil had put it into the heart of Judas to betray Jesus (Jn 13:2). Luke's reference to the role of Satan discloses that more than human decisions are involved in the passion of Jesus. There are forces present which surpass the human characters of the story. Thus during the course of the meal Jesus tells Peter that Satan desires to sift him and his fellow apostles like wheat (22:31). On the Mount of Olives Jesus warns the apostles to pray lest they enter into temptation (22:40). And at the moment of his arrest he says to his captors, "But this is your hour, and the power of darkness" (22:53). Luke gives his passion story the character of a great eschatological struggle. Satan has found the opportune time to assault Jesus and his followers, the opportune time for which he has been searching since the temptations in the desert (4:13).[3]

But one must not overemphasize the role which Satan plays. He enables the passion story to move forward but his activity does not absolve the human actors of guilt as Luke makes clear. In the final analysis, Judas betrays Jesus for the sake of money (22:4–5). He has not understood Jesus' missionary discourse (9:1–6) or his instructions not to be absorbed with anxiety for possessions (12:22–34).[4] In like fashion, Peter and the rest of the apostles will have to assume the responsibility for their own failures, because they have not heeded Jesus' injunction to pray lest they enter into temptation (22:40).

The Lucan passion is the moment of darkness which foreshadows the great eschatological trial that comes at the end of time. Forces greater than the human characters of the story are involved. In order to withstand this trial and all future trials, Jesus' disciples must heed his teaching: "Take heed, and beware of all covetousness; for a man's life does not consist in the abundance of his possessions" (12:15); and "pray that you may not enter into temptation" (22:40).

II.
THE LAST SUPPER 22:7–30

This section consists of two parts and several subsections. When compared to the accounts of Matthew and Mark, Luke's narration of Jesus' last meal is longer and differs at several points. The Lucan version has some affinities with the Johannine tradition and several elements of what has been called a Farewell Testament.

A. *Preparations for the Meal (22:7–13)*

This brief incident stands in contrast to what has just taken place. In vv. 3–6, Luke describes one of the twelve betraying his master. Now he depicts two of the twelve (Peter and John) obeying the Lord's command. Although Jesus has been betrayed by one of the twelve, the rest of the apostles still remain faithful to him.

The incident occurs on the Day of Unleavened Bread, "on which the Passover lamb had to be sacrificed." Once more it is clear that Luke views the two festivals, Unleavened Bread and Passover, as one. Strictly speaking the Day of Unleavened Bread began after Passover, on the fifteenth of Nisan, but Luke dates it with the beginning of Passover. Preparations for Passover began on the fourteenth. At midday of the fourteenth the lambs for the Passover supper were slain. The supper, eaten after sunset, would then be celebrated on the fifteenth since the Jewish day began after sundown.

According to Matthew, Mark and Luke, Jesus' last meal with his disciples was a Passover supper. According to John, the Passover supper had not yet taken place (see Jn 18:28; 19:14). The Johannine Last Supper, therefore, was not a Passover meal.[5] This discrepancy between John and the Synoptics derives, in part, from different theological views. John wants to emphasize that Jesus dies as the new Passover Lamb. So Pilate condemns Jesus to death on Preparation Day, at the very hour the Passover lambs were being slain for the Passover meal (19:14).[6] By contrast, the Synoptic writers seem more intent upon showing the connection between the Eucharist and the Passover tradition. According to them, the Passover lambs had already been sacrificed and Jesus' Last Supper was a Passover meal. Whereas John wants to stress that Jesus dies as the Passover lamb, the purpose of Luke and the other Synoptic writers is to emphasize that Jesus' last meal with his apostles was a Passover supper, the meal which recalled Israel's freedom from bondage (see Ex 12:3–20 for a description of how and why the meal was to be observed).

This section also underlines Jesus' prophetic knowledge. The final events of Jesus' life do not catch him by surprise. His death is not unexpected nor does he resist it. He carefully plans this final and important meal with his closest friends to whom he will give the Eucharist and deliver a farewell address. As regards Jesus' prophetic knowledge, the story is similar to the account of his triumphal entry into Jerusalem (19:29–35). Then he sent two of his disciples to find a colt in a predetermined spot. Now he sends Peter and John to follow a man to a predetermined house. Then he told the two disciples that if anyone questioned them they were to respond, ''the Lord has need of it.'' Now he tells Peter and John to say, ''Where is the guest room, where I am to eat the passover with my disciples?'' Finally, both stories note that the disciples ''found it as he had told them.'' In both incidents Luke portrays Jesus as a Prophet fully aware of the events which will take place.

The Lucan version of the story is similar to that in Matthew and Mark except that Luke attributes the initiative for this final meal to Jesus. It is not the disciples who come to the Lord and ask where they should prepare the Passover supper (Mk 14:12, Mt 26:17); it is Jesus who calls two of them by name and tells them what to do: ''So Jesus sent Peter and John, saying. . . .'' Luke places Jesus in the role of Teacher and Lord. Not only is Jesus aware of the events which will transpire, he remains Lord over them. Although his Jerusalem ministry has come to a close, he continues to teach his chosen ones and remains their Teacher.

B. The Supper and Jesus' Farewell Discourse (22:14–38)

Having described the careful and prophetic manner in which Jesus prepares for the Passover meal, Luke narrates the events of the Last Supper. In doing so he presents a slightly different account from that found in Matthew and Mark. Put briefly, Luke's narrative is longer than that of the other two evangelists. Jesus engages in table talk[7] with his apostles which prepares them for the events of the passion and the period after his death. As regards the farewell discourse, Luke is again similar to John in whose passion account there is an even longer farewell address (see John 13–17).

Most studies of the Last Supper concentrate upon the Eucharist and the words of institution. As a result, many readers do not appreciate the new emphasis present in Luke's story. Whereas Mark and Matthew focus upon the supper as the moment when Jesus institutes the Eucharist, Luke employs the meal as an opportunity not only to narrate the words of institution but also as an occasion for Jesus' farewell discourse to his disciples.

In light of this insight scholars suggest that Luke casts his narrative of the Last Supper in the genre of the Farewell Testament.[8] The Farewell Testament is a common genre found in the Old Testament and much of the literature of late Judaism. In the Old Testament, for example, the dying Jacob assembles his sons and tells them what will befall them in the time after his death (Gen 47:29—49:33). Joshua (Jos 23:1—24:30) and David (1 Kgs 2:1–10) do much the same. The genre came to its maturity in the literature of late Judaism during the period of the second temple. Among its best examples is the *Testament of the Twelve Patriarchs*. The authors of the New Testament also knew and employed the genre (Jn 13–17; Acts 20:17–38; 2 Tim; 2 Pet).

Among the important elements of the genre are the following. The hero determines that his death is imminent. He assembles a group such as his family, his kinsmen or the leaders of the people and announces this fact. This announcement takes place during the course of a speech in which the hero retraces the course of history or of his past life, and then speaks of the future. By this speech he prepares them and their descendants for the future and encourages them to live a life of justice. Finally, there is usually an account of the hero's death and burial.

Luke does not slavishly follow this literary form, but several of the elements characteristic of farewell testaments are present in this section and the genre is helpful for understanding the material. It is evident from Luke's second volume, the Acts of the Apostles, that he is acquainted with the genre. In Acts 20:17–38, Paul delivers a farewell speech to the elders of Ephesus at Miletus. Nearly all authors agree that the speech is an outstanding example of the Farewell Testament. In light of the frequent parallels between the lives of Jesus and Paul in Luke-Acts,[9] it is not surprising that Luke employs elements of the same genre in what is Jesus' final discourse to his apostles. This section may be organized in the following manner.

> Jesus, the testator, announces his death (14–23)
>> by explaining that this is his last Passover (15–18)
>> by miming his death (19–20)
>> by announcing his betrayer (21–23)
> Jesus, the testator, recalls his past life (24–30)
>> during which he acted as servant (24–27)
>> during which the apostles remained with him (28–30)
> Jesus, the testator, looks to the future (31–38)
>> when Peter will momentarily fail (31–34)
>> when a time of struggle will begin (35–38)

The advantage of this arrangement is that it puts Jesus' table talk with his apostles in sharper focus. Jesus delivers a final instruction to the apostles who, in the Acts of the Apostles, will become the new rulers of the reestablished Israel.[10]

(1) *Jesus Announces His Death (22:14–23)*. This section consists of three distinct units (see chart above). The first is vv. 15–18. Three of the verses (15–17) are special to Luke. He notes that when the "hour" arrived Jesus sat at table and his apostles with him. The hour is no ordinary one; it is the hour of the passion predicted by Jesus (9:22) and the goal of his Jerusalem journey begun at 9:51. At the moment of Jesus' arrest, Luke will again refer to this hour but then he will describe it as the hour of Jesus' enemies and of the power of darkness (22:53).

Having set the scene, Luke once more portrays Jesus as a prophet fully conscious of his destiny. Jesus has earnestly desired to eat this Passover meal with his apostles because he knows that it is the last he will share with them before the final establishment of the kingdom of God. The sayings of vv. 15–18 are a prophetic announcement of Jesus' death, but the prophecy already carries a note of victory. In two references to the kingdom, Jesus makes it clear that death will not conquer him. The next Passover which Jesus shares will be in the kingdom of God (22:16), and the next time he drinks wine, God's kingdom will have arrived (22:18).[11]

The cup of wine mentioned in v. 18 does not have anything to do with the Eucharist. Rather, vv. 15–18 refer to the Passover meal which Jesus is celebrating.[12] It is important to keep this unit distinct from what follows.

Verses 19–20 form the second unit. They narrate the institution of the Eucharist. In their present context they also serve to announce Jesus' death. Jesus mimes his impending death and interprets its meaning by pointing to the broken bread and the cup of wine. The precise text of these verses is disputed since one important manuscript omits vv. 19b–20. The majority of manuscripts, however, witness to this longer text.[13]

The words of institution recorded by Luke appear to come from a tradition similar to that found in 1 Corinthians 11:23–26, especially verses 24–25: "*and when he had given thanks, he broke it,* and said, '*This is my body which is for you. Do this in remembrance of me.*' In the same way also the cup, after supper, saying, 'This cup is the new covenant in my blood. Do this, as often as you drink it, in remembrance of me.' " The italicized words correspond with Luke's account.

The Lucan tradition differs from the Marcan in the following ways. First, Luke emphasizes that Jesus gives his body and blood on behalf of his disciples: ". . . my body . . . given for you . . . this cup which is poured out for you." The "for you" formula, *hyper hymōn,* demonstrates that Luke attaches salvific value to the death of Jesus (see Acts 20:28 which also points to the significance of Jesus' death).[14] Second, Luke makes the cup the sign of the new covenant whereas Mark speaks of the blood of the covenant. In doing this Luke alludes to a rich Old Testament background. On the one hand, the words recall the incident at Sinai when Moses sprinkled the blood of the covenant upon the people of Israel (Ex 24:8). But Luke also has in mind the new covenant announced in Jeremiah 31:31, "Behold the days are coming, says the Lord, when I will make a new covenant with the house of Israel and the house of Judah." It is this covenant that the death of Jesus establishes.

Verses 21–23 form the final unit. By announcing that one of the twelve will betray him, Jesus points to his death a third time. In Mark and Matthew the announcement of the betrayer occurs before the institution of the Eucharist, perhaps to avoid the impression that Judas shared in the meal. Luke, however, heightens the treachery of this action by saying that the betrayer's hand rests upon the Passover table (22:21). By this rearrangement Luke warns his community that everyone who partakes of the Eucharist is capable of betraying the Lord. Mere presence at the Eucharist is no assurance of perseverance.[15] Indeed, only Jesus' intimates can betray him!

Jesus' prophecy shows that death does not catch him off guard. He knows his betrayer and understands that the events of the passion have been determined (*ōrismenon*) by the Father. Consequently, the risen Christ will ask the two disciples on the road to Emmaus, "Was it not necessary that the Christ should suffer these things and enter into his glory?" (24:26). And at Pentecost Peter will declare that Jesus was "delivered up according to the definite (*ōrismenē*) plan and foreknowledge of God" (Acts 2:23).

(2) *Jesus Recalls His Past Life (22:24–30).* In this second section of the Farewell Testament, Jesus delivers a final address to his apostles. The discourse is occasioned by an unexpected dispute among the disciples over greatness (22:24). Such a dispute is ironic since Jesus has just announced his death. Nonetheless it provides an opportunity for Jesus' table talk just as Peter's refusal to allow Jesus to wash his feet (Jn 13:3–11) occasions, in part, the Farewell Discourse in John's Gospel.

Mark has a scene similar to Luke's, but he does not place it at this point. In his Gospel it occurs before the passion narrative, after the request by James and John for seats of honor at Jesus' right and left (Mk 10:35–40). Their request causes an argument among the other disciples. Because of this dispute, Jesus teaches them anew the meaning of discipleship with words similar to, but not exactly the same as, those found in Luke (Mk 10:41–45).

In its Lucan setting this scene serves two functions. First it provides Jesus with an occasion to recall his own life. It has been one of service (22:27) which is about to come to a climax in the passion. Jesus is the master who serves his own servants (12:37). In this regard the Lucan passion is again similar to John's passion narrative since, as in John, Jesus takes up the role of a servant and washes his disciples' feet (Jn 13:1–20). Second, the scene has a clear exhortative value insofar as it reminds the Church that Eucharistic celebration must issue in communal service. In Jesus' community traditional roles of leadership are recast so that the greatest becomes as the youngest and the leader as a servant (cf. 9:48 for a similar saying and 14:7–11 for proper banquet behavior). In other parts of the New Testament the words employed here "youngest" (*neōteros*) and "leader" (*hēgoumenos*) appear to be terms for Church offices (Acts 5:6; 1 Tim 5:1; I Pet 5:5 *neōteros;* Acts 15:22, Heb 13:7,17,24, *hēgoumenos*). Their presence here suggests that Luke may be directing this lesson to Church leaders of his day.

For all of their faults the apostles are the ones who have stood by Jesus in all of his trials. In vv. 28–30, Jesus promises to reward his faithful disciples. These trials of Jesus should not be confused with the temptations he suffered in the desert (4:1–13). They refer to the trials Jesus endured during his earthly ministry.[16] During that critical period the Pharisees and scribes accused Jesus of blasphemy (5:21), criticized him for eating with sinners (5:30), asked for signs from heaven (11:16), etc., but the apostles stood by their Lord. Because of this, Jesus fulfills a promise made earlier in the Gospel: "Fear not, little flock, for it is your Father's good pleasure to give you the kingdom" (12:32). He "assigns" (*diatithemai;* the Greek also has the sense of "to will") them a kingdom so that they can judge the twelve tribes of Israel (cf. Mt 19:28 for a similar saying). This promise has an eschatological dimension seen in the reference to eating and drinking at Jesus' table (22:30). But it will find a more immediate fulfillment in the first part of the Acts of the Apostles where Luke portrays the apostles as the new rulers of the reestablished Israel. It is this future role of the apostles which accounts for Luke's benevolent treatment of Jesus' followers throughout the Gospel and the passion. Unlike the Marcan disciples, they will not completely abandon their master.

(3) *Jesus Looks to the Future (22:31–38).* Having recalled the course of his life, Jesus plays the prophet by warning the apostles of what lies ahead. In vv. 31–34 he predicts the denial of Peter. In doing so, he employs Peter's old name, Simon, perhaps to indicate that Peter will temporarily fall back to his former way of life (cf. 5:8). Luke stresses that Peter's denial involves more than human failure; Satan is at work. The reference to Satan who "demanded to have you [*hymas,* plural in Greek, therefore referring to all of the apostles]," recalls the opening chapter of Job (1:6–12) where Satan makes a similar request for Job. It is only the prayer of Jesus, a constant factor in Luke's Gospel, which prevents Peter's faith from falling short. Again, Luke is similar to John who also portrays Jesus praying for his disciples during the passion (Jn 17:9,11,15). Peter protests that he is ready to go to prison and to death for Jesus, and in the Acts of the Apostles he will undergo imprisonment (5:18; 12:4).

Having spoken to Peter, Jesus addresses all of the apostles (22:35–38). This second prediction concerns the hostility which they can expect to encounter. In the period that Jesus was with them, they enjoyed his divine protection. Thus the twelve returned from their missionary journey unharmed (9:1–6,10), although they carried nothing for the journey

(9:3). Likewise, the seventy experienced Jesus' protection during their mission (10:1–20), even though they did not carry purse, bag, or sandals (10:4). Satan fell as lightning from heaven before them (10:18). But with the passion a different period begins. In accordance with Scripture Jesus will be "reckoned with transgressors" (22:37), a prophecy that will be fulfilled literally when Jesus is crucified between two criminals (23:33). The apostles, because of their association with him, will also be reckoned as transgressors.

To emphasize this coming period of struggle, Jesus tells the apostles to take purse and bag and to purchase a sword.[17] The instructions are precisely the opposite of those given for the missionary journeys (9:3; 10:4). The disciples take Jesus' words literally and produce two swords, but Jesus does not intend such a literal interpretation, as can be seen from his remark, "It is enough." The sense is not that the swords are sufficient, but "enough of such foolishness, you have misunderstood me." A somewhat similar expression occurs in Deuteronomy 3:26 where the Lord angrily speaks to Moses, "Let it suffice you; speak no more to me of this matter." Jesus is not encouraging violence, but employing metaphorical language to indicate that a time of persecution is about to begin. Fitzymer writes: "The introduction of the 'sword' signals the difference in the periods; the Period of the Church will be marked with persecution, as the later Lucan story makes clear."[18]

III.
AT THE MOUNT OF OLIVES, 22:39–53

The scene changes from the Passover supper to the Mount of Olives where Jesus prays before his passion (22:39–46) and then submits to arrest (22:47–53). Luke ties the events of this episode to those of the previous scene in two ways. First, at the beginning of the passion (22:3), and then during the supper (22:31), he points to the activity of Satan. At the end of this section he alludes to Satan's power when he speaks of "the power of darkness" (22:53). Second, Luke employs the sword motif to draw a contrast between the behavior of Jesus and that of his disciples. In the final verse of the last scene, the disciples proudly produce two swords (22:38), and at the moment of Jesus' arrest one of his followers tries to defend him with a sword (22:49–50). Jesus, by contrast, refuses such protection. He finds his strength in prayer to the Father.

A. *Jesus at Prayer (22:39–46)*

Luke's portrayal of Jesus' agony differs significantly from the narratives of Matthew and Mark.[19] In examining those accounts, I indicated that they contain a threefold structure determined by the three times Jesus prays to his Father. In Luke the structure is different as the following outline makes clear.[20]

> Introduction: Jesus and his disciples come to the Mount of Olives (39).
> A. He tells them to pray lest they enter into temptation (40).
> B. He leaves his disciples (41a).
> C. He kneels down (41b).
> D. He prays that the Father's will be done (41c–42). [An angel comforts him, 43–44.]
> C' He rises from prayer (45a).
> B' He returns to the disciples (45b).
> A' He finds them asleep. He tells them to pray lest they enter into temptation (45c–46).

It is evident from this outline that there is one basic movement in Luke's account. Jesus encourages the disciples to pray lest they enter into temptation, then goes off to his own prayer. Upon returning he asks why they sleep and encourages them to pray lest they enter into temptation. Luke does not report, as does Mark, that Jesus returns three times only to find the disciples asleep.

The outline forms a chiasma in which admonitions to pray enclose the portrait of Jesus at prayer, the central point of the account. I have placed vv. 43–44 in brackets because there is doubt about their authenticity.[21] On the one hand, their presence in many manuscripts, as well as their citation by Justin, Irenaeus, Hippolytus, Eusebius and many other Church Fathers, points to their antiquity. But on the other, the verses are not found in ancient and widely diversified manuscripts. Many argue that the verses were deleted because early scribes felt that this account of Jesus, overwhelmed by grief, was incompatible with his divine nature. It is just as likely, however, that they were added in the second century when the Church was preoccupied with Jesus' real humanity in the face of various strands of Docetism, a heresy which denied Jesus' true humanity.

There are two foci in this story. The first and most important is Jesus. Luke presents him as obedient to the Father's will. He goes to the Mount of Olives "as was his custom" even though the place was known to his betrayer who will lead the arresting party there. This Mount of Olives plays an important role in Luke's Gospel. It is the place to which Jesus retires each evening during the period of his Jerusalem ministry (21:37).

Once at the Mount, Jesus prays that his Father's will might be done (see Acts 21:14 where a similar prayer is offered on behalf of Paul). Luke does not dwell upon Jesus' agony as do Mark and Matthew. Instead he stresses his submission to God's will. The cup which Jesus asks the Father to remove is the cup of suffering, a metaphor found in Matthew 20:22, Mark 10:38, and John 18:11. It may also have some relationship to the Old Testament imagery where the cup serves as a symbol of judgment and retribution (Ps 75:8; Is 51:17; Jer 25:15–26).[22] The cup of Jesus' suffering entails the judgment and wrath of God which he endures for others.

The second focus of this story is the behavior of the disciples. Mark and Matthew concentrate upon the failure of Peter, James, and John, but Luke brings all of the disciples into play. They are to pray lest they enter into temptation (*peirasmon*). In the parable of the sower (8:5–15), Jesus refers to temptation as the prelude to apostasy: "And the ones on the rock are those who, when they hear the word, receive it with joy; but these have no root, they believe for a while and in time of temptation fall away" (8:13). In the Our Father he employs the word in reference to the great eschatological struggle that will come at the end of time: "and lead us not into temptation" (11:4). The passion is the prelude to that eschatological struggle. The disciples must pray not to enter into temptation lest the moment of the passion lead to apostasy.

The disciples momentarily fail. Instead of praying, they sleep "for sorrow." The last phrase, peculiar to Luke, is his way of softening the judgment against the disciples.[23] This more benign attitude toward the disciples is a Lucan theme which culminates in the role the twelve play in the Acts of the Apostles. The result of their failure to pray manifests itself in the next scene when one of the disciples defends Jesus with a sword. The failure, however, does not lead to apostasy[24] since Jesus has prayed for Peter who, in turn, will strengthen his brethren (22:31).

While Mark's story is calculated to emphasize Jesus' agony and sense of abandonment, Luke is more intent upon presenting this incident as a lesson in prayer. Jesus is the model of what it means to persevere in prayer in order to avoid temptation. The disciples, by contrast, exemplify what can happen to those who do not pray. The manner in which Luke brackets his account with admonitions to pray is the major clue to the narrative's meaning. Christians must pray as did Jesus lest they enter into temptation.

B. Jesus Arrested (22:47–53)

In this scene Luke continues to portray Jesus as one who accepts the Father's will and is in control of the situation. When Judas approaches to kiss him, Jesus asks with prophetic knowledge, "Judas, would you betray the Son of Man with a kiss?" In Luke's account, Judas does not appear to kiss or even touch Jesus as he does in Mark's (14:45). When one of the disciples strikes the ear of the high priest's slave, Jesus orders him to desist and then heals the servant. The passion does not limit Jesus' power to heal or to call sinners to conversion (see 23:39–43).

The arrest of Jesus (22:54) does not occur until he finishes speaking and says, "But this is your hour, and the power of darkness" (22:53). It is as if Jesus gives permission for his own arrest. Luke's arrest scene is similar to John 18:2–12 where Jesus, not the arresting party, is in control. Such behavior on the part of Jesus results from his faithfulness to prayer[25] and his acceptance of the Father's will.

Once more Luke manifests a benevolent attitude toward the disciples by not mentioning their flight (cf. Mk 14:50 where everybody abandons Jesus). He places the onus for the arrest more squarely upon the shoulders of the religious leaders than does Mark. Whereas in Mark the arresting party *comes from* the chief priests, scribes and elders (Mk 14:43), in Luke the party is *composed of* chief priests, temple officers, and elders (22:52). It is as though the whole Sanhedrin comes out to apprehend Jesus! Such a situation is historically improbable, but it is part of Luke's theology which consistently places the people in a better light than their leaders. After all, it was the people who heard Jesus with approval in the temple while their leaders sought to destroy him (19:47–48).

IV.
DENIAL, MOCKERY, TRIAL, 22:54–71

The most important difference between Luke and Mark in this section is the change in the order of events. Whereas the Marcan order is arrest, night trial before the Sanhedrin, mockery and denial, Luke's order is arrest, denial, mockery and morning trial.

MARK	LUKE
Arrest	Arrest
Trial	Denial
Mockery	Mockery
Denial	"Trial"

I place the last event in quotation marks because there is no formal condemnation of Jesus in Luke as there is in Mark (see 14:64). In Luke it is more accurate to speak of a hearing before the Sanhedrin than of a trial. However, because I shall compare Luke's account of the incident with Mark's, I retain the traditional terminology.

This different order of events has given rise to a number of literary and historical questions. In terms of literary criticism, scholars ask if Luke is dependent upon Mark or if he is drawing from other sources, e.g., another passion narrative or independent traditions.[26] Regarding the question of history, scholars seek to determine which account is closer to the events which took place. There is no unanimous agreement on the answers to these questions, but it does seem probable that Luke was drawing from some other traditions, although not necessarily another passion narrative, in his composition of the denial, mockery, and trial scenes. Moreover, his version may be more accurate when it describes a morning hearing rather than a night trial before the Sanhedrin.[27]

A. Peter's Denial (22:55–62)

The story occurs immediately after Jesus' arrest (22:54) and just before the mockery scene. This new rearrangement of events (arrest, denial and mockery) allows Luke to accomplish several goals. First, he can draw a comparison between the behavior of Jesus and Peter. On the Mount of Olives Jesus gives permission for his arrest (22:53), but Peter, recognized because of his association with Jesus, denies that he knows him (22:57). The difference, of course, is that Jesus has prayed and so does not fall at the moment of temptation. Peter, on the other hand, fails because he has not prayed. Second, by placing Peter's denial before the mockery, Luke dissociates the chief apostle from the cruelty which follows. In fact, immediately after the denial, Peter remembers the words of the Lord and repents (22:61–62). This is in sharp contrast to Mark's account where the denial occurs after the mockery, thereby adding to Peter's guilt. In Luke, Peter denies his Lord, but his behavior does not add to the humiliation of the mockery.

Apart from this new order of events, Luke's account is similar to Mark's, leading most commentators to believe that at this point Mark is his only source. Nonetheless there are some important differences. First, in Mark it is two maids and a bystander who accuse Peter, whereas Luke speaks of one maid and two men. Some authors see a forensic element[28] here, that is, the witness of two women did not count in court whereas that of two men did. Second, in Luke the entire scene takes place in the courtyard, whereas in Mark, Peter moves from the courtyard to the gateway after the first denial (14:68). This detail is important because it highlights that in Luke, Peter's denial takes place in the presence of the Lord. After the third denial Luke writes, "And the Lord turned and looked at Peter" (22:61), a phrase not found in Mark or Matthew. The denial now functions as a way to intimidate Jesus.[29] His chief apostle has denied him. Will he lose heart? Finally, in Mark the denials are stronger than those in Luke. For example, after Peter's third denial Mark writes, "But he began to invoke a curse on himself and to swear, 'I do not know this man of whom you speak' " (14:71). By contrast Luke reads, "But Peter said, 'Man, I do not know what you are saying' " (22:60). This is a part of Luke's wider theology which lessens the guilt of Peter and the other apostles.[30]

Despite these differences, Luke and Mark agree that Peter's denial is the fulfillment of Jesus' prophecy made at the Last Supper, "I tell you, Peter, the cock will not crow this day, until you three times deny that you know me" (22:34). Luke emphasizes the fulfillment of this prophecy in two ways. First, the content of Peter's denial before the maid is precisely what Jesus said it would be. Peter denies that he *knows* Jesus: "Woman, I do not know him." Second, Peter is still uttering the words of his third denial when the cock crows: "and *immediately,* while he was still speaking, the cock crowed." It is at this point that Peter remembers the words of the Lord. Remembering the words of the Lord is an important theme in Luke-Acts. At the empty tomb the angel tells the women, ''Remember how he told you, while he was still in Galilee, that the Son of Man must be delivered into the hands of sinful men'' (24:6–7). And in Acts both Peter and Paul remember the words of the Lord (11:16; 20:35). The message is clear. By recalling the words of the Lord, believers will be saved from the fate which befell Peter.

B. *The Mockery (22:63–65)*

In the next incident Luke narrates how those charged with guarding Jesus deride him as a Prophet. In Mark and Matthew there is a connection between the mockery and Jesus' prophecy that he will return as the Son of Man to judge his judges. There is no such connection in Luke's passion since the trial before the Sanhedrin has not yet taken place. Then why do Jesus' captors mock him as a false prophet? The answer is not difficult to discern if one remembers that Luke portrays Jesus as a Prophet throughout the Gospel. Furthermore, at the Last Supper Jesus foretells his death, his betrayal, and Peter's denial. The mockery by Jesus' captors should not surprise the attentive reader. As in Mark and Matthew, the irony of the situation is patent. Jesus' enemies mock him as a false prophet immediately after one of his prophecies, Peter's denial, has been fulfilled. The reader can now expect that any prophecy Jesus has made or will make, for example the destruction of Jerusalem (23:28–31), will come to pass.

C. *The ''Trial'' (22:66–71)*

In Luke it appears that the mockery continues throughout the night since the formal hearing before the religious council does not take place until morning (22:66). Trial is not the best description for this scene since there is no formal judgment or condemnation. Luke, like John, sees the scene before Pilate as *the* trial. Nonetheless, this preliminary hearing before the Sanhedrin allows Luke to emphasize the central charge directed against Jesus: his messianic claims.

The Lucan trial differs from its Marcan counterpart in several ways. First, it takes place early in the morning rather than at night. Second, Luke does not mention the false witnesses who testify that Jesus threatened to destroy the temple (Mk 14:57–59). But Luke is aware of the charge since a like accusation is raised at Stephen's trial:

> And they stirred up the people and the elders and the scribes, and they came upon him and seized him and brought him before the council, and set up false witnesses who said, "This man never ceases to speak words against this holy place and the law; for we have heard him say that this Jesus of Nazareth will destroy this place [the temple], and will change the customs which Moses delivered to us" (Acts 6:12–14).

Why Luke does not include the charge in the passion is a puzzle. Part of the reason may be his benevolent attitude toward the temple[31] since the temple still has a role to play in the Acts of the Apostles. Luke avoids any impression that Jesus spoke against the temple. The absence of the temple charge allows him to focus more sharply upon the messianic question. Finally, whereas the dialogue occurs between Jesus and the high priest in Mark (14:60–62), in Luke it takes place between Jesus and the whole council, giving the impression that Jesus stands before the entire religious establishment.

The scene begins with a sharp command that borders on a challenge, "If you are the Christ, tell us" (22:67). In Mark it is phrased as a question (14:61). The statement is reminiscent of the temptation account: "If you are the Son of God" (4:3,9); and it foreshadows the mockery by the rulers: "if he is the Christ of God, his Chosen One!" (23:35), and by the soldiers: "If you are the King of the Jews" (23:37). Jesus responds, "If I tell you, you will not believe; and if I ask you, you will not answer" (22:67–68). The style is that of the prophetic refusal to answer such as is found in Jeremiah 38:15: "If I tell you, will you not be sure to put me to death? And if I give you counsel, you will not listen to me." By responding in this fashion Jesus points to the futility of further discussion, recalling other occasions in the Gospel (20:3–7, 41–44) when he did ask and answer to no avail. Instead of answering as the religious council demands, Jesus utters a prophecy, "But from now on the Son of Man shall be seated at the right hand of the power of God" (22:69). The statement is different from Mark 14:62 where Jesus says, "and you will see the Son of Man seated at the right hand of Power, and *coming* with the clouds of heaven.'' Mark refers the prophecy to Jesus' imminent parousia, whereas Luke says that from this point forward (*apo tou nyn;* see the same expression in Lk 1:48, 5:10, 12:52, 22:18, Acts 18:6, where it points to a new beginning) Jesus will be enthroned at God's right hand. Jesus prophesies that as a result of the passion, he will be enthroned in glory, an idea similar to that found in John's passion where Jesus' crucifixion is his enthronement in glory. Since Jesus' other prophecies have come true, the reader can rely on this prophetic word. And, in fact, it proves reliable. In the Acts of the Apostles Jesus ascends into heaven (1:6–11), and at his martyrdom Stephen cries out, ''Behold, I see the heavens opened, and the Son of Man standing at the right hand of God'' (7:56).

The religious leaders understand all too clearly the significance of Jesus' prophecy and respond, ''Are you the Son of God, then?'' The words are improbable upon their lips since ''Son of God'' is a Christian confession. But Luke places it in their mouths to establish that the religious leaders condemn Jesus as a false messiah. The dialogue between Jesus and the religious leaders may seem confusing, but there is a logical progression which moves from Christ to Son of God by means of the Son of Man prophecy.

> If you are the Christ . . .
> But from now on the Son of Man . . .
> Are you the Son of God, then?

In this movement Luke equates Messiah with Son of God. As Messiah, Jesus is God's Son (1:35). In the fulfillment of the Son of Man prophecy, God will vindicate him.

V.
JESUS BEFORE PILATE AND HEROD, 23:1–25

Luke's report of Jesus' trial before Pilate has a different setting than Mark's account. First, in Mark the trial occurs after Peter's denial, but in Luke it follows the hearing before the Sanhedrin during which Jesus prophesies that he will be enthroned at God's right hand. The consequence of this different arrangement is that Luke achieves a greater unity between the hearing before the Sanhedrin, where Jesus is accused of being a messianic pretender, and the trial before Pilate, where he is accused of calling himself a king. Second, in Mark the trial before Pilate is followed by a scene in which the Roman soldiers mock Jesus as the King of the Jews (Mk 15:16–20a). In Luke there is no such episode. Instead, Luke immediately begins the narration of the crucifixion. This new arrangement is important because it gives the impression that it is the Jews who lead Jesus out to be crucified (see Lk 23:25–26).

MARK	LUKE
Trial before Jews	Hearing before Jews
Denial by Peter	
Trial before Pilate	Trial before Pilate
Mockery	
Crucifixion	Crucifixion

In addition to this change of setting, there are other differences between the two narratives. In fact, at this point there are differences between all four Gospels. Matthew, for example, includes the events of Judas' death (27:3–10), the dream of Pilate's wife (27:19), Pilate's dramatic gesture of personal innocence (27:24), and the people's cry of responsibility (27:25). John presents a highly stylized scene in which there is an extended dialogue between Jesus and Pilate (18:28–19:16).[32] But Luke is the only writer to tell of an encounter between Jesus and Herod. Moreover, while all four evangelists report the Barabbas incident, the scene is least developed in Luke.

There is a great deal of debate concerning Luke's source or sources. Several authors are convinced that he is working with a non-Marcan passion account, while others argue that they can explain the entire scene in light of Luke's editorial activity. Whatever the answer, it is evident that his account has a slightly different emphasis from that found in Mark.

It is easy to determine the structure of this section inasmuch as there are two changes of scene. In vv. 1–5 Jesus stands before Pilate. In vv. 6–12 Pilate sends Jesus to Herod. In vv. 13–25 Jesus once more stands before Pilate. Luke ties the first two scenes to each other by references to Galilee (23:5,6), and the last two by references to Herod and Pilate

(23:12,13,15). In addition, he relates the first and third scenes to each other in two ways. First, in both of them he has Pilate declare Jesus' innocence (23:4,14,22). Second, in both he makes a reference to Jesus as "stirring up" (23:5) and "perverting" (23:2,14) the people. The material forms a tightly knit section.

A. *Jesus Before Pilate (23:1–5)*

The first unit begins with the "whole company of them" (the elders of the people, the chief priests and scribes; see 22:66), bringing Jesus to Pilate. Whereas Mark mentions that Jesus was bound, Luke does not report any such detail because of his sensitivity to Jesus' dignity which he heightens throughout the passion. Arrested, Jesus can still perform miracles of healing (22:51). Crucified, he can still promise paradise to a repentant criminal (23:43).

In Mark the scene opens abruptly with Pilate asking Jesus if he is the King of the Jews. Luke, by contrast, carefully lays out the charges before Pilate's question. Although the RSV gives the impression that there are three distinct charges, the Greek implies one major charge ("perverting our nation") which is specified in two ways: "forbidding us to give tribute to Caesar, and saying that he himself is Christ a king." The first of these two specifications refers to the incident at 20:20–26 when the chief priests and scribes sent spies to trap Jesus by asking if it is lawful to pay taxes to Caesar. The outcome of that incident demonstrates that the charge is false. The second specification recalls Jesus' triumphal entry into Jerusalem (19:28–40) and the hearing before the Sanhedrin (22:67–70) when the religious leaders interpreted Jesus' Son of Man prophecy as a messianic claim. This charge is both true and false. On the one hand, Luke presents Jesus as a royal figure from his birth (1:32). He is the King of Israel and the King of the Jews. But the latter title has political overtones which Luke never attributes to Jesus. Consequently, when Pilate asks if Jesus is the King of the Jews, Jesus gives an ambiguous response found in all of the Gospels, "You have said so." It implies a guarded yes. Jesus is the King of the Jews inasmuch as he is David's royal descendant. But Jesus himself would prefer another title due to the political connotations inherent in King of the Jews. Jesus is not a political rebel who sets himself against Rome.

Pilate seems to understand Jesus' partial disclaimer because he says that he finds no crime in the man (23:4). This statement of innocence is peculiar to Luke, and it is the first of three such declarations in this section; see 23:14,22 for the others. Luke stresses that Jesus is not a political rebel and that even the Roman Pilate testifies to this.

Jesus' accusers are insistent and in 23:5 they charge him with stirring up the people from Galilee to Judea. The accusation points to the scope of Jesus' ministry (Lk 4:44, 7:17; Acts 10:37). The reference to Galilee, a hotbed of revolutionary activity (Acts 5:37), underlines the political overtones. On one level the charge is true. Jesus' teaching has aroused the people so that the religious leaders have become fearful (20:19; 22:2). But on another level the charge is false. Jesus' message has not been political; there is no danger to Rome.

B. Jesus Before Herod (23:6–12)

This scene is peculiar to Luke. The only element which has some relationship to Marcan material is the silence of Jesus and the accusations of the chief priests and scribes. These verses, 23:9–10, have a certain similarity to Mark 15:3–4 where Jesus is also accused by the priests but remains silent.

Herod plays a minor but important role in Luke's Gospel. The birth of Jesus takes place during the days of his father Herod the Great (1:5). The word of God comes to John the Baptist while Herod is tetrarch of Galilee (3:1). It is this same Herod who throws John into prison (3:19). When Herod hears of Jesus, he seeks to see him (9:7–9), and later the Pharisees warn Jesus that Herod wants to destroy him (13:31–33). The present encounter between Herod and Jesus is not a chance occurrence; it has been well prepared for throughout the Gospel.

Herod, however, desires to meet Jesus for the wrong reason. He hopes to see a sign. Jesus is a mighty Prophet, and throughout the Gospel he performs many miracles. But as for signs, others have already tested Jesus seeking a sign from heaven (11:16), but Jesus replied that the only sign this generation will receive is the sign of Jonah (11:29–30). Like Jonah, Jesus is a sign which calls for conversion. Herod will not receive such a sign, and so Jesus becomes a sign of contradiction (2:34) for him. Because Jesus falls short of Herod's expectations, he and his soldiers mock Jesus by dressing him in gorgeous apparel, *esthēta lampran* (see Acts 10:30 where an angel appears to Cornelius in similar garb; although the RSV translates "bright apparel," the Greek is the same). The magnificent apparel is meant to mock the pitiful Jesus who Herod concludes is not a King. Ironically, the gorgeous apparel is proper to Jesus' true dignity.

The result of this strange incident is that Herod and Pilate become friends. This is Luke's way of suggesting that the power of Jesus is such that even during his passion he reconciles enemies.[33]

This incident establishes Jesus' innocence. Not only does the Roman governor, Pilate, find Jesus innocent, but even Herod, the murderer of John the Baptist, does not condemn him. Here there is a parallel with what happens to Paul in the Acts of the Apostles where neither the Roman governor, Festus, nor the Jewish king, Herod Agrippa (not the same Herod), finds Paul guilty (26:30–32).

In Acts 4:25–31 Luke refers to the Herod-Pilate incident but interprets it differently. In Acts 4 the Sanhedrin releases Peter and John, commanding them not to preach in the name of Jesus (4:18). When the two apostles return to the Church, the Church prays for boldness (Acts 4:29), the same boldness that Peter and John manifested before the Sanhedrin (4:13). In its prayer for boldness the Church, in the light of Psalm 2, remembers Jesus' appearance before Pilate and Herod.

> Sovereign Lord, who didst make the heaven and the earth and the sea and everything in them, who by the mouth of our father David, thy servant, didst say by the Holy Spirit, "Why did the Gentiles rage, and the peoples imagine vain things? The kings of the earth set themselves in array, and the rulers were gathered together, against the Lord and against his Anointed" [Ps 2:1], for truly in this city there were gathered together against thy holy servant Jesus, whom thou didst anoint, both Herod and Pontius Pilate, with the Gentiles and the peoples of Israel (4:24–27).

In this interpretation, Luke portrays Pilate and Herod in a more negative light. No longer are they witnesses to Jesus' innocence; they have become his opponents. But all of this, according to Luke, was part of God's plan as prophesied by David in Psalm 2. No incident of the passion occurs which is not a part of God's plan.

C. Jesus Before Pilate (23:13–25)

In the third and final scene Jesus stands before Pilate once more. This time Luke stresses the innocence of Jesus by having Pilate summon the chief priests, the rulers and the people. For a second time (23:14–15) Pilate testifies to Jesus' innocence. This is the first occasion that Luke introduces the people (*laos*) by whom he understands the covenant people of Israel. Throughout the Gospel Luke is usually benevolent toward the people. And later, in Acts 3:17, he excuses them and their rulers by saying that they acted in ignorance. Moreover, at the conclusion of the passion, the multitudes return home beating their breasts (23:48). But at this supreme moment of decision, Luke wants all of Israel present to witness Pilate's declaration of Jesus' innocence.

Luke's version of the Barabbas incident is the shortest of those recorded in the Gospel passion stories. It is as if Luke, so sensitive to Jesus' dignity, cannot bear to compare Jesus with one accused of murder. He only mentions Barabbas by name once (23:18) compared with three times in Mark and five in Matthew. The incident provides Luke with a third opportunity to have Pilate declare Jesus innocent (23:22). But the declaration is to no avail, and Pilate must release Barabbas, "the man who had been thrown into prison for insurrection and murder."

I noted that trial is not the correct description for the events which transpire before the Sanhedrin. For Luke the trial of Jesus takes place before Pilate. Nonetheless, Pilate does not formally condemn Jesus or pronounce the judgment of death. Instead he delivers up (*paredōken*) Jesus to their will. The word "deliver up" has a technical sense in Luke, as in the other Synoptic Gospels, and refers to God's divine will for his Messiah (9:44; 18:32; 22:22; 24:7). In delivering up Jesus to the Jews, Pilate unwittingly becomes part of God's plan for the Messiah (24:26).

VI.
Crucifixion and Death, 23:26–49

The events described in this section are very similar to those found in Mark. Nonetheless, because there are important differences, it is helpful to compare the two accounts.[34]

MARK	LUKE

CRUCIFIXION

MARK	LUKE
Simon of Cyrene	Simon of Cyrene
_____	Women of Jerusalem
_____	two criminals
Golgotha	Skull Place
refuses wine with myrrh	_____
they crucified him	they crucified him
_____	with two criminals
_____	["Father, forgive them"]
divided his garments	divided his garments
third hour	_____
inscription, King of the Jews	_____

MOCKERY

MARK	LUKE
two robbers	_____
_____	people watch
passers-by deride him as	_____
temple destroyer	_____
chief priests and scribes mock	rulers scoff
Christ, King of Israel	Christ of God, Elect
_____	soldiers mock (vinegar)
_____	King of the Jews
_____	Inscription, This One is
_____	the King of the Jews
robbers reviled him	_____
_____	first criminal rails him
_____	as the Christ
_____	second criminal repents

DEATH

MARK	LUKE
darkness, 6–9th hours	darkness 6–9th hours
_____	sun's light fails
_____	temple curtain is torn

Psalm 22	Psalm 31
Elijah . . . vinegar	_____
loud cry and dies	_____
temple curtain is torn	_____
Son of God	Innocent/Just man
	Crowd repents
_____	
women afar	acquaintances and women
list of women	_____

It is clear from this comparison that Luke differs from Mark in three ways: the presence of new material, the absence of certain Marcan material, and a different order of events. These data again give rise to the question of Luke's sources. Is he following another passion story in addition to Mark? Is he making use of isolated traditions? Is he simply rewriting Mark? Scholars have not solved the source question, but I am inclined to the position that Luke's editorial activity explains most of the differences since this section reflects the theology present in the rest of the Gospel.[35] The section forms a literary unit, but for the sake of clarity I divide it into six parts.

A. *Simon of Cyrene (23:26)*

In the first unit "they" require Simon to help Jesus with the cross. The text is ambiguous at this point and does not identify who "they" are. Read in context, it seems to refer to the chief priests, rulers, and people (23:13). Luke knows that it was the Romans who crucified Jesus, and in 23:36 he refers to the soldiers who are evidently Roman. He purposely leaves the text ambiguous in order to heighten the responsibility of the Jews.[36]

As in Matthew, Alexander and Rufus, the sons of Simon, have disappeared from the narrative, perhaps because they were not known to Luke's community. But Luke does have a phrase not found in Mark or Matthew. In referring to the cross, he says that Simon was forced "to carry it behind Jesus (*opisthen tou Iēsou*)." The phrase is reminiscent of 9:23, "If any man would come after me, let him deny himself and take up his cross daily and *follow me*." It also has a close, literary contact with 14:27, "Whoever does not bear his own cross and come *after me* (*opisō mou*) cannot be my disciple.'' In this Gospel, Simon becomes a model of discipleship, and Luke expects his readers to follow this example.

B. *The Women of Jerusalem (23:27–31)*

Next Luke narrates a story not found in any other Gospel, the weeping women of Jerusalem. The point of this story is not easy to determine. Some commentators, in the light of Zechariah 12:10–14, read the account in terms of the women's compassion.

> And I will pour out on the house of David and the inhabitants of Jerusalem a spirit of compassion and supplication, so that, when they look on him whom they have pierced, they shall mourn for him, as one mourns for an only child, and weep bitterly over him, as one weeps over a first-born.

The connection between this text and the women of Jerusalem, however, is not especially strong (cf. Jn 19:37 which explicitly refers to Zech 12:10). Others suggest, therefore, that the point of the text is Jesus' prophetic oracle of doom over Jerusalem.[37]

Earlier in the Gospel, Jesus issued warnings to Jerusalem (13:34–35; 19:41–44) in which he pronounced a sentence:

> Behold your house is forsaken (13:35).
> Your enemies will cast up a bank about you
> and surround you,
> and hem you in on every side,
> and dash you to the ground,
> you and your children within you,
> and they will not leave
> one stone upon another in you (19:43–44).

Jesus identified the city's crimes as:

Killing the prophets (13:34).
Not knowing the time of your visitation (19:44).

The present text is of the same genre. Jesus predicts the city's destruction because of what is taking place, his crucifixion.

Here the crime is expressed by the proverb, "For if they do this when the wood is green, what will happen when it is dry?" The meaning is: if these things have been done to me who am innocent, what will happen to you who are guilty?[38] Similar sayings can be found in Proverbs 11:31 and 1 Peter 4:17–18.

Jesus points to the fate which awaits the inhabitants of Jerusalem because of their crime: "For behold the days are coming when they will say, 'Blessed are the barren, and the wombs that never bore, and the breasts that never gave suck!' " The background for this text is Hosea 10:8: "The high places of Aven, the sin of Israel, shall be destroyed. Thorn and thistle shall grow up on their altars; *and they shall say to the mountains, Cover us, and to the hills, Fall upon us.*" In this passage the people of Samaria ask the mountains and hills to protect them from the wrath of God's judgment. Jesus says that Jerusalem's punishment will be so great that her own inhabitants will do the same.

The point of this story is not the compassion of the women, but Jesus' final prophetic word to the inhabitants of Jerusalem. Once more Luke portrays Jesus as a prophet who calls his people to conversion. Upon entering the city, he wept over it and prophesied its destruction (19:41–44). Now, as he leaves (Jesus was crucified outside the city walls), he pronounces his last prophetic word.

C. The Two Criminals (23:32–33)

Luke notes that two criminals were also led out to be crucified. Here he employs the work *kakourgos* which means criminal or evil-doer, whereas Mark uses *lēstēs* which can refer either to a robber or to a revolutionary. By this choice of words, Luke avoids any intimation that Jesus was a political rebel. The Greek expression *kai heteroi kakourgoi duo* is imprecise and may also be translated "and two other criminals [were led away to be put to death with him]," thereby implying that Jesus was a criminal! Some Christian scribes, embarrassed by this, inverted the word order to avoid this interpretation as does the RSV which reads "Two others also, who were criminals, were led away to be put to death with him." It may be that Luke takes the bold step of calling

Jesus a criminal, thereby fulfilling the prophecy of 22:37, "and he was reckoned with transgressors." In later Christian tradition, one author, writing in the name of Paul,[39] says that he was suffering "like a criminal" (2 Tim 2:9). Luke, of course, does not believe that Jesus is a criminal, but he does know that a repentant criminal was among the first to enter the kingdom of God (23:43). It is precisely those whom the world counts as criminals, therefore, that Jesus comes to save.

D. Jesus' Prayer (23:34)

This verse ("And Jesus said, 'Father, forgive them; for they know not what they do' ") presents a textual problem. The words are not found in the best manuscripts, but the text is testified to as early as the second century by Hegesippus, Tatian and Irenaeus, and is in accord with Luke's general portrait of Jesus. It is difficult to come to a decision.[40] Some scholars argue that the text entered the manuscript tradition through Stephen's words in Acts 7:60, "Lord, do not hold this sin against them." But others suggest that it was dropped in a later, more anti-Semitic period of the Church's history, when Christian scribes were shocked by Jesus' leniency toward the Jews. The verse has an old and venerable tradition and presents an authentically Lucan picture of Jesus. The second half of the verse, "And they cast lots to divide his garments," is accepted by all as authentic, and is a clear allusion to Psalm 22:18.

E. The Mockery (23:35–43)

Most commentators believe that the next scene is composed of vv. 35–38, the mockery of Jesus, and that vv. 39–43 form another unit, the story of the good thief. I suggest, however, that vv. 35–43 comprise a single unit in which there is a threefold mockery of Jesus which concludes with the repentance of one of the criminals. Luke composes the scene in a careful manner. Three strata of society, beginning with the most important, mock Jesus: the rulers, the soldiers, a criminal. The content of each mockery is the same: Jesus cannot save himself. Each mockery refers to Jesus by a specific title: the Christ of God, his Chosen One (23:35); the King of the Jews (23:37); the Christ (23:39). Throughout the mockery the people (*laos*) watch,[41] but do not participate. After the death of Jesus, Luke refers to them once more (23:48), saying they returned home beating their breasts.

	people watch	
rulers scoff	let him save himself	Christ of God
		Chosen One
soldiers mock	save yourself	King of the Jews
criminal rails	save yourself and us	Christ
	criminal repents	

It is clear from this outline that all of the individual mockeries focus upon the same point. Jesus claims to be the Messiah but cannot save himself. All of the mockers challenge Jesus to save himself if he is who he claims to be. The challenges here are similar to those Jesus faced from the devil while in the desert: "If you are the Son of God" (4:3,9). They are also reminiscent of what Jesus said about the inhabitants of Nazareth on the occasion of his inaugural sermon: "Doubtless you will quote to me this proverb, 'Physician, heal yourself' " (4:23). The irony of the situation is that if Jesus tries to heal or save himself, he will lose his life: "For whoever would save his life will lose it; and whoever loses his life for my sake, he will save it" (9:24). The paradox of the Gospel is that the only way in which Jesus, or any Christian, can save his life is by relying upon God. Jesus still has the power to save others, even while on the cross, as is seen in his promise to the repentant criminal, "today you will be with me in paradise." But the mockers speak an ironic truth, even though they do not realize the full implication of what they are saying. Jesus will not save himself, because he trusts in the power of God to rescue him. By refusing to save his life, Jesus will save his life!

All of the titles attributed to Jesus here play a prominent role in the Gospel. When the rulers say that Jesus is the Christ of God, his Chosen One, they unwittingly recall two of the most important moments in the Gospel. In 9:20 Peter confesses that Jesus is "the Christ of God." And in 9:35, at the transfiguration, the Father declares, "this is my Son, my Chosen." The mockery of Jesus as King of the Jews recalls the scene before Pilate, but it is also the culmination of Luke's royal theology which begins when the angel tells Mary that "the Lord God will give to him the throne of his father David" (1:32). Jesus is everything that the rulers, soldiers, and criminal mockingly call him. But they do not understand the truth of their own speech since they cannot comprehend the paradox of the cross.

One criminal does acknowledge Jesus' kingship by asking him to remember him when he enters his kingdom. In return Jesus promises that "today you will be with me in paradise."[42] Paradise refers to the king's royal garden. The word "today" emphasizes the present reality of salvation which characterizes Luke-Acts, and it is the completion of a theme which runs thoughout the Gospel (2:11; 4:21; 5:26; 19:9). In this scene Luke portrays Jesus as the Messiah who refuses to save himself, but continues to save others even at the moment of death.

F. Jesus' Death (23:44–49)

Luke's portrayal of Jesus' death differs significantly from the scene in Mark. As in Mark there is darkness over the whole land from the sixth to the ninth hours, and the temple curtain is torn. However, this last incident occurs before rather than after Jesus' death. Jesus does not utter the opening words of Psalm 22 nor does the centurion acclaim him as God's Son. Instead he dies with the peaceful words of Psalm 31:5, and the centurion testifies that Jesus was a just (*dikaios*) man. As a result of this spectacle (*theōrian*, 23:48) the crowd returns home beating their breasts. There is a dramatic shift in mood here. Jesus no longer dies as the abandoned Son of God, but as the suffering righteous one who peacefully entrusts his soul to the Father.

The darkness recalls a series of texts from the minor prophets used to describe the Day of Yahweh: "a day of darkness and gloom" (Zeph 1:15); "the sun and the moon are darkened" (Jl 2:10); "I will make the sun go down at noon, and darkened the earth in broad daylight" (Am 8:9). Luke couples this darkness with the tearing of the temple curtain, thereby providing two dramatic signs at the threshold of Jesus' death.[43] That Luke places the tearing of the temple curtain before the death of Jesus may be his way of indicating, contrary to Mark, that the temple cult does not end at Jesus' death. The temple will play a role in the Acts of the Apostles (2:46). Instead, the torn curtain, especially if it refers to the outer curtain,[44] may symbolize that the Gentiles now have access to God's grace since it was that curtain that veiled the mystery of Israel's religion from them. Thus the first to acknowledge Jesus after his death is a Gentile, the centurion.

Luke next reports that at his death Jesus prayed the words of Psalm 31:5. But whereas the psalm verse reads, "Into thy hand I commit my spirit," Jesus says "*Father,* into thy hands I commit my spirit," thereby emphasizing the Father–Son relationship so prominent in this Gospel (2:49; 9:26; 10:21–22; 11:2,13,; 12:30,32; 22:29,42; 23:34; 24:49). Whereas Mark proclaims Jesus as Son by the centurion's confession, Luke does so by Jesus' final words.

Having witnessed the events of the crucifixion, the centurion "praised God, and said, 'Certainly this man was innocent!' " At first this seems a weaker statement than that found in Mark. But it has a deeper meaning than is first apparent. When Luke has the centurion call Jesus innocent, he intends more than the mere legal innocence already established at Jesus' trial. The underlying Greek word (*dikaios*) contains the Old Testament notion of righteous (*sedeq*). The meaning is that a person is in the right relationship to God because he stands within God's covenant practicing torah, the Mosaic law. Thus Luke describes Zechariah, Elizabeth and Simeon as righteous Israelites (1:6, 2:25). He says that the purpose of John the Baptist's ministry is to prepare a people for the Lord by turning "the disobedient to the wisdom of the just" (1:17, *dikaion*). The ultimate sense of the centurion's statement is that Jesus, not his persecutors, stands in the correct covenant relationship to God; he is the truly righteous person portrayed in the psalms of the righteous sufferer. It is not surprising, therefore, that in the Acts of the Apostles Luke eventually describes Jesus as the Just/Righteous One, a messianic title (3:14; 7:52; 22:14). The best translation of the centurion's cry, then, is "Truly this man was righteous."[45]

Luke says that in making this statement the centurion praised (*edoxazen*) God. The wording is important, since praise plays an important role in Luke-Acts. Of the nine times that Luke uses the verb, in eight instances the object of praise is God (2:20; 5:25,26; 7:16; 13:13; 17:15; 18:43; 23:47). In six of these cases (5:25,26; 7:16; 13:13; 17:15; 18:43), the reason for praising God is miraculous activity on the part of Jesus. In the other two instances people praise God at the major events of Jesus' life, his birth (2:20) and his death (23:47). The same pattern continues in Acts where God is praised because of a miracle worked in the name of Jesus (Acts 4:21) and because salvation comes to the Gentiles (Acts 11:18; 13:48; 21:20). In other words, in Luke's Gospel people praise God because he manifests his salvific activity in Jesus the Savior. The centurion praises God because he sees in Jesus one whose life is just, that is, in the right relationship to God. Jesus manifests that righteousness by refusing to save his own life (23:35,37,39), and by trustfully placing it in the hands of the Father (23:46).

But it is not only the centurion who acknowledges the quality of Jesus' life. In Luke the crowd, after witnessing these events, returns home beating their breasts. The expression is the same as that found in 18:13 where a tax collector prays in the temple beating his breast and is declared justified (*dedikaiomenos*) by Jesus (18:14). The implication is that because of the manner of Jesus' death, the crowd already begins to repent. Jesus' death is salvific.

The acquaintances of Jesus and the women who stand at a distance recall the words of Psalm 38:11, "My friends and companions stand aloof from my plague, and my kinsmen stand afar off" (also see Ps 88:8). Here the psalmist speaks of the predicament of the righteous sufferer. Luke and the first believers saw the messianic fulfillment of this psalm in Jesus.

Luke does not specify who the acquaintances are, but in Greek the noun is masculine (*hoi gnōstoi*), thereby suggesting that they include the disciples.[46] This suggestion is probable, if we remember the benevolent manner in which Luke treats the disciples throughout the passion. They do not abandon Jesus, and Jesus does not die as the forsaken Son of God.

VII.
THE BURIAL OF JESUS, 23:50–56

The final episode of Luke's passion narrative contains two scenes. In the first Joseph of Arimathea asks Pilate for the body of Jesus, and in the second the women who were present at the crucifixion (23:49) become witnesses that Jesus' body was truly laid in the tomb. The two scenes prepare for the story of the empty tomb (24:1–11) and establish beyond doubt that Jesus died and was buried. The episode becomes a transition between the passion and the resurrection.

Luke describes Joseph of Arimathea as a member of the council (*bouleutēs*), a good and righteous (*dikaios*) man who was looking for (*prosedexeto*) the kingdom of God. Although Luke does not specify the council, the logic of the story suggests that he is referring to the Sanhedrin. This reveals that although Luke places the burden of responsibility upon the leaders, he is aware that not all of them agreed to Jesus' death. Thus in the Acts of the Apostles, Luke narrates that Gamaliel counsels caution in dealing with the apostles (5:34–39) and that a great number of priests joined the faith (6:7). The references to Joseph's character and his hope for the kingdom of God serve two purposes. First, they recall qualities found in the pious Israelites of the infancy narrative, Zechariah, Elizabeth, Simeon and Anna. The first three are described as righteous (1:6; 2:25). Simeon is further portrayed as waiting for (*prosdexomenos*) the consolation of Israel (2:25). And Anna announces the Messiah to all those who were looking for (*prosdexomenos*) the redemption of Jerusalem (2:38). Luke places Joseph in that long line of faithful Israelites who practiced the law and patiently awaited God's redemption. Second, Luke establishes Joseph as a reliable witness to Jesus' death and burial. It was not one of Jesus' own circle who buried him. Nor was it a Gentile, or a Jew who did not practice torah. It was a member of the Sanhedrin, a faithful and pious Israelite.

Luke describes the place of Jesus' burial as "a rock-hewn tomb, where no one had ever yet been laid" (23:53). He is close to John who says that it was "a new tomb where no one had ever been laid" (Jn 19:41). The reference to a tomb "where no one had ever yet been laid" is a way of paying honor to Jesus. It may also be a subtle allusion to the royal nature of Jesus' burial, especially since John, who also emphasizes the royal theme, makes a similar allusion. Jesus lies in a tomb in which no one had ever been laid just as he made his royal entrance into Jerusalem on a colt upon which no one had yet sat (19:30).

All of this occurs on the Day of Preparation, Friday, the day before the sabbath. It is imperative that Jesus be buried as quickly as possible since the sabbath began at sundown. According to Deuteronomy 21:22–23, a crucified person had to be buried before sundown lest his body defile the land:

> And if a man has committed a crime punishable by death and he is put to death, and you hang him on a tree [an expression which later referred to crucifixion], his body shall not remain all night upon the tree, but you shall bury him the same day, for a hanged man is accursed by God; you shall not defile your land which the Lord your God gives you for an inheritance.

The story of the burial has a double edge. The burial is a kindness to Jesus, but it also fulfills the prescription of Deuteronomy, thereby recalling the shameful circumstances surrounding Jesus' death.

The final scene of this episode concerns the women who followed Jesus from Galilee (see 8:1–3). Unlike Mark, Luke does not name them here, but in 24:10 he does. They are Mary Magdalene, Joanna, Mary the mother of James, and some other unnamed women. These are the same women who stood at a distance with Jesus' acquaintances (23:49). There they served as witnesses to Jesus' death. Here they are witnesses to his burial, and they will be the first witnesses to the resurrection when they announce (*apēggeilan*) to the apostles the empty tomb and the angel's message (24:9).

Women play an active role in Luke's Gospel. Mary, Elizabeth, and Anna are prominent figures in the infancy narrative. Women from Galilee accompany Jesus during his public ministry (8:1–3), and Martha and Mary offer him hospitality (10:38–42).

The women in this scene prepare to anoint Jesus' body with spices and ointments, but first they must rest on the sabbath according to the commandment of the Mosaic law (Ex 12:16). Jesus the Messiah does not come to destroy the law but to reestablish Israel in righteousness. Luke presents Jesus' life as one that begins by following the prescriptions of the law (2:22–24) and ends with his followers doing the same.

CONCLUSION

A review of Luke's passion narrative reveals how multi-faceted it is. Surely the evangelist presents Jesus as an example of innocent suffering, but he does much more. At the Last Supper, Luke portrays Jesus as a prophetic and royal figure who delivers a Farewell Discourse to his chosen apostles. He is a prophetic figure because he is fully aware of what is about to take place. He is a royal figure because he prepares to enter his kingdom and promises a kingdom to his followers. At the Mount of Olives, Luke depicts Jesus as the obedient Son of God who accepts the will of the Father. Luke shows that the passion involves more that the plotting of human beings against a martyr. It is an hour of darkness which ironically coincides with God's will for his anointed Messiah. At the hearing before the Sanhedrin and the trial before Pilate, Jesus' royal character comes into sharper focus. Jesus predicts that he will be seated in royal splendor at God's right hand. The religious leaders deliver him to Pilate as a messianic pretender, the King of the Jews, but both Pilate and Herod do not find evidence to condemn Jesus to death. Nonetheless, he is led out to crucifixion. In the midst of that awful agony, Jesus shows himself a Prophet to the women of Jerusalem and a Savior to the repentant criminal. He is mocked as the Messiah, the King of the Jews, the Savior who cannot save himself. Despite these humiliations, he dies as the Son of God who confidently places his spirit in the hands of the Father. The manner of his death and the quality of his life lead a Gentile centurion to praise God because of Jesus' righteousness. The crowds return home repentant, and Joseph of Arimathea provides Jesus with a royal burial.

Throughout this ordeal, Jesus' disciples play a prominent role. They have persevered with him during the trials of his ministry; they do not completely abandon Jesus during the passion. It is true that they dispute about greatness at the Last Supper. It is true that Judas betrays him and that Peter denies him. Nonetheless, Jesus assigns the apostles a kingdom. He prays for them, and especially for Peter that his faith will not fail. Jesus prepares them for the difficult period which lies ahead. Although they will only understand the events of the passion in the light of his resurrection, they stand by him as best they can, even to the point of trying to defend him at the Mount of Olives. With the women, they watch the crucifixion from a distance and become witnesses of these events.

It is difficult to choose one theme by which to express all that occurs in Luke's passion. Although the martyr motif is attractive, it is not comprehensive. In light of this investigation, I propose four vantage points from which to view Luke's narrative. First, Luke presents the passion as Jesus' divinely appointed destiny. The hour of darkness and the fulfillment of the Scriptures coincide at the passion. Second, the hour of the passion becomes Jesus' last and greatest lesson for discipleship. He serves as a model for his followers. His example is more than one of martyrdom; it is a model of discipleship for the kingdom. Third, the passion is the rejection of Jesus the Prophet. The city of Jerusalem, especially its leaders, rejects the last and the greatest of the prophets. Finally, the passion is the death of God's royal Son: the King of the Jews, the Messiah, the Savior. The next chapter shows how each of these themes is present in the Gospel, and how each leads to the passion.

Chapter Nine

LUKE'S GOSPEL THEOLOGY

In chapter seven I suggested that to appreciate the full meaning of Luke's passion narrative, it is important to situate it within the wider context of his Gospel theology. At the conclusion of chapter eight, I identified four vantage points from which to view Luke's account of Jesus' passion: the passion as the destiny of Jesus; the passion as a model for discipleship; the passion as the rejection of Jesus the Prophet; the passion as the death of God's royal Son. In this chapter, I examine these themes in light of Luke's Gospel story. I will show that Luke prepares for the major themes of the passion narrative throughout the Gospel. To a lesser extent, I will also explain how many of these themes continue in the second part of Luke's work, the Acts of the Apostles.

I.
THE PASSION AS THE DESTINY OF JESUS

On several occasions I have made the point that the events of the passion do not catch Jesus by surprise. Everything seems to occur according to a predetermined plan. The room for the Passover supper has been decided in advance (22:10–13). Judas betrays his Lord, but Jesus announces that "the Son of Man goes as it has been determined" (22:22). Jesus proclaims that the Scripture from Isaiah 53:12 ("And he was reckoned with transgressors") must (*dei*) be realized in him, because everything written about him has its fulfillment (22:37). At the Mount of Olives, he prays that the will of his Father will be done (22:42), and at his arrest he does not resist his enemies because "this is your hour, and the power of darkness" (22:53). Finally, during his crucifixion Jesus tells the women of Jerusalem not to weep for him but for themselves and pronounces an oracle of doom over the city's inhabitants (23:29–30). Jesus is not surprised at what is happening because the passion is his destiny.

Luke can present this portrait of Jesus during the passion because he has prepared for it throughout the Gospel in two ways. First, he develops the theme of Jerusalem, the city of Jesus' destiny. Second, he speaks of the divine necessity (*dei*, "it is necessary") which impels Jesus' journey to this city.

The city of Jerusalem plays an important role in Luke's Gospel. References to the city and its temple bracket Luke's story. It is there that the Gospel begins with the pious Zechariah offering incense in the temple (1:5–23), and it is there that the Gospel concludes with the apostles praising God in the temple (24:53). Within the narrative, Jerusalem and its temple appear again and again. In what follows I review the story of Luke's Gospel in light of the Jerusalem theme and the divine necessity which guides Jesus to this city.

A. *The Infancy Narrative (1:5–2:52)*

The infancy narrative features the city of Jerusalem.[1] The Gospel begins in the temple of Jerusalem, thereby relating the story of Jesus to the center of Israelite piety. Following the annunciation to Zechariah (1:5–20), Luke narrates the annunciation to Mary (1:26–38) during which the angel tells Mary that her child will sit on David's throne and rule over the house of Jacob (1:32–33). At the beginning of the story the reader discovers that Jerusalem is destined to be Jesus' royal city.

After the birth of Jesus his parents, as law-abiding Israelites, bring him to the temple and present him to the Lord (2:22). There a pious Israelite, Simeon, recognizes the child as the Lord's Messiah (2:26). In the temple Simeon foretells that Jesus will be a sign of contradiction (2:34), and Anna speaks of the child to all who are awaiting the redemption of Israel (2:38). Thus these two pious Israelites point to the passion.

Jesus' parents, having fulfilled all the prescriptions of the law, return to Nazareth. But as pious Israelites, they make pilgrimages to Jerusalem every year for the Passover (2:41), thereby foreshadowing Jesus' final Passover, the passion. On one occasion they find the child in the temple of Jerusalem, and he says to them, "Did you not know that

I must (*dei*) be in my Father's house?'' (2:49) The incident prefigures Jesus' Jerusalem ministry (19:45–21:38) when, as Messiah, he takes possession of Jerusalem's temple and teaches the people (19:45–48). The infancy narrative points to the conclusion of the Gospel and the events of Jesus' passion.

B. The Threshold of Jesus' Ministry (4:1–13)

Following the infancy narrative, Luke relates the preaching of John, the baptism of Jesus, and his temptations in the desert (3:1–4:13). It is the last event (4:1–13), the temptations, which concerns us. Luke narrates the story so that the third of Jesus' temptations takes place at the pinnacle of Jerusalem's temple (4:9).[2] In doing this he makes the climax of Jesus' struggle with the devil occur in the very city where Jesus will undergo his passion. Satan departs from Jesus, but he returns at the "opportune time," the time of the passion (cf. 4:13)

C. Ministry in Galilee (4:14–9:50)

The next section of Luke's Gospel consists of Jesus' Galilean ministry. In this section Luke mentions Jerusalem three times. In 5:17 and 6:17 he notes that people come from all over, including Jerusalem, to witness Jesus' deeds and words. Jerusalem will not be able to claim ignorance of Jesus' words and deeds at the time of the passion.

The third notice of Jerusalem occurs toward the end of Jesus' Galilean ministry, at the transfiguration (9:28–36). Luke narrates that on that occasion Jesus stood between Moses and Elijah and "spoke of his departure (*exodon*, literally "exodus"), which he was to accomplish at Jerusalem." Jesus' first and second passion predictions (9:22,44) bracket this incident. In these Jesus says it is necessary (*dei*) for the Son of Man to suffer many things (9:22) and to be handed over (*paradidosthai*) into the hands of men (9:44). Jesus' "exodus" in Jerusalem is divinely appointed. He must suffer many things.

There is yet another way in which the material of this section serves the Jerusalem theme. In Mark 6:45–8:26, the second evangelist narrates Jesus' journeys into pagan lands outside of Galilee (Bethsaida, Mk 6:45; Tyre and Sidon, Mk 7:24,31; Decapolis, Mk 7:31). Luke, who employs Mark as a major source for his Gospel, omits this portion of Mark from his account. As a result, in Luke's Gospel, Jesus does not venture outside of Galilee during the first part of his ministry. His mission is only to Israel, and the course of his divinely predetermined life moves, without interruption, from Galilee to Jerusalem (see Lk 23:5, Acts 10:37).

D. Journey to Jerusalem (9:51–19:44)

The most distinctive portion of Luke's Gospel, however, is Jesus' journey to Jerusalem.[3] Matthew and Mark are aware of this journey (Mt 19:1–2; Mk 10:1), but neither of them describes it with the detail or mastery of Luke. All three evangelists share common material (Mt 19:13–21:9 = Mk 10:13–11:10 = Lk 18:15–19:40), but Luke has a section peculiar to himself (9:51–18:14)[4] which contains several stories and parables found only in his Gospel (good Samaritan, prodigal son, rich man and Lazarus, Martha and Mary). This material forms the heart of Jesus' Jerusalem journey as recorded by Luke.

Although scholars refer to this section as Jesus' Jerusalem journey, it is a strange journey during which there is little movement. Although Jesus is supposedly on journey, he appears to pass most of his time instructing his disciples and arguing with his opponents. Consequently, as if to remind the reader that Jesus is really on a journey, Luke provides five notices that Jesus is making his way to Jerusalem (9:51; 13:22; 17:11; 18:31; 19:28).

Jesus' journey begins with the majestic verse, "When the days drew near for him to be received up, he set his face to go to Jerusalem" (9:51). Behind the English phrase "to be received up" stands the Greek noun *analēmpsis* which can also be translated as "ascension." In the Acts of the Apostles its verbal form (*analambanein*) is employed in reference to Jesus' ascension: "This Jesus, who was taken up (*analēmphtheis*), will come in the same way as you saw him go into heaven" (Acts 1:11; cf. 1:22). By this introductory verse Luke intimates that the ultimate goal of Jesus' life is his ascension to the Father. The verse might be translated as follows: "When the days drew near for his ascension, he set his face to go to Jerusalem." But this should not be interpreted in too restrictive a manner. Jesus can only ascend to the Father after he has undergone his passion. The Jerusalem journey is the beginning of the exodus (9:31) which Jesus will accomplish at Jerusalem, an exodus which will result in his ascension.[5]

In 13:22 Luke mentions Jesus' journey for the second time: "He went on his way through towns and villages, teaching, and journeying toward Jerusalem.'' A few verses later some Pharisees warn Jesus to leave the area because Herod seeks to kill him (13:31). Jesus refuses to heed their advice since he has undertaken this journey under divine necessity: ''Nevertheless I must (*dei*) go on my way today and tomorrow and the day following; for it cannot be that a prophet should perish away from Jerusalem'' (13:33). Jesus goes to Jerusalem to die, and there he will meet Herod! Jesus concludes this encounter with the Pharisees with the first of four prophecies against the city: ''O Jerusalem, Jerusalem, killing the prophets and stoning those who are sent to you! How often would I have gathered your children together as a hen gathers her brood under her wings, and you would not! Behold your house is forsaken'' (13:34–35; for the other prophecies, see 19:41–44; 21:20–24; 23:28–31).

In 17:11 Luke provides a third notice of Jesus' Jerusalem journey: ''On the way to Jerusalem he was passing along between Samaria and Galilee.'' A few verses later the Pharisees ask him when the kingdom of God is coming (17:20). After answering them, he turns to his disciples and delivers a discourse on the Day of the Son of Man (17:22–37). In the midst of that discourse he once more points to his passion: ''For as the lightning flashes and lights up the sky from one side to the other, so will the Son of Man be in his day. But first he must (*dei*) suffer many things and be rejected by this generation'' (17:24–25). Jesus cannot return as the glorious Son of Man until he has journeyed to Jerusalem, the city which will reject him.

In the next chapter Luke recounts the fourth notice of the journey as Jesus pronounces his most detailed passion prediction: ''And taking the twelve, he said to them, 'Behold we are going up to Jerusalem, and everything that is written of the Son of Man by the prophets will be accomplished. For he will be delivered to the Gentiles, and will be mocked and shamefully treated and spit upon; they will scourge him and kill him, and on the third day he will rise' '' (18:31–33). The prediction comes after an incident in which a rich ruler asks Jesus what he must do to inherit eternal life (18:18–30), and it precedes the declaration by a blind beggar that Jesus is the Son of David (18:35–43). The central position of the prediction suggests that Jesus will inherit eternal life, and that he is the Son of David, precisely because he makes this journey to Jerusalem where he willingly surrenders his life. The emphasis that all of this happens according to what has been written by the prophets demonstrates the divine necessity of the journey.

A few verses later, 19:11, Luke makes a fifth reference to the city as he introduces one of Jesus' parables: "As they heard these things, he proceeded to tell a parable, because he was near to Jerusalem, and because they supposed that the kingdom of God was to appear immediately." Those traveling with Jesus think that his journey will bring the immediate arrival of God's kingdom. They have not understood the necessity of his passion. Therefore, Jesus tells the parable of the ten pounds (19:11–27), in which "a nobleman went into a far country to receive a kingdom and then return." The parable is an allegory in which the "nobleman" represents Jesus and the journey to the "far country" corresponds to the passion Jesus must endure in Jerusalem before his return as King.

Having concluded the parable, Jesus continues his journey: "And when he had said this, he went on ahead, going up to Jerusalem" (19:28). When he reaches the Mount of Olivet (19:29), he sends two of his disciples to find a colt, and seated upon it he makes his triumphal procession toward the city. For all practical purposes, the journey is ended. Having arrived at the outskirts of Jerusalem, Jesus prophesies the city's destruction because it did not know the time of its visitation (19:41–44). Jerusalem will reject Jesus, and his visitation will result in judgment.

E. Jesus in Jerusalem (19:45–24:53)

The final portion of Luke's Gospel concerns Jesus' activity in the city. The material can be divided into three sections: (1) Jesus' temple ministry (19:45–21:38); (2) Jesus' passion and death (22:1–23:56); (3) Jesus' resurrection and ascension (24:1–53). Luke begins the first of these sections with Jesus cleansing the temple (19:45–46), and then notes that he was "teaching daily in the temple" (19:47). He repeats the statement a few verses later, saying that Jesus "was teaching the people in the temple and preaching the Gospel" (20:1). He concludes the entire section with a similar verse: "And every day he was teaching in the temple, but at night he went out and lodged on the mount called Olivet. And early in the morning all the people came to him in the temple to hear him" (21:37–38). This section portrays Jesus, the royal Messiah, teaching the people in his Father's house (cf. 2:46–49). At the same time, the shadow of the passion falls upon this period as the religious leaders engage Jesus in controversy (20:1–8,20–40) and plot to destroy him (19:47; 20:19). Jesus delivers a major discourse in which he foretells the destruction of Jerusalem (21:20–24) for the third time. The Jerusalem ministry becomes the immediate occasion for his passion and death.

There is no need to repeat the material of the passion narrative. By now it is clear that Jesus' death in Jerusalem, and his words to the women of that city (23:28–31), are the outcome of a theme Luke has carefully crafted. In chapter 24 he brings the theme to a close by situating all of Jesus' resurrection appearances in or near Jerusalem. Here Luke diverges from Matthew and Mark who locate the appearances of the Risen One in Galilee. Thus at the empty tomb the angel does not say to the women "tell his disciples and Peter that he is going before you to Galilee" (Mk 16:7). Instead the women tell the eleven, who are still in Jerusalem (24:9), what they have seen. Likewise the two disciples who encounter the Lord on the way to Emmaus return to Jerusalem and report the news to the eleven (24:33), and at Jerusalem Jesus appears to all of them (24:36–49). In all of these appearances, Luke takes up the theme of divine necessity (24:7 *dei,* 24:26 *edei,* 24:44 *dei*). Finally, after Jesus' ascension, the eleven return to Jerusalem where they continually bless God in the temple (24:53). Thus the story ends where it begins, in the temple of Jerusalem. Jerusalem, the center of salvation in the Old Testament, remains so in the New Testament. Indeed, the geographical importance of Jerusalem will continue in the Acts of the Apostles. There the Risen Lord will commission the disciples to be his "witnesses in Jerusalem and in all Judea and Samaria and to the end of the earth" (Acts 1:8).

II.
THE PASSION AS A MODEL FOR DISCIPLESHIP

Luke presents his version of the passion story as a model for discipleship. In the suffering of Jesus the reader discovers the full meaning of what it means to take up one's cross daily and follow Jesus (9:23). By his passion Jesus gives the disciples a final lesson in discipleship. At the Last Supper he delivers a Farewell Discourse which explains the nature of leadership (22:24–27) and prepares the disciples for the trials which lie ahead (22:35–38). On the Mount of Olives he becomes a model of what it means to persevere in prayer (22:39–46). At his arrest, he does not resist but continues to do good, healing the servant of the high priest (22:47–53). At his crucifixion, he prays for his persecutors (23:34), and by his example he leads others to repentance. Josef Ernst puts it well when he says that following Jesus in the way of suffering finds its high point in the passion narrative.[6]

But it is not only Jesus who plays an important role in the passion story. In chapter 22 Luke features the disciples who, with Jesus, are principal characters in the narrative. In his treatment of them Luke is especially benevolent. For example, Jesus says that he has earnestly desired to eat this Passover with his disciples before he suffers (22:15). He points to the bread and the wine as his body and blood given *for them,* his disciples (22:19–20). When they argue about greatness Jesus reproves them, but then promises that they will sit on thrones judging the twelve tribes of Israel (22:24–30). He predicts Peter's denial, but also notes that he has prayed for him lest his faith fail (22:31–32). At the Mount of Olives the disciples fall asleep, but a sleep which Luke explains as resulting from sorrow (22:45). At Jesus' arrest, Luke says nothing of the disciples fleeing (cf. Mk 14:50). To the contrary, he hints that they stand with the women watching the events of the crucifixion (23:49).

Luke's portrait of the disciples can be explained, in part, by the role they play in the Acts of the Apostles. There they become witnesses to everything that Jesus did: "And we are witnesses to all that he did both in the country of the Jews and in Jerusalem. They put him to death by hanging him on a tree; but God raised him on the third day and made him manifest" (Acts 10:39–40). The disciples (and here I mean the apostles as I shall explain below) become the rulers of a reestablished Israel.[7] As is apparent from the opening chapters of Acts, they replace Israel's former leaders as the true shepherds of the people.

This picture of the disciples is firmly rooted in the rest of the Gospel. What happens at the passion is the culmination of a theme that Luke develops throughout his narrative. Joseph Fitzmyer writes, "To be a disciple of Christ one has to follow him along the road that he walks to his destiny in Jerusalem, his *exodus,* his transit to the Father."[8] In other words, discipleship means not only learning from Jesus, but following him on the way that leads to Jerusalem. The theme of discipleship is akin to that of Jesus' destiny as expressed in his journey to Jerusalem. This journey is more than Jesus' way, it becomes the way for all would-be disciples.

A. Who Are the Disciples?

In Luke's Gospel the disciples represent a variety of people: a fisherman, Simon Peter, and his companions, James and John (5:1–11); a tax collector named Levi (5:27); an unnamed group of people (9:23); Martha and Mary (10:38–42); a rich ruler (18:18); a chief tax collector named Zacchaeus (19:1–9); a group of women (8:2–3; 23:55–24:11). The disciples of Jesus do not form a small, select group. Jesus offers the invitation of discipleship to everybody: "And he said to *all*, 'If any man would come after me, let him deny himself and take up his cross daily and follow me' " (9:23). Thus Luke can speak of "a great crowd of his disciples" (6:17) and of "the whole multitude of the disciples" (19:37). Those who follow Jesus constitute a great number from the whole of Israel.[9]

In time, however, Luke makes a distinction between those who follow Jesus as his disciples and the crowd which continually accompanies him. This occurs for the first time at the Sermon on the Plain, Luke's counterpart to Matthew's Sermon on the Mount. "And he came down with them and stood on a level place, with a great crowd of his disciples *and a great multitude of people from all Judea and Jerusalem and the seacost of Tyre and Sidon*" (6:17; see also 12:1). This multitude (*ochlos*) follows and accompanies Jesus (7:9,11; 9:11), but such people are not his disciples. This is not necessarily a negative judgment since Luke tends to treat favorably the crowd which follows Jesus. Although the people of the crowd are not his disciples, they witness his deeds and words with approval (7:16; 11:14,27; 13:17; 18:43).

Luke makes a further distinction between the disciples, who constitute a great number, and the apostles whom he, and only he among the evangelists, identifies with the twelve. Thus before the Sermon on the Plain, Jesus prays all night, "And when it was day, he called his disciples, and chose from them twelve, whom he named apostles" (6:13). Later Luke, like Mark and Matthew, describes the mission of the twelve (9:1–6). But then in 10:1–12, he narrates a mission of the seventy which has no parallel in the other Gospels, thereby further distinguishing the apostles from the disciples. The apostles are and remain disciples, but not all disciples are apostles.

Throughout Jesus' public ministry, Luke does not make much of this distinction between apostle and disciple. On a few occasions he employs the titles rather indiscriminately. A good example is found in chapter 9 where Jesus sends the twelve on mission and then, upon their return, feeds the five thousand (9:1–17). In 9:1 Luke refers to them as the twelve, and in 9:10 he calls them apostles. In 9:12 he reverts to the terminology of the twelve, but in 9:14 he calls them disciples. It is apparent that Luke is still thinking of the twelve apostles in 9:14 because he notes in 9:17 that they gathered up *twelve* baskets of broken pieces. A final example is found in 17:1–5, a collection of sayings about scandal, forgiveness, and faith. In 17:1 Luke refers to the disciples, but in 17:5 he calls the same group apostles.

During Jesus' public ministry, except for the different missions which he entrusts to them and the seventy, the apostles do not perform a role different from that of the disciples. They are disciples in the process of learning what it means to follow Jesus. They, like the rest of the disciples and the multitudes, witness all that Jesus says and does. Because of their faithfulness during this period Jesus commends them at the Last Supper: "You are those who have continued with me in my trials" (22:28).

When Luke speaks about the disciples, in most instances he does not specify if he means the twelve or the wider group which follows Jesus. Sometimes the reader suspects that Luke means the twelve when he refers to the disciples, for example, the first and second passion predictions (9:22, 9:44), since the third (18:31) is directed to the twelve. But Luke leaves the matter open, thereby suggesting that Jesus directs his teaching to an audience wider than the twelve. But in the passion Luke makes it clear that the disciples with Jesus are the twelve apostles: "And when the hour came, he sat at table, and the apostles with him" (22:14). Having followed Jesus on his journey to Jerusalem, they follow him to the end, because in the Acts of the Apostles they must be witnesses to *all* that Jesus did. Thus the risen Lord says to them, "Thus it is written, that the Christ should suffer and on the third day rise from the dead. . . . You are witnesses of these things" (24:46,48).

B. What Is Required of a Disciple?

On several occasions Luke describes the requirements of discipleship.[10] At the beginning of the Gospel he explains that true disciples, like Peter, James, John and Levi, leave everything in order to follow Jesus (5:11,28). They accompany him on his journeys (8:1–3). During his Galilean ministry (4:14–9:50), Jesus delivers a major sermon, the Sermon on the Plain (6:17–49). Although the multitudes hear the sermon, Luke makes it clear that Jesus directs it to his disciples: "And he lifted up his eyes on his disciples, and said . . ." (6:20). However, it is in the section which narrates Jesus' Jerusalem journey (9:51–19:44) that Luke gives the fullest picture of discipleship. Indeed, the journey to Jerusalem becomes a model for discipleship.[11]

Prior to the journey, Jesus makes two passion predictions (9:22,44) so that the disciples will understand why he is undertaking it. After the first of these, he tells *everybody*, "If any man would come after me, let him deny himself and take up his cross daily and follow me" (9:23). From the outset it is clear that discipleship entails suffering. After the second prediction, the full implications of which are hidden from the disciples, Jesus' followers argue about who is the greatest. As a result, he teaches that the least among them will be the greatest (9:46–48). Discipleship demands self-effacement. A somewhat similar point is made in the next incident in which the disciples forbid someone to cast out demons in Jesus' name (9:49–50). Jesus instructs them not to exclude from their company anyone who is not against them.

The journey opens with a number of discipleship stories which set the tone for what follows. After introducing the journey (9:51–56), Luke recounts three stories which explain the demands of discipleship (9:57–62). In the first (9:57–58) and the third (9:61–62), would-be disciples say that they will follow Jesus, but in each case he explains that they do not understand the full implications of what they are undertaking. In the central story (9:59–60), Jesus calls someone to discipleship and demands an immediate response: "Leave the dead to bury their own dead; but as for you, go and proclaim the kingdom of God." Discipleship entails making the journey to Jerusalem with Jesus, and no one should undertake this vocation unprepared to suffer with the Lord.

Following these discipleship stories, Luke recounts the mission of the seventy (10:1–11). He warns all future disciples of the dangers which lie ahead: "I send you out as lambs in the midst of wolves" (10:3). Discipleship requires missionary work done in complete dependence upon God: "Carry no purse, no bag, no sandals" (10:4). Just as Jesus was rejected by the Samaritans while on his journey to Jerusalem (9:52–53), so disciples can expect rejection in the course of their missionary endeavors: "But whenever you enter a town and they do not receive you, go into its streets and say, 'Even the dust of your town that clings to our feet, we wipe off against you' " (10:10–11). When the disciples return triumphant (10:17–20), Jesus explains the true reason for rejoicing; their names "are written in heaven." Jesus rejoices that the Father has revealed such things to "babes" (10:21–22), that is, to his disciples. The purpose of these opening stories is to relate discipleship to Jesus' Jerusalem journey, a journey which leads to the passion.

As the journey progresses Jesus offers his disciples a wide variety of teaching to aid them in the way of discipleship. In chapter 11 a disciple asks Jesus to teach them to pray as John taught his disciples (11:1). In response, Jesus teaches the Our Father (11:2–4) and instructs them on the necessity of praying with perseverance (11:5–13). Prayer is one of the ways in which disciples follow Jesus.

After these instructions, Luke presents Jesus engaged in controversy with the Pharisees and scribes (11:14–54). But in chapter 12 he resumes his picture of the Lord instructing the disciples: "In the meantime, when so many thousands of the multitude had gathered together that they trod upon one another, he began to say to his disciples . . ." (12:1). The instruction is briefly interrupted in 12:13–21, but it resumes in 12:22: "And he said to his disciples. . . ." It continues until 12:54 when Jesus turns to the multitude: "He also said to the multitudes. . . ." The chapter prepares disciples for the difficulties which lie ahead: "And when they bring you before the synagogues and the rulers and the authorities" (12:11); and "henceforth in one house there will be five divided, three against two and two against three" (12:52).

Jesus tells disciples who will face such trials not to be anxious, because "the Holy Spirit will teach you in that very hour what you ought to say" (12:12). He instructs them not to be anxious for their lives, because it is the Father's "good pleasure to give you the kingdom" (12:32). And he warns them to be ready, "for the Son of Man is coming at an unexpected hour" (12:40). The disciples must think of themselves as a "little flock" (12:32), and as men "waiting for their master to come home from the marriage feast'' (12:36). Discipleship is a journey that demands trust in God, the kind of trust Jesus manifests at his passion.

As the journey progresses, Jesus continues to explain the demands of discipleship. In 14:25–33, while a great multitude accompanies him, he turns to the crowd and sets down three conditions for would-be followers: the need to place discipleship before family (14:26); the need to bear one's cross (14:27); the need to calculate the cost of discipleship (14:28–33). Each of the sayings concludes with the same phrase. If a person is not willing to accept the particular condition, he ''cannot be my disciple.'' The middle saying about bearing one's cross and coming after Jesus points to the passion. It finds a model in Simon of Cyrene who does carry the cross behind Jesus (23:26).

In the last saying Jesus proclaims, ''So, therefore, whoever of you does not renounce all that he has cannot be my disciple'' (14:33). This saying points to a major theme in Luke's theology of discipleship, the use of possessions. A disciple's attitude toward wealth is a barometer of commitment to Jesus. Thus in chapter 16 Jesus tells his disciples the parable of the dishonest servant (1–9). Isolated the parable is difficult to understand since it gives the impression that Jesus approves of the steward's dishonest behavior. But in the sayings which follow (10–13), Luke relates the parable to discipleship. Disciples who are faithful in small matters will be faithful in greater; it is impossible to serve two masters.

The same theme occurs in chapter 18 when a rich ruler asks Jesus what he must do to inherit eternal life. Jesus responds, ''Sell all that you have and distribute to the poor, and you will have treasure in heaven; and come, *follow* me'' (18:22). After this incident, Peter boasts that he and the other disciples have left all in order to follow Jesus (18:28). Jesus promises Peter that he, and those like him, will ''receive manifold more in this time, and in the age to come, eternal life'' (18:30). But then, as if to place this promise in proper perspective, Jesus takes the twelve aside and gives them the most detailed prediction of his passion (18:31–33). Discipleship will ultimately lead to the cross, and in order to undertake such discipleship one must have the proper attitude toward possessions.

Luke describes discipleship as a way, a journey to Jerusalem. Discipleship is open to all, but no one should undertake it lightly, since it entails a total commitment to Jesus manifested in a willingness to leave all things behind and follow him. In this regard Luke is not much different from the other evangelists. But he does bring a distinctive contribution to the theology of discipleship by relating it to Jesus' Jerusalem journey. That journey is an expression of Jesus' destiny to suffer in Jerusalem. It manifests what lies in store for every disciple. The disciple must stand united with the Lord and his destiny. The journey Jesus makes to Jerusalem is a model of the way every disciple must tread. If Jesus' journey led to the passion, the disciple can expect no less. In the Acts of the Apostles the lives of Stephen and Paul show this.

III.
THE PASSION AS THE REJECTION OF JESUS THE PROPHET

On several occasions in the passion narrative, Luke presents Jesus as a man with prophetic insight. For example, Jesus instructs Peter and John to prepare the Passover supper and with prophetic knowledge tells them where it will be held (22:12). At the supper Jesus prophesies that this is the last Passover he will share with the disciples until it is fulfilled in the kingdom of God (22:16,18). He foretells his betrayal (22:21,22) and predicts Peter's denial (22:34). As the meal draws to a close, he reveals that the disciples will face a time of persecution because of their association with him (22:35–37). At the Mount of Olives, his prayer discloses that he knows the suffering which lies before him (22:42), and when Judas approaches, he recognizes him as the betrayer (22:48). Finally, when he stands before the Sanhedrin, Jesus prophesies that from this point forward he will be seated at the right hand of the power of God (22:69).

On two other occasions Luke is even more explicit in his portrait of Jesus as Prophet. First while held in custody, Jesus is mocked as a Prophet (22:64). Second as Jesus is being led out to be crucified, he makes a prophetic statement:

Daughters of Jerusalem do not weep for me,
but weep for yourselves and for your children.
For behold the days are coming when they will say,
"Blessed are the barren, and the wombs that never bore,
and the breasts that never gave suck!"
Then they will begin to say to the mountains,
"Fall on us"; and to the hills, "Cover us."

> For if they do this when the wood is green,
> what will happen when it is dry? (23:28–31).

This portrait of Jesus as a rejected Prophet is not limited to the passion narrative. Scholars remark that the theme of the rejected Prophet plays a major role in the rest of the Gospel as well as the Acts of the Apostles.[12] What happens in the passion is the climax of a theme which Luke has carefully crafted throughout his two-volume work.

A. *The Return of the Spirit of Prophecy (1:5–2:52)*

In terms of salvation history the time prior to Jesus' birth belongs to the final period of the old covenant. It was a period during which many believed that the gift of prophecy had ceased.[13] So the First Book of Maccabees, describing the period after the death of Judas Maccabeus (160 B.C), says, "Thus there was great distress in Israel, such as had not been since the time that prophets ceased to appear among them" (9:27). There was an expectation, however, that a prophet would arise. So, the same Book of Maccabees, commenting on the appointment of Simon Maccabeus as leader and high priest, says, "And the Jews and their priests decided that Simon should be their leader and high priest for ever, until a trustworthy prophet should arise" (14:41). Who this trustworthy prophet would be was a matter of dispute, but many associated him either with Elijah come back to life, or with the prophet like Moses promised in Deuteronomy 18:15: "The Lord your God will raise up for you a prophet like me from among you, from your brethren—him you shall heed."

One of the striking aspects of Luke's infancy narrative, is its proclamation that the spirit of prophecy has returned. Luke portrays all of the major figures of the narrative as filled with the prophetic spirit. For example, the angel who announces the birth of John to Zechariah says that the child will be "filled with the Holy Spirit" (1:15) and that "he will go before him in the spirit and power of Elijah" (1:17). At the birth of John, Luke writes that Zechariah "was filled with the Holy Spirit, and prophesied" (1:67). What follows is the *Benedictus* (1:68–79). Within that canticle, Zechariah says of John, "And you, child, will be called the Prophet of the Most High" (1:76). In a similar fashion, the spirit of prophecy comes upon other characters. Elizabeth, "filled with the Holy Spirit" (1:41), says to Mary, "Blessed are you among women" (1:42). In turn, Mary proclaims her prophetic canticle, the *Magnificat* (1:46–55), in which she prophesies, "henceforth all generations will call me blessed" (1:48). Earlier in the story, the angel had said of Mary, "The Holy Spirit will come upon you, and the power of the Most High will overshadow you" (1:35). Finally, when Jesus' parents present him in the temple, they encounter the aged Simeon and Anna. Luke says of the first that "the Holy Spirit was upon him. And it had been revealed to him by the Holy Spirit that he should not see death before he had seen the Lord's Christ. And inspired by the Spirit he came into the temple" (2:25–27). Of Anna he writes, "And there was a prophetess, Anna, the daughter of Phanuel" (2:36). The birth of the Messiah marks the beginning of a new age; the spirit of prophecy returns to Israel.

Within the infancy narrative Luke does not present Jesus as a Prophet since he is drawing a parallel between the birth of John, the prophetic forerunner of the Messiah, and Jesus, God's royal Son. Although the births of John and Jesus have many parallels, Luke makes it clear that Jesus is the greater of the two.[14] But once John is imprisoned (3:19–20) and Jesus begins his public ministry (4:14), Luke portrays Jesus as a mighty Prophet, powerful in word and deed. He does not forget Jesus' royal identity, but he does not emphasize it as much as he did in the infancy narrative. But when Jesus reaches Jerusalem, Luke again highlights Jesus' royal lineage, thereby merging the prophetic and royal themes.

B. *The Inaugural Sermon and Galilean Ministry (4:14–9:50)*

Having overcome the temptations of Satan in the wilderness (4:1–13), Jesus returns to Galilee "in the power of the Spirit" (4:14) and initiates his public ministry with an inaugural sermon at Nazareth (4:16–30).[15] Nearly all commentators agree that this is a key text for understanding the Gospel since it provides a programmatic statement of Jesus' ministry. The scene is filled with prophetic imagery and presents Jesus as the Prophet who proffers salvation for his people only to be rejected by them. So Luke sets the stage for the rest of his story. Jesus is a Prophet destined for rejection.

The scene has two parts. In the first (4:14–22), Jesus, filled with the prophetic spirit, proclaims the text of Isaiah 61:1–2 and declares that it finds fulfillment in his person.

> The Spirit of the Lord is upon me,
> because he has anointed me to preach good news to the poor.
> He has sent me to proclaim release to captives
> and recovering of sight to the blind,
> to set at liberty those who are oppressed,
> to proclaim the acceptable year of the Lord.

Jesus identifies himself as a Prophet who brings salvation to his people. The initial reaction to the sermon is favorable. Although the people are puzzled because of Jesus' origins ("Is not this Joseph's son?"), they acknowledge his gracious words. The irony, of course, is that Jesus is God's Son (3:22; 3:38), a fact of which the people are not aware.

In the second half of the scene (4:23–30), the mood unexpectedly changes. Jesus, the Prophet, knows what the people are thinking and says, "Doubtless you will quote to me this proverb, 'Physician, heal yourself; what we have heard you did at Capernaum, do here also in your own country' " (4:23). In face of the people's opposition, Jesus identifies himself with Elijah and Elisha, two Old Testament prophets who brought salvation to non-Israelites because their own people rejected them (1 Kgs 17; 2 Kgs 5). At these words the people in the synagogue are filled with wrath and try to destroy Jesus. The scene serves as a parable for the rest of the Gospel. Jesus comes to Israel with salvation for his people. There will be an initial favorable reaction, but ultimately Israel will reject him. As a result, salvation will be offered to those outside of Israel as the story of Acts will show.

In the chapters which follow, Jesus carries out the program of his ministry announced in the sermon. He performs several healings and he delivers his Sermon on the Plain (6:17–49). The sermon is the announcement of good news to the poor, the hungry, the sorrowing, and the despised (6:20–23). Following this sermon, Jesus performs two mighty deeds: the healing of the centurion's servant (7:1–10) and the raising of the widow's son at Nain (7:11–17). The first borders on a miracle of resurrection while the second is such a miracle. Furthermore, the raising of the widow's son recalls how Elijah raised the son of the widow of Zarephath (1 Kgs 17:8–24). At this point the crowd spontaneously cries out, "A great Prophet has arisen among us!" and "God has visited his people!" (7:16).

But not everybody is convinced that Jesus is a Prophet. After these events, a Pharisee named Simon invites Jesus to his home (7:36–50). When Jesus allows a sinful woman to kiss and anoint his feet, Simon says to himself, "If this man were a Prophet, he would have known who and what sort of woman this is who is touching him, for she is a sinner" (7:39). Prophet that he is, Jesus knows Simon's innermost thoughts and confronts him with the question of the two debtors (7:41–42).

This confusion about Jesus' identity continues in chapter 9.[16] Herod the tetrarch hears about Jesus and is perplexed (9:7–9) because people are identifying Jesus with prophetic figures: John the Baptist, Elijah, one of the prophets of old. In the next scene Jesus feeds five thousand people in the wilderness (9:10–17), thereby associating himself with Moses, the greatest prophet of the Old Testament, who fed the children of Israel with manna (Ex 16).[17] After this miracle, Jesus asks his disciples who people say that he is (9:18). He receives the same answer that Herod heard, "John the Baptist; but others say, Elijah; and others, that one of the prophets has risen" (9:19). Next, Jesus asks their opinion and Peter responds, "The Christ of God" (9:20). At this critical moment of Jesus' ministry, Luke discloses that although Jesus is a Prophet, he is greater still.

The prophet theme, however, does not disappear after Peter's confession. To the contrary, Luke intensifies it by insisting that Jesus is the Prophet who must die at Jerusalem. In the next scene, the transfiguration (9:28–36), Jesus stands between Moses and Elijah, the two greatest prophets of the Old Testament, and discusses with them "his departure (*exodon*), which he was to accomplish at Jerusalem" (9:31). The Father identifies Jesus as "my Son, my Chosen" and says "listen to him!" (*autou akouete*, 9:35). The words recall those spoken by Moses in Deuteronomy 18:15, "The Lord your God will raise up for you a prophet like me from among you, from your brethren—him you shall heed (*autou akousesthe*)." Luke suggests that, as God's Messiah and Son, Jesus is the Prophet like Moses. And like Moses, he is destined for rejection (see Acts 7:35–43 where Stephen explains this).

C. A Prophet's Journey to Jerusalem (9:51–19:44)

In the section which deals with Jesus' Jerusalem journey (9:51–19:44), Luke develops the theme of the suffering Prophet foreshadowed at the transfiguration. In 9:51 he announces the journey: "When the days drew near for him to be received up, he set his face to go to Jerusalem." Although Luke does not employ the word prophet at the opening of the journey, 9:51–62 is filled with prophetic imagery. For example, the expression "he set his face" (9:51) is reminiscent of a similar phrase in the Book of Ezekiel where God tells the prophet, "Son of man, set your face toward the mountains of Israel, and prophesy against them" (6:2; also see 13:17). When a Samaritan village refuses to receive Jesus because he has set his face toward Jerusalem, James and John want to "bid fire come down from heaven and consume them" (9:54). The two apostles recognize that their Lord is a kind of Elijah, and they expect him to react in the same way as Elijah did when he called fire upon the messengers of the Samaritan King Ahaziah (2 Kgs 1:1–16). But Jesus does not agree to their wishes. Finally, in 9:61 someone says that he will follow Jesus, but first he must say farewell to those at home. Jesus responds, "No one who puts his hand to the plow and looks back is fit for the kingdom of God" (9:62). This response is reminiscent of 1 Kings 19:19–21 where Elisha asks to follow Elijah. The difference, however, is that Elijah allows Elisha to return home and kiss his father and mother before coming after him. The demands for following Jesus, the new Elijah, are greater than those for following the old Elijah. This opening section makes it clear that Jesus undertakes his journey to Jerusalem as a Prophet. Although similar to Ezekiel and Elijah, he surpasses them, especially in what he demands of his disciples.

At the midpoint of the journey, Pharisees tell Jesus to flee from Herod. In response, Jesus says that it would be unseemly for a prophet to perish away from Jerusalem (13:31–33). Next Jesus pronounces an oracle over Jerusalem: "O Jerusalem, Jerusalem, killing the prophets and stoning those who are sent to you! . . . Behold, your house is forsaken. And I tell you, you will not see me until you say, 'Blessed is he who comes in the name of the Lord!' " (13:34–35). By this incident Luke shows that Jesus perceives himself to be a Prophet in a long line of prophets who have died at Jerusalem.

The final verse, "you will not see me until you say, 'Blessed is he who comes in the name of the Lord,' '' points to Jesus' triumphal approach to Jerusalem (19:37–40). Immediately after his entry into Jerusalem, Jesus weeps over the city and pronounces yet another oracle of doom (19:43–44):

> For the days shall come upon you,
> when your enemies will cast up a bank about you
> and surround you, and hem you in on every side,
> and dash you to the ground,
> you and your children within you,
> and they will not leave one stone upon another in you;
> because you did not know the time of your visitation.

The journey has ended and the Prophet has arrived.

D. *The Prophet like Moses (Dt 18:15–20)*

Earlier I indicated the several prophetic motifs present in the passion narrative. Most dealt with Jesus' foreknowledge and his prophetic predictions. In light of Luke's Gospel story, it is evident that there is another aspect to Jesus' prophetic identity. According to Luke, Jesus is the Prophet who must suffer and die at Jerusalem. The passion of Jesus is foreshadowed by Jesus' rejection at Nazareth (4:16–30). It is the fulfillment of the conversation he had with Moses and Elijah at the transfiguration (9:31). It is the outcome of his journey to Jerusalem (9:51–19:44) undertaken in his capacity as Prophet. But the theme continues even after Jesus' death.

The last time that Luke refers to Jesus as Prophet occurs in 24:19, the appearance of the Risen Lord to the two disciples on the road to Emmaus.[18] When the Risen One asks them what things they are discussing, they reply, "Concerning Jesus of Nazareth, who was a Prophet mighty in deed and word before God and all the people" (24:19). Their answer shows that the disciples still identify Jesus as a Prophet. What they have not grasped, however, is the necessity of his death. They understand him as a Prophet "mighty in word and deed," just as the crowd did when Jesus raised the son of the widow at Nain. But the disciples have not comprehended that as a Prophet Jesus was destined to be rejected and put to death. This is the mystery that the Risen Christ explains when he says, "Was it not necessary that the Christ should suffer these things and enter into his glory?" (24:26).

The Prophet theme, however, does not find its resolution until the Acts of the Apostles where Luke discloses the precise nature of Jesus' prophetic identity. He does this on two occasions. The first comes in a speech which Peter delivers to the inhabitants of Jerusalem (3:12–26) after he has cured a crippled man in the temple. In that speech Peter reviews the events of the passion (3:12–16), reminding the people that they delivered up the Holy and Righteous One and asked for a murderer instead. Next he acknowledges that the people and their leaders acted in ignorance and calls them to repentance (3:17–26), In doing this, he tells them that the events of the passion had been foretold by the prophets. Peter gives a free quotation of verses taken from Deuteronomy 18:15–20: "Moses said, 'The Lord your God will raise up for you a prophet from your brethren as he raised me up. You shall listen to him in whatever he tells you. And it shall be that every soul that does not listen to that prophet shall be destroyed from the people' " (Acts 3:22–23). It now becomes clear that Jesus is "that Prophet." He is none other than *the* Prophet like Moses.

The identification of Jesus as the Prophet like Moses occurs a second time in Stephen's speech at his martyrdom (7:2–53). In that speech Stephen reviews the course of Israel's history and reveals a pattern of rejected prophet-saviors. Throughout history, according to Stephen, God has sent savior-prophets such as Joseph and Moses to the people, only to have them rejected. The last and the greatest of these is Jesus, the Prophet like Moses. Speaking of Moses, Stephen alludes to the text from Deuteronomy 18:15. "This is the Moses who said to the Israelites, 'God will raise up for you a prophet from your brethren as he raised me up' " (Acts 7:37). Further on he says, "Which of the prophets did not your fathers persecute? And they killed those who announced beforehand the coming of the Righteous One, whom you have now betrayed and murdered" (7:52). The Righteous One is Jesus. He stands in the line of the prophets; he is the Prophet Moses promised long ago.

For Luke, Jesus is part of a long line of prophets God sent to his people with the offer of salvation. Like them he has been rejected. But the distinguishing trait of Jesus is that he is more than a Prophet; he is *the* Prophet, God's final Prophet. He is the Prophet Moses promised long ago. To reject him is to be cut off from the people.

IV.

THE PASSION AS THE DEATH OF GOD'S ROYAL SON

On several occasions during the passion narrative, Luke presents Jesus as King, Messiah, Savior, God's Son. For example, in his version of the Last Supper, Luke portrays him as a royal figure who has received a kingdom from his Father and now promises a kingdom to his followers (22:29–30). Before assigning this kingdom to his disciples, Jesus warns them not to rule as do "the kings of the Gentiles." They must pattern their rulership after his example of humble, royal service (22:26–27). Jesus eats this supper with the firm expectation that he will enter the kingdom of God (22:16,18).

On the Mount of Olives, Jesus prays in his capacity as Son, confidently calling God "Father" (22:42). At the moment of his arrest, he manifests that he is still Savior by healing the ear of the high priest's servant (22:51). At the hearing before the Sanhedrin, Luke brings together three titles: Christ (Messiah), Son of Man, and Son of God (22:67–70). The Son of Man prophecy shows that Luke understands these titles in a royal sense. Jesus, the Son of Man, will be seated at God's right hand; as Messiah and Son of God he will assume royal authority.

This claim to royal authority becomes the charge against Jesus in the hearings before Pilate and Herod. The leaders assert that Jesus calls himself "Christ a King" (23:2). Pilate asks Jesus if he is the "King of the Jews" (23:3), and Herod mocks him as a royal pretender by dressing him in "gorgeous apparel" (23:11). At his crucifixion Jesus calls God "Father" and asks him to forgive his persecutors (23:34). In the mockery which follows (23:35–39), the leaders, the soldiers, and one of the criminals deride Jesus in his royal capacity as Messiah and King of the Jews. All of them implicitly mock Jesus as the Savior who cannot save himself. One of the criminals, however, recognizes that Jesus is about to enter into his kingdom and asks him to remember him (23:42). As a result Jesus promises that "today" the criminal will be in paradise, the royal garden (23:43).

In Luke the centurion does not acclaim Jesus as the Son of God, but Luke still emphasizes Jesus' sonship by recording that he addresses God as "Father" at the moment of his death: "Father, into thy hands I commit my spirit!" (23:46). Finally, the burial of Jesus in a tomb "where no one had ever yet been laid'' (23:53) suggests that Jesus receives the dignity of a royal burial.

If the reader keeps in mind that titles such as Messiah, Savior, and Son of God have a royal content, it is apparent that a royal motif runs through Luke's passion narrative. This is not surprising inasmuch as Jesus is crucified as the King of the Jews: ''There was also an inscription over him, 'This is the King of the Jews' '' (23:38). As with the the other themes we have seen, the royal theme is not limited to the passion. Luke weaves it into the fabric of the Gospel. In what follows I tell Luke's story of Jesus once more, but this time from the perspective of Jesus' kingship.[19]

A. *Jesus' Royal Lineage (1:5–2:52)*

In tracing the royal motifs of Luke's Gospel, it is important to recall that royal theology is found in more places than where the title King appears. Messiah, for example, is a royal appellation inasmuch as every king of Israel was God's anointed, his Christ (*christos*). The Messiah was to be a royal descendant of the great king, David. Thus the title Son of David is also royal in scope; it is another way of saying king. In a similar fashion, Son of God has royal connotations inasmuch as every Israelite king was seen as God's adopted son. Psalm 2, sung on the day of the king's enthronement, reads, ''You are my son, today [the day of enthronement] I have begotten you.'' To be sure, the meaning of Son of God in Luke and the other Gospels is not limited to this dimension.[20] Jesus is not God's ''adopted'' Son; he is Son in a unique fashion. But it would be unfortunate to overlook the royal dimension of sonship present in Son of God. As God's beloved Son, Jesus is King.

There is an important aspect of kingship in the title that is peculiar to Luke among the Synoptic writers, the title Savior. The kings of the Hellenistic world looked upon themselves as saviors and benefactors.[21] In a well-known inscription, the Provincial Assembly of Asia Minor passed a resolution recognizing Caesar Augustus as savior and benefactor. It reads in part as follows.

Whereas the Providence which has guided our whole existence
and which has shown such care and liberality, has brought our
life to the peak of perfection in giving us Augustus Caesar,

whom it (Providence) filled with virtue (*aretē*) for the welfare
of mankind, and who, being sent to us and to our descendants
as a savior (*sōtēr*), has put an end to war and has set all things
in order . . . Caesar has fulfilled the hopes of all earlier times
. . . not only in surpassing all the benefactors (*euergetai*) who
preceded him but also in leaving to his successors no hope of
surpassing him.[22]

The world in which Luke wrote was familiar with benefactor kings who
styled themselves as saviors of the people.

From the opening of his story Luke demonstrates that Jesus is a
King. The angel Gabriel comes to a virgin betrothed to Joseph, of the
royal house of David (1:27), thereby suggesting that Jesus' credentials
are in order. The angel tells Mary that she will bear a child who will be
called "the Son of the Most High" (1:32) and "the Son of God" (1:35).
In describing the child, the angel says that God will give him the throne
of his father David and there will be no end to his kingdom.

He will be great, and will be called the Son of the Most High;
and the Lord God will give to him the throne of his father
David, and he will reign over the house of Jacob *for ever; and
of his kingdom there will be no end* (1:32–33).

In these verses Luke alludes to two important messianic texts. The first
is God's promise to David that his dynasty will endure forever. "I will
be his father, and he shall be my son. . . . *And your house and your
kingdom shall be made sure for ever*" (2 Sam 7:14–16). In time, this
prophecy was interpreted in terms of the Messiah. The second text comes
from Isaiah and concerns the birth of a royal son. Like the first, it also
took on messianic overtones. "Of the increase of his government and of
peace *there will be no end,* upon the throne of David, and over his kingdom, to establish it, and to uphold it with justice and with righteousness
from this time forth and for evermore" (Is 9:7).

The birth of Jesus takes place in Bethlehem, the city of King David
(2:4). The first to hear of the birth are shepherds (2:8), men practicing
the same occupation David did before he became king. In announcing
Jesus' birth, the angels describe him as "a Savior, who is Christ the
Lord" (2:11). That is, he is a King from his birth. Luke heightens the

royal character of Jesus the Savior by mentioning Caesar in 3:1, thereby implying a contrast between the two savior-kings. From the outset of his narrative, Luke reveals that as Son of God, Jesus will fulfill the royal, messianic expectations of old. He is King from his birth.

When Jesus' parents bring him to the temple, the aged Simeon recognizes him as the Lord's Messiah (2:26), the one who will bring God's salvation (2:30). Simeon points to the child's destiny when he says, "Behold, this child is set for the fall and rising of many in Israel, and for a sign that is spoken against" (2:34). The prophetess Anna also recognizes that Jesus is God's royal Messiah and speaks of him to all who were looking for the redemption of Jerusalem (2:38). The infancy narrative concludes with the story of the twelve year old child in the temple (2:41–51). In that episode Jesus identifies the temple as his Father's house (2:49), implicitly claiming that he is the Messiah. From start to finish the infancy narrative announces that Jesus is the Savior, the Messiah, David's royal Son, the Son of God.

B. Genealogy and Temptations (3:1–4:13)

In the period between the infancy narrative and Jesus' public ministry, Luke describes the preaching of John, the baptism of Jesus, Jesus' genealogy, and Jesus' temptations in the desert. In this intermediate period Luke continues to emphasize Jesus' royal background. First, he narrates that after Jesus' baptism the Holy Spirit descends upon him and that the Father identifies Jesus as his Son: "Thou art my beloved Son; with thee I am well pleased" (3:22). Behind this declaration is an allusion to Psalm 2:7 ("I will tell of the decree of the Lord: He said to me, 'You are my son, today I have begotten you' "), the royal psalm sung on the day of the king's enthronement. While the baptism emphasizes Jesus' unique sonship, the allusion to the psalm places Jesus in the line of Israel's anointed kings.

Following the baptism, Luke gives his version of the genealogy (3:23–38). The genealogy traces Jesus' lineage through his supposed father, Joseph (3:23), to King David (3:31), Abraham (3:34) and Adam (3:38). In doing this, Luke makes several points. First, Jesus is a Son of David. Second, he appears as the new Adam: the beginning of a new humanity. Finally, he is Son of God.

It is as Son of God that Jesus is led into the wilderness by the Spirit to be tempted (4:1). Twice during these temptations, the devil addresses Jesus as God's Son. "If you are the Son of God, command this stone to become bread" (4:3). "If you are the Son of God, throw yourself down from here" (4:9). By overcoming these temptations Jesus shows that he is truly God's Son, the royal Messiah, and that his kingdom is not of this world.

C. Jesus' Public Ministry (4:14–19:44)

The opening chapters of Luke's Gospel, 1:5–4:13, helps the reader to understand Jesus' identity. After reading this section there is no doubt who Jesus is; he is the royal Son of God. Consequently, when Jesus embarks upon his public ministry in 4:14, Luke no longer needs to emphasize the royal theme, because the reader knows Jesus' identity. Instead, Luke develops another aspect of Jesus' person: the rejected prophet. To be sure, the theme of Jesus' royal sonship does not disappear from Luke's account of Jesus' public ministry. The demons refer to him as the Son of God and the Son of the Most High God (4:41; 8:28). Luke 4:41 is especially important because it makes a connection between Messiah and Son of God: "And demons also came out of many, crying, 'You are *the Son of God!*' But he rebuked them, and would not allow them to speak, because they knew that he was *the Christ.*" In addition, Peter makes his confession that Jesus is "the Christ of God" (9:20), and at the transfiguration the Father declares, "This is my Son, my Chosen" (9:35). But on balance, the royal theme is kept in the background during Jesus' Galilean ministry.

During the period of Jesus' Jerusalem journey (9:51–19:44), the theme is even more muted as Luke expands upon the motif of Jesus the Prophet. Nonetheless, at three important moments Luke gives the reader an insight to the nature of Jesus' sonship. These incidents are important since they highlight Jesus' unique relationship to the Father. The first occurs after the return of the seventy from their mission. Jesus rejoices in the Spirit and prays in a manner which reveals the intimate relationship he enjoys with the Father. "All things have been delivered to me by my Father; and no one knows who the Son is except the Father, or who the Father is except the Son and any one to whom the Son chooses to reveal him" (10:22). The second moment comes when a disciple sees Jesus at prayer and asks him to teach the disciples to pray. In response, Jesus teaches them his own prayer in which he addresses God as "Father" (11:1–4). The boldness of this address should not be overlooked. Only someone with a unique relationship to God would dare call him Father and teach others to do the same. Finally, in 12:22–34 Jesus gives his disciples an extended instruction on the foolishness of care and anxiety. He discloses the intimacy he enjoys with God. "Fear not, little flock, for it is your Father's good pleasure to give you the kingdom. Sell your possessions, and give alms" (12:32). Only someone who has experienced a unique sonship could make such demands and promises. As God's royal Son, Jesus is far more than God's adopted Son.

When Jesus approaches Jerusalem, Luke again takes up the royal theme with the result that there is a convergence of prophetic and royal motifs. As Jesus draws near to Jericho, a blind man addresses him as Son of David (18:38–39). Jesus accepts the title and heals the man. After leaving the city, Jesus delivers the parable of the ten pounds (19:11–27). Matthew reports a similar parable (in 25:14–30), but Luke's version takes on a new meaning because of the manner in which he introduces it. He writes, "As they heard these things, he proceeded to tell a parable, because he was near to Jerusalem, and because they supposed that the kingdom of God was to appear immediately." Luke's editorial comment suggests that some misunderstand Jesus' kingship, perhaps by confusing it with worldly power. Because of this, Jesus tells a parable to discourage false expectations. The parable involves a nobleman who goes into a far country to receive a kingdom. The nobleman is Jesus, and the point of the parable is that before he can receive his kingdom, he must go on a long journey, the journey to suffering and death which is symbolized by the Jerusalem journey. The Lucan version of the parable points to Jesus' death. He will receive his kingdom only after he has made his exodus at Jerusalem, his passage through death.

Having explained the nature of his kingship, Jesus makes his royal approach to Jerusalem (19:28–40). The scene is reminiscent of Solomon's royal procession when he was proclaimed king (1 Kgs 1:38–40). In addition, there is an allusion to the humble king mentioned in Zechariah 9:9, "Rejoice greatly, O daughter of Zion! Shout aloud, O daughter of Jerusalem! Lo, your king comes to you; triumphant and victorious is he, humble and riding on an ass, on a colt the foal of an ass." The Old Testament allusions show that this is a royal entry, but they also warn that the nature of Jesus' kingship must not be misunderstood. He has not come to replace Caesar.

As Jesus descends from the Mount of Olives, the mountain at which the Messiah was expected to make his appearance (Zech 14:1–5), the whole multitude of his disciples say, ''Blessed is the King who comes in the name of the Lord! Peace in heaven and glory in the highest!'' (19:38). The last phrase alludes to the song of the angels at Jesus' birth: ''Glory to God in the highest, and on earth peace among men with whom he is pleased!'' (2:14) As Jesus prepares to enter into his kingdom, Luke recalls incidents from the infancy narrative which is so filled with royal allusions. Thus a few verses later, Jesus cleanses the temple and takes possession of it (19:45–46), an event foreshadowed when the twelve year old child called the temple his Father's house (2:49).

The end of Jesus' Jerusalem journey becomes the time of his royal visitation. But the city's inhabitants do not accept him (19:39), and Jesus makes his prophetic lament (19:41–44). Royal and prophetic themes converge here, and Jesus enters his passion as God's royal Son, the Prophet like Moses destined to be rejected. The royal theme, like the prophet theme, leads to the passion.

As was the case in the prophet theme, the full dimensions of Jesus' kingship are not understood until Easter. In chapter 24 the Risen Lord explains to his disciples that God's royal Messiah had (*dei*) to suffer such things before he could enter into his glory (24:26,44). After explaining the Scriptures to his disciples, Jesus is taken up to the Father's right hand to be exalted with kingly glory (Lk 24:51; Acts 1:9–10). Thereafter in the Acts of the Apostles, the Church proclaims Jesus as God's royal Messiah (2:32–36).[23] At his martyrdom, Stephen sees a vision of the Lord enthroned in glory: ''Behold, I see the heavens opened, and the Son of Man standing at the right hand of God'' (Acts 7:56).

CONCLUSION

This chapter has examined four themes from the passion narrative: the passion as the destiny of Jesus; the passion as a model for discipleship; the passion as the rejection of Jesus the Prophet; the passion as the death of God's royal Son. Luke sees the passion as Jesus' divine destiny, but he expresses this destiny throughout the narrative by the prominent role given to Jerusalem and by the simple phrase "it is necessary" (*dei*). Luke views the passion as the fulfillment and model of discipleship. He develops this throughout his story, but especially in the instructions given to the disciples in chapter 9 and during the Jerusalem journey. Finally, Luke views the passion as the rejection of Jesus the Prophet who is God's royal Son. He develops these themes in his Christology throughout the narrative. These themes often find their best expression in the infancy narrative and the Jerusalem journey section. This is no coincidence since these sections, as well as chapters 9 and 24, form the most distinctive parts of Luke's Gospel. To be sure, the passion narrative and the Gospel contain other common themes but these are among the most representative of Luke's passion narrative and Gospel theology.

CONCLUSION

This study has emphasized the distinctive aspects of each passion narrative. There is no need for a detailed summary here; a few words will be sufficient.

In the passion narrative according to Mark, the emphasis is upon the forsaken Son of God. Jesus dies betrayed by one of the twelve, denied by Peter, and abandoned by the rest of his disciples. At the moment of his death, he cries the opening words of Psalm 22, "My God, my God, why hast thou forsaken me?" On the cross Jesus even experiences the absence of his Father. But in Mark's Gospel, the death of Jesus becomes the moment of revelation. For the first time a human character within the story confesses that Jesus was truly the Son of God.

Mark's message is as clear as it is simple. No one can confess that Jesus is the Son of God until he has acknowledged the crucified Messiah. No one can be Jesus' disciple unless he accepts the scandal of the cross. The passion narrative is the climax of Mark's Gospel because it is the moment when the secret of Jesus' identity is fully revealed. It is the proper understanding of this secret which makes discipleship possible.

The passion narrative according to Matthew develops the great themes of Mark's story. This is not surprising since Mark's Gospel is Matthew's primary source. Matthew also views Jesus as the crucified Messiah and stresses the abandonment he suffered during his passion. But Matthew's careful editorial activity serves to heighten Mark's Christological portrait of Jesus as the Son of God. In various ways, Matthew emphasizes Jesus' divine Sonship. He stresses that the passion does not catch Jesus unaware. To the contrary, Jesus is in full control of the events. He knows what will take place before it happens. He even seems to grant permission for the events of the passion to occur. The genius of Matthew is his ability to highlight the dignity of Jesus' person without diminishing the sense of suffering and abandonment he experiences.

But the distinctive aspect of Matthew's passion is found in his ecclesiological and ethical outlook. For Matthew the passion becomes the moment when Israel definitively rejects her Messiah and the Gentiles enter the Church. Jesus is the model of righteousness and an example for would-be disciples. Ecclesiology and ethical concerns do not overpower Matthew's Christological vision; they are founded upon it. In comparison to Mark, they are the distinctive concerns of his passion narrative.

In the passion according to Luke the emphasis is altered once more. Jesus is the model of innocent suffering. In the midst of trial and persecution, he is God's righteous sufferer. At the moment of Jesus' death, the centurion glorifies God, saying, ''Certainly this man was innocent.'' Pilate's triple acknowledgement of Jesus' innocence and the repentance of a criminal support this judgment. But Luke's passion account is more than the agony of an innocent sufferer, and Jesus' dying is more than a martyr's death. Jesus dies as King and Prophet. He is the royal Son of God, the one who promises a kingdom to his followers. He is the royal Son of David, the one announced by Gabriel. He is the Prophet who pronounces a final judgment over Jerusalem, the rejected Prophet foreshadowed by the inaugural sermon at Nazareth, and later revealed as the Prophet like Moses.

The centurion's cry is best understood as, ''Certainly this man was righteous.'' The death of Jesus is the culmination of a life of righteous behavior manifested throughout the Gospel story.

Although the passion narratives are distinctive in their theological outlooks, they offer a common witness.

1. The passion did not surprise Jesus. On several occasions he predicted that he would suffer and die at Jerusalem. He celebrated a final meal with his disciples during which he announced his betrayer and by the Eucharist explained the significance of his death. His death would be salvific.

2. Jesus willingly embraced the passion when it occurred. In Gethsemane, on the Mount of Olives, he prayed to accept God's will.

3. Jesus refused to resist his enemies at the moment of his arrest. Although he had done nothing meriting arrest, he accepted it as the fulfillment of Scripture.

4. The Jewish leaders accused Jesus of claiming to be the Messiah, the Son of God. This religious charge was turned into a political one before Pilate. Jesus was accused of claiming to be the King of the Jews.

5. The Romans crucified Jesus as the King of the Jews with criminals at his right and left.

6. During his crucifixion, Jesus was mocked as a Savior who was powerless to save himself. But in accordance with his own teaching, he refused to save his life, trusting instead in the power of God to deliver him from death.

7. Miraculous signs accompanied Jesus' death (darkness, the tearing of the temple veil), and his death led to a confession on the part of the centurion. Jesus' death became the occasion for the Gentiles to enter the Church.

8. Faithful women witnessed Jesus' death, and Joseph of Arimathea provided him with a dignified burial.

This common witness of the Gospel writers is impressive, but the theology of each evangelist is even more beautiful than this common witness. The passion narrative is like a jewel with many facets. The gem is always the same, but changes of light make its many facets shine in ever new ways.

NOTES

INTRODUCTION

1. See the article by J. Schneider, s.v. *stauros* in *Theological Dictionary of the New Testament,* vol. 7, ed. Gerhard Friedrich, trans. and ed. Geoffrey W. Bromiley (Grand Rapids, Michigan: Eerdmans, 1971), pp. 572–584, esp. p. 573.

2. Martin Hengel, *Crucifixion in the Ancient World and the Folly of the Message of the Cross,* trans. John Bowden (Philadelphia: Fortress, 1977), p. 46. Hengel's work is indispensable for a knowledge of crucifixion in the ancient world. It contains numerous bibliographical references to authors both ancient and modern.

3. *Ibid.,* pp. 46–63.

4. *Ibid.,* pp. 41–42.

5. *Ibid.,* p. 52.

6. *Ibid.,* p. 51.

7. The RSV reads "servant," but the Greek *doulos* may also be translated as "slave."

8. Hengel, *Crucifixion,* p. 8. For a description of crucifixion, see the article by J.F. Strange, s.v. Crucifixion, in *The Interpreter's Dictionary of the Bible Supplementary Volume,* ed. Keith Crim (Nashville: Abingdon, 1976), pp. 199–200.

9. The material is discussed by Joseph A. Fitzmyer, "Crucifixion in Ancient Palestine, Qumran Literature, and the New Testament," *CBQ* 40 (1978): 493–513.

10. *Ibid.,* p. 503.

11. *Ibid.,* p. 507.

12. For a discussion of the historical events surrounding the death of Jesus see E.P. Sanders, *Jesus and Judaism* (Philadelphia: Fortress, 1985), pp. 294–318.

1. THE PASSION ACCORDING TO MARK: OVERVIEW

1. For a reliable account of Marcan scholarship, see Ralph Martin, *Mark Evangelist and Theologian* (Grand Rapids, Michigan: Zondervan, 1972). For an account of more recent literature, see Daniel J. Harrington, ''A Map of Books on Mark,'' *BTB* 15 (1985): 12–16. For a survey of approaches to Mark, see Cilliers Breytenbach, *Nachfolge und Zukunftserwartung nach Markus: Eine methodenkritische Studie,* AbhTANT, no. 71 (Zurich: Theologischer Verlag, 1984), pp. 16–74.

2. The history of the life of Jesus movement has been chronicled in the classic work of Albert Schweitzer, *The Quest of the Historical Jesus: A Critical Study of Its Progress from Reimarus to Wrede,* trans. F.C. Burkitt (New York: Macmillan, 1968). The history of the life of Jesus movement also serves as a review of Marcan scholarship in the nineteenth century.

3. The method of form criticism was pioneered by Rudolf Bultmann (*The History of the Synoptic Tradition,* trans. John Marsh [New York: Harper & Row, 1963]), Martin Dibelius (*From Tradition to Gospel,* trans. Bertram Lee Woolf [New York: Scribners, n.d.]), and Karl Ludwig Schmidt (*Der Rahmen der Geschichte Jesu: Literarkritische Untersuchungen zur ältesten Jesusüberlieferung* [Berlin: Trowitzsch & Sohn, 1919]).

4. The method of redaction criticism was pioneered by Willi Marxsen, *Mark the Evangelist: Studies on the Redaction of the Gospel,* trans. James Boyce, Donald Juel, William Poehlmann, with Roy A. Harrisville (New York: Abingdon, 1969).

5. For an introduction to literary criticism as applied to the New Testament, see Norman R. Petersen, *Literary Criticism for New Testament Critics* (Philadelphia: Fortress, 1978).

6. *From Tradition to Gospel,* p. 193.

7. This point is discussed by Nils A. Dahl, ''The Crucified Messiah,'' in *The Crucified Messiah and Other Essays* (Minneapolis, Minnesota: Augsburg, 1974), pp. 10–36.

8. This point is made by Donald Juel, *Messiah and Temple: The Trial of Jesus in the Gospel of Mark,* SBLDS, no. 31 (Missoula, Montana: Scholars Press, 1977), and in my own work *The Kingship of Jesus: Composition and Theology in Mark 15,* SBLDS, no. 66 (Chico, California: Scholars Press, 1982).

9. Donald Senior (*The Passion of Jesus in the Gospel of Mark* [Wilmington, Delaware: Glazier, 1984]) takes a similar approach. He relates the passion to Mark's portrait of Jesus (pp. 139–147) and to Mark's portrayal of the Church (pp. 148–156).

10. *From Tradition to Gospel,* p. 180.

11. *The History of the Synoptic Tradition,* p. 279.

12. The question of the growth and development of Mark's passion nar-

rative has given rise to several scholarly hypotheses. Much of this scholarship has been summarized by John R. Donahue ("Introduction: From Passion Traditions to Passion Narrative," in *The Passion in Mark: Studies on Mark 14–16,* ed. Werner H. Kelber [Philadelphia: Fortress, 1976], pp. 1–20), and myself (*The Kingship of Jesus,* pp. 1–5).

13. *Das Markusevangelium, II. Teil: Kommentar zu Kap. 8,27–16,20.* HTKNT, vol 2 (Freiburg: Herder, 1977). A more popular presentation of Pesch's position can be found in *Das Evangelium der Urgemeinde,* Glaubensinformation, no. 748 (Freiburg: Herder, 1979).

14. *Das Evangelium,* pp. 89–91, and *Das Markusevangelium,* pp. 15–16.

15. *Das Markusevangelium,* pp. 15–16.

16. This is the position I defend in *The Kingship of Jesus.*

2. THE PASSION ACCORDING TO MARK: COMMENTARY

1. The arrangement of material in this fashion is a common Marcan technique sometimes called intercalation. For an explanation of its implications for interpreting Mark, see Howard Clark Kee, *Community in the New Age: Studies in Mark's Gospel* (Philadelphia: Westminister, 1977), pp. 55–56, and John R. Donahue, *Are You the Christ? The Trial Narrative in the Gospel of Mark,* SBLDS, no. 10 (Missoula, Montana: Scholars, 1973), pp. 77–84.

2. On the chronology of the passion, see Rudolf Pesch, *Das Markusevangelium II Teil: Kommentar zum Kap. 8,27–16:20,* HTKNT, vol 2 (Freiburg: Herder, 1977), pp. 323–328. I have learned much from Pesch's commentary and make use of his insights in this chapter.

3. So Joachim Gnilka, *Das Evangelium nach Markus: 2. Teilband Mk 8:27–16:20,* EKK (Zürich: Benziger, 1979), p. 220. I have learned much from Gnilka's commentary and make use of his insights in this chapter.

4. Gnilka, *Das Evangelium,* p. 220.

5. Josef Ernst, *Das Evangelium nach Markus,* RNT (Regensburg: Pustet, 1981), 401–402. Note that in Mark 10:21 Jesus says, "sell what you have, and give to the poor."

6. *Ibid.,* p. 400. It should be noted that the royal theme is secondary to the theme of Jesus' impending death.

7. See the remarks of Paul J. Achtemeier, *Mark* (Philadelphia: Fortress, 1975), pp. 48–50.

8. The passage is quoted by Xavier Léon-Dufour, *Le partage du pain eucharistique: Selon le Nouveau Testament* (Paris: Éditions du Cerf, 1982), pp. 223–224.

9. Pesch notes that the whole scene is influenced by the theme of the *passio justi* ("passion of the just man"), *Das Markusevangelium,* p. 349.

10. Bread (*artos,* which the RSV often translates as "loaf") is an important theme in Mark's Gospel. The word occurs seventeen times in chapters 6–8. The theme comes to a climax in 8:14–21 when the disciples fail to comprehend the meaning of Jesus' two feeding miracles. For an explanation of the theme, see Werner H. Kelber, *Mark's Story of Jesus* (Philadelphia: Fortress, 1979), pp. 30–42, and Donald Senior, *The Passion of Jesus in the Gospel of Mark* (Wilmington, Delaware: Glazier, 1984), pp. 53–59.

11. Léon-Dufour (*Le partage du pain eucharistique,* pp. 230–231) makes this point.

12. Gnilka (*Das Evangelium,* p. 254) makes this point.

13. *New Testament Theology: The Proclamation of Jesus,* trans. John Bowden (New York: Scribners, 1971), pp. 61–75.

14. The Old Testament employs the cup as an image for God's judgment and salvation. Ernest Best (*Mark The Gospel as Story* [Edinburgh: T & T Clark, 1983], p. 70) notes "men drink the cup of salvation which is reached to them in the eucharist. Because Jesus has borne God's wrath they will enjoy God's salvation."

15. I am indebted to Pesch, *Das Markusevangelium,* p. 400, for these references.

16. Gnilka, *Das Evangelium,* p. 269.

17. *Ibid.,* pp. 271–272.

18. On this point see Donald Juel, *Messiah and Temple: The Trial of Jesus in the Gospel of Mark,* SBLDS, no. 31 (Missoula, Montana: Scholars, 1977), pp. 127–136.

19. For a comprehensive listing of these psalms, see Pesch, *Das Markusevangelium,* pp. 13–14.

20. The Mishna is a collection of rabbinic legal and procedural material edited by Judah ha-Nasi. It often represents oral traditions which date from the time of Jesus. Donald Juel (*Messiah and Temple,* pp. 59–74) discusses the trial of Jesus in light of these Jewish legal requirements.

21. For an historical investigation of the trial of Jesus see Josef Blinzler, *The Trial of Jesus,* trans I.F. McHugh (Westminster, Maryland: Newman, 1959), Paul Winter, *On the Trial of Jesus,* Studia Judaica, I, rev. and ed. T.A. Burkill and G. Vermes (Berlin: de Gruyter, 1974), and Ellis Rivkin, *What Crucified Jesus? The Political Execution of a Charismatic* (Nashville: Abingdon, 1984).

22. See Pesch (*Das Markusevangelium,* pp. 431–432) for a more complete listing.

23. See Juel (*Messiah and Temple,* pp. 169–209) for a discussion of this topic.

24. Quoted from 1 Enoch, trans. E. Isaac, in *The Old Testament Pseudepigrapha, vol 1, Apocalyptic Literature and Testaments*, ed. James H. Charlesworth (New York: Doubleday, 1983), p. 71.

25. Quoted by Juel, *Messiah and Temple*, p. 181.

26. *Ibid.*, p. 181.

27. On the Son of Man see Barnabas Lindars, *Jesus Son of Man: A Fresh Examination of the Son of Man Sayings in the Gospels in the Light of Recent Research* (Grand Rapids, Michigan: Eerdmans, 1984), pp. 101–114.

28. So Gerhard Lohfink, *The Last Days of Jesus: An Enriching Portrayal of the Passion*, trans. Salvator Attanasio (Notre Dame, Indiana: Ave Maria, 1984), pp. 35–43; and August Strobel, *Die Stunde der Wahrheit: Untersuchungen zum Strafverfahren gegen Jesus*, WUNT, no. 21 (Tübingen: Mohr, 1980), pp. 43–45.

29. For an insight to the political climate of Jesus' day see Richard A. Horsley, "Popular Messianic Movements around the Time of Jesus," *CBQ* 46 (1984): 471–495.

30. Nils A. Dahl makes this point in "The Crucified Messiah," in *The Crucified Messiah and Other Essays* (Minneapolis, Minnesota: Augsburg, 1974), pp. 10–36.

31. See my discussion of this in *The Kingship of Jesus: Composition and Theology in Mark 15*, SBLDS, no. 66 (Chico, California: Scholars Press, 1982), pp. 125–135.

32. On the use of the psalms in the passion narratives see U.P. McCaffrey, "Psalm Quotations in the Passion Narratives of the Gospels," *Neotestamentica* 14 (1981): 73–89, and Douglas J. Moo, *The Old Testament in the Gospel Passion Narratives* (Sheffield: Almond Press, 1983), pp. 225–300.

33. Gnilka (*Das Evangelium*, p. 315) makes this point.

34. Pesch (*Das Markusevangelium*, p. 477) makes this point.

35. Quoted by Lohfink, *The Last Days of Jesus*, p. 59.

36. Gnilka (*Das Evangelium*, pp. 317–318) speaks of an apocalyptic determinism when discussing the hours marking the crucifixion.

37. So Pesch, *Das Markusevangelium*, p. 487.

38. Ernesto Martinez made this point in an unpublished paper delivered at the Catholic Biblical Association Meeting (1984).

39. For a discussion of this question, see R. Alan Culpepper, "The Passion and Resurrection in Mark," *RevExp* 75 (1978): 583–600, esp. pp. 589–92; John R. Donahue, *Are You the Christ? The Trial Narrative in the Gospel of Mark*, SBLDS, no. 10 (Missoula, Montana: Scholars Press, 1973), pp. 202–203; Juel, *Messiah and Temple*, pp. 140–142; Paul Lamarche, "La mort du Christ et le voile du temple selon Marc," *NRT* 106 (1974): 583–599; and Senior, *The Passion of Jesus*, pp. 126–128.

3. MARK'S GOSPEL THEOLOGY

1. Morna Hooker (*The Message of Mark* [London: Epworth, 1983], pp. 1–16) explains the importance of the beginning of Mark's Gospel.

2. In recent years scholars have begun to study Mark's Gospel as a story. As a story it can be investigated with the techniques of literary criticism. For a brief presentation of Mark's Gospel as a story, see Werner H. Kelber, *Mark's Story of Jesus* (Philadelphia: Fortress, 1979). For an introduction to literary criticism as applied to Mark's Gospel, see Robert M. Fowler, *Loaves and Fishes: The Function of the Feeding Stories in the Gospel of Mark,* SBLDS, no. 54 (Chico, California: Scholars, 1981), pp. 149–180; David Rhoads and Donald Michie, *Mark as Story: An Introduction to the Narration of the Gospel* (Philadelphia: Fortress, 1982); and Augustine Stock, *Call to Discipleship: A Literary Study of Mark's Gospel,* Good New Studies, no. 1 (Wilmington, Delaware: Glazier, 1982).

3. There is need for a word of caution here. Although the reader knows that Jesus is the Son of God, the reader must discover *how* Jesus shows himself to be the Son of God: through his passion, death, and resurrection. Thus at the beginning of the narrative the reader does not know *everything* about Jesus.

4. Hooker (*The Message of Mark,* pp. 8–10) stresses that John only prepares the way for Jesus.

5. Ernest Best (*Mark the Gospel as Story* [Edinburgh: T. & T. Clark], pp. 81–83) seems to favor the background of Genesis 22:2 for interpreting Jesus' sonship. He argues that in Jewish thought contemporary to Jesus' day, Isaac was depicted as willingly consenting to his own sacrifice. By alluding to Genesis 22, Mark would be stressing the sacrificial nature of Jesus' death. I agree with this general interpretation but would argue that the reference to Psalm 2:7, the great messianic psalm, is primary.

6. The remark in 1:13, "and he was with the wild beasts," suggests that Jesus has overcome Satan and restored the original harmony of God's creation—at least in a proleptic manner.

7. See Mark 10:24,32 where the same word occurs. The context makes it clear that those around Jesus find it difficult to believe in his words and actions.

8. *The Christology of Mark's Gospel* (Philadelphia: Fortress, 1983), pp. 86–87. In this presentation of Mark's Christology I am indebted to many of Kingsbury's insights. I have also profited from a manuscript which Paul J. Achtemeier has generously forwarded to me. It represents the revised chapter on Christology for his volume on Mark in the Proclamation Commentaries series (Fortress).

9. *Ibid.,* p. 87.

10. *Ibid.,* pp. 89–91.

11. The interpretation of Peter's confession presents a major challenge for students of Mark. Does Mark intend that Jesus firmly rejects the title of Messiah in favor of Son of Man? Or does he mean that Jesus approves of the title but cautions that it cannot be understood apart from his passion? On this point, see Hooker (*The Message of Mark,* pp. 51–63). She argues, and I agree, that the title Messiah is acceptable but needs to be understood in the light of Jesus' passion and death.

12. The healing of the blind man in Mark 8:22–26 symbolizes how the disciples slowly come to faith. Just as the former blind man at first saw poorly and then received full sight, so the disciples see poorly at this point in the Gospel, but they will see clearly when they meet the Risen Lord.

13. That Jesus accepts Bartimaeus' confession does not mean that Bartimaeus has come to the fullness of faith. Like the other characters in the story, he has not yet experienced Jesus' passion and death.

14. See Klyne Snodgrass (*The Parable of the Wicked Tenants: An Inquiry into Parable Interpretation,* WUNT, no. 27 [Tübingen: Mohr, 1983]) for a discussion of this parable.

15. The Greek word for "reject" is *apodokimazein.* It is the same word employed in the first passion prediction (8:27). By using the same word in the passion prediction as is found in Psalm 118:22, Mark (or the tradition he employs) shows that Jesus' rejection is in accordance with Scripture.

16. See Psalms of Solomon 17 and 18 for an insight into how the people of Jesus' day viewed the Davidic Messiah.

17. The centurion represents the *ideal* member of Mark's community. Such a member confesses Jesus as God's Son in the light of Jesus' passion and death. It is not coincidental that a Roman centurion makes the confession since Mark's congregation seems to have been composed primarily of Gentiles.

18. On discipleship in Mark see Ernest Best, *Following Jesus: Discipleship in the Gospel of Mark.* JSNTSS, no. 4 (Sheffield, JSOT, 1981), and R.C. Tannehill, "The Disciples in Mark: The Function of a Narrative Role," *JR* 57 (1977): 386–405.

19. See Norman Perrin, "Towards an Interpretation of the Gospel of Mark," in *Christology and a Modern Pilgrimage: A Discussion with Norman Perrin,* ed. Hans Dieter Betz (Missoula, Montana: Scholars Press, 1974), pp. 1–52, esp. pp. 6–21.

20. So Best, *Mark,* pp. 68–71.

21. Paul J. Achtemeier (*Mark* [Philadelphia: Fortress, 1975], p. 100) makes this point well.

22. I do not agree with Theodore J. Weeden (*Mark: Traditions in Conflict* [Philadelphia: Fortress, 1971], p. 117) who argues that the disciples did not see

the risen Lord because the women did not report the angel's message to them (see Mk 16:8b).

23. This is one of the major contributions of Donald Juel's work, *Messiah and Temple: The Trial of Jesus in the Gospel of Mark,* SBLDS, no. 31 (Missoula: Montana: Scholars Press, 1977).

24. For an explanation of the temple theme see John R. Donahue, *Are You the Christ? The Trial Narrative in the Gospel of Mark,* SBLDS, no. 10 (Missoula, Montana: Scholars Press, 1973), pp. 113–138; Juel, *Messiah and Temple,* pp. 127–142; Donald Senior, *The Passion of Jesus in the Gospel of Mark* (Wilmington, Delaware: Glazier, 1974), pp. 155–156.

25. This point is made by Werner H. Kelber in *The Kingdom in Mark: A New Place and a New Time* (Philadelphia: Fortress, 1974), pp. 92–97.

26. See Achtemeier, *Mark,* pp. 23–26.

27. *Messiah and Temple,* pp. 159–168. For the image of the Church as temple, see Best, *Following Jesus,* pp. 213–225.

28. See Psalms of Solomon 17.

29. Mark, unlike the other evangelists, makes a point of noting that Jesus was seated *opposite* the temple (cf. Mt 24:3), thereby heightening his temple polemic.

30. For a helpful introduction to this difficult chapter see Achtemeier, *Mark,* pp. 101–117.

31. Vincent Taylor, *The Gospel According to Mark: The Greek Text with Introduction, Notes, and Indexes,* 2nd ed. (New York: St. Martin's Press, 1966), p. 511.

32. The temple of Jerusalem was destroyed in August of 70 A.D. by the Roman general Titus. Its destruction had major consequences both for Judaism and Christianity. The former was reorganized by Johanan ben Zakkai into rabbinic Judaism; the latter became primarily a Gentile movement since Jewish Christianity lost its capital.

33. Aloysius M. Ambrozic, *The Hidden Kingdom: A Redaction-Critical Study of the References to the Kingdom of God in Mark's Gospel,* CBQMS, no. 2 (Washington: CBA, 1972), p. 106.

34. A helpful presentation of the Son of Man is found in Hooker, *The Message of Mark,* pp. 64–73.

35. The Son of Man in Daniel (whether an individual or a corporate figure) is presented as a royal figure; see Dan 7:14,18,22,27.

4. THE PASSION ACCORDING TO MATTHEW: OVERVIEW

1. "The Passion Narrative in Matthew," in *Jesus in the Memory of the Early Church* (Minneapolis, Minnesota: Augsburg, 1976), p. 37.

2. 26:1–2,25,52–54; 27:3–10,19,24–25,29,51b–53,62–66. I discuss these verses below.

3. Jack D. Kingsbury makes this point in *Matthew* (Philadelphia: Fortress, 1977), pp. 27–28. He writes on p. 28: "These passages express the thought that *in the person of Jesus Messiah, his Son, God has come to dwell to the end of time with his people, the church, thus inaugurating the eschatological age of salvation.*"

4. Hans-Ruedi Weber (*The Cross: Traditions and Interpretation,* trans. Elke Jessett [Philadelphia: Fortress, 1977], p. 114) writes: "According to Matthew, it is not at his resurrection that Jesus is enthroned as the Son of God and King. He is the Son from the beginning and remains so even during the crucifixion."

5. The spectrum of opinions is surveyed by Donald Senior, "The Passion Narrative in the Gospel of Matthew," in *L'Évangile selon Matthieu,* ed. M. Didier, *BETL,* no. 29 (Gembloux: Éditions J. Duculot, 1972), pp. 343–357.

6. *From Tradition to Gospel,* trans. Bertram Lee Woolf (New York: Scribners, n.d.), p. 197.

7. The translation of 26:50 may also be rendered, "Friend, why are you here?" But given Matthew's emphasis upon Jesus' foreknowledge, the translation I have provided is to be preferred.

8. Weber, *The Cross,* p. 114.

9. "The Passion Narrative in Matthew," p. 48.

10. Matthew's ecclesiology and the ecclesial setting for his Gospel are major topics of discussion for Matthean scholars. For a review of the literature, see Donald Senior, *What Are They Saying about Matthew?* (New York: Paulist, 1983), pp. 5–15, 67–76; and Graham Stanton, "The Origin and Purpose of Matthew's Gospel: Matthean Scholarship from 1945 to 1980," in *Aufstieg und Niedergang der römischen Welt* II,25,3, ed. H. Temporini and W. Haase (Berlin: de Gruyter, 1984), pp. 1910–1920, 1925–1929.

11. Gerhard Schneider, *Die Passion Jesu nach den drei älteren Evangelien* (Munich: Kösel-Verlag, 1973), p. 169.

12. Dahl, "The Passion Narrative in Matthew", p. 48.

13. This point is emphasized by Birger Gerhardson, "Jesus livré et abandonné d'après la Passion selon saint Matthieu," *RB* 76 (1969): 206–227; and Georg Strecker, *Der Weg der Gerechtigkeit,* 3rd ed. (Göttingen: Vandenhoeck & Ruprecht, 1971).

14. At the conclusion of his study on Matthew's passion narrative, Donald Senior (*The Passion Narrative according to Matthew: A Redactional Study,* BETL, no 39 [Louvain: Louvain University Press, 1975], pp. 337–339) says that the primacy of place belongs to Christology. Albert Descamps ("Redaction et christologie dans le recit matthéen de la Passion" in *L'Évangile selon Matthieu,* pp. 359–415) supports this position.

15. Senior, *The Passion Narrative,* p. 334.

16. Senior (*The Passion Narrative*), in my view, establishes that Matthew's passion narrative is a redaction of Mark's account.

17. Not all authors espouse the two-source hypothesis. For several years William R. Farmer has argued that Matthew was the first Gospel to be written. His position has not enjoyed wide acceptance.

18. This seems to be the position of Dahl (*The Passion Narrative in Matthew,* p. 29) and Dibelius (*From Tradition to Gospel,* p. 196).

5. The Passion According to Matthew: Commentary

1. Donald Senior, *The Passion Narrative according to Matthew: A Redactional Study,* BETL no. 39 (Louvain: Louvain University, 1975), p. 12.

2 Eduard Schweizer, *The Good News according to Matthew,* trans. D.E. Green (Atlanta: John Knox, 1975), p. 486.

3. See G. Barth, "Matthew's Understanding of the Law," in Günther Bornkamm, Gerhard Barth, and Heinz Joachim Held, *Tradition and Interpretation in Matthew,* trans. P. Scott (Philadelphia: Westminster, 1963), pp. 105–112.

4. Senior, *Passion,* p. 40.

5. Jack D. Kingsbury, *Matthew,* (Philadelphia: Fortress, 1977), p. 23.

6. Senior, *Passion,* p. 40.

7. See my comments in chapter 2, section 1b.

8. Note that Matthew employs the proper name "Jesus" whereas Mark simply uses the pronouns "him" and "he." Cf. Mt 26:17,19 with Mark 14:12,16

9. On the question of the date of Passover, see my discussion in chapter 2, section 2a.

10. Senior, *Passion,* p. 59.

11. Kingsbury, *Matthew,* p. 79.

12. John Meier, *Matthew,* New Testament Message, no. 3 (Wilmington, Delaware: Glazier, 1980), p. 317.

13. For a discussion of the title "Lord," see Jack D. Kingsbury, *Matthew: Structure, Christology, Kingdom* (Philadelphia: Fortress, 1975), pp. 103–113, hereafter cited as *Structure.*

14. On the significance of "Rabbi," see Kingsbury, *Structure,* pp. 92–93.

15. For a discussion of the relation between the accounts of the Last Supper see I. Howard Marshall, *Last Supper and Lord's Supper* (Grand Rapids, Michigan: Eerdmans, 1980), pp. 30–56.

16. See Kingsbury, *Structure,* 40–83.

17. Schweizer, *Good News,* 491.

18. Senior, *Passion,* p. 113, and David Stanley, *Jesus in Gethsemane: The*

Early Church's Reflection on the Sufferings of Jesus (New York: Paulist, 1980), p. 177.

19. Stanley, *Gethsemane*, p. 177.

20. *Gethsemane*, p. 179.

21. See the discussion on prayer in Matthew by Stanley, *Gethsemane*, pp. 161–166.

22. *Passion*, p. 120.

23. See Meier, *Matthew*, p. 327.

24. Pierre Bonnard, *L'Évangile selon Saint Matthieu*, Commentaire du Nouveau Testament, no. 1 (Neuchatel: Delachaux & Niestle, 1963), p. 386.

25. *Matthew*, p. 329.

26. Senior, *Passion*, p. 26.

27. Schweizer, *Good News*, p. 498.

28. Senior, *Passion*, p. 168.

29. Meier, *Matthew*, p. 332.

30. In Mark Jesus says that the Son of Man will come *with* the clouds of heaven (14:62). In Matthew Jesus says that the Son of Man will come *on* the clouds of heaven (26:64).

31. So, Barnabbas Lindars, *Jesus Son of Man: A Fresh Examination of the Son of Man Sayings in the Gospels in the Light of Recent Research* (Grand Rapids, Michigan: Eerdmans, 1983), p. 121.

32. Matthew uses the same expression *ap' arti* in 23:39 and 26:29 where he also implies an imminent fulfillment of Jesus' words.

33. For differing views of the role which the Son of Man plays in Matthew's Gospel see Kingsbury, *Structure*, pp. 113–122, and John Meier, *The Vision of Matthew: Christ, Church and Morality in the First Gospel* (New York: Paulist, 1978), esp. pp. 210–219. On Matthew's development of the Son of Man traditions he received, see Lindars, *Son of Man*, pp. 115–131.

34. See Lindars, *Son of Man*, pp. 122–131.

35. See Senior, *Passion*, p. 190.

36. *Passion*, pp. 343–397, esp. p. 397.

37. Douglas Moo, *The Old Testament in the Gospel Passion Narratives* (Sheffield: Almond Press, 1983), p. 195.

38. Senior, *Passion*, pp. 368–369.

39. Lindars, *Son of Man*, p. 121.

40. Senior, *Passion*, pp. 227–228.

41. For an explanation of this motif see Birger Gerhardson, ''Jesus livré et abandonné d'après la Passion selon Saint Matthieu,'' *RB* 76 (1969): 206–227, and Frank J. Matera, ''Matthew 27:11–54,'' *Int* 38 (1984): 55–59.

42. Some texts preserve Barabbas' name as ''Jesus Barabbas.'' Although the textual evidence for this reading is slim, there are good arguments in support

of the reading. See Bruce M. Metzger, *A Textual Commentary on the Greek New Testament: A Companion Volume to the United Bible Societies' Greek New Testament,* (United Bible Societies, 1971), pp. 67–68.

43. Nils A. Dahl, "The Passion Narrative in Matthew," in *Jesus in the Memory of the Early Church* (Minneapolis, Minnesota: Augsburg, 1976), p. 48.

44. See Raymond E. Brown, *The Gospel according to John (XIII-XXI),* The Anchor Bible, no. 29A (New York: Doubleday, 1970), pp. 857–859 for the chiastic structure of this scene.

45. For the political nature of the scene see David Rensberger, "The Politics of John: The Trial of Jesus in the Fourth Gospel," *JBL* 103 (1983): 395–411.

46. Meier, *Matthew,* p. 344.

47. O. Lamar Cope, *Matthew: A Scribe Trained for the Kingdom of Heaven,* CBQMS no. 5 (Washington: CBA of America 1976), pp. 102–110 defends this interpretation of Jesus as the royal Son of God.

48. On the meaning of crucifixion at the time of Jesus see Martin Hengel, *Crucifixion: In the Ancient World and the Folly of the Message of the Cross,* trans. John Bowden (Philadelphia: Fortress, 1977), and Joseph A. Fitzmyer, "Crucifixion in Ancient Palentine: Qumran Literature and the New Testament," *CBQ* 40 (1978): 493–513.

49. See Colpe, *A Scribe Trained,* pp. 102–110.

50. Senior (*Passion,* p. 338) calls it a "terminal point in the Passion narrative." Meier (*Matthew,* p. 353) sees the presence of the woman and what follows as a preparation for the resurrection.

51. See Metzger (*Textual Commentary,* p. 70) for a discussion of the textual problems.

52. On the significance of the temple curtain, see my discussion in chapter 2, section 6c.

53. For a thorough discussion of these verses, see Maria Riebl, *Auferstehung Jesu in der Stunde seines Todes? Zur Botschaft von Mt 27,51b–53,* Stuttgarter biblische Beitrage (Stuttgart: Katholisches Bibelwerk, 1978), and Donald Senior, "The Death of Jesus and the Resurrection of the Holy Ones," *CBQ* 38 (1976):312–29.

54. Riebl, *Auferstehung Jesu,* pp. 25–29.

55. The threefold use of the passive voice, "the rocks *were* split," "the tombs also *were* opened," "many bodies . . . *were* raised," indicates divine intervention.

56. *Auferstehung,* p. 40.

57. A translation can be found in *New Testament Apocrypha: vol 1, Gospels and Related Writings,* ed. Wilhelm Schneemelcher, trans. R. McL. Wilson (Philadelphia: Westminster, 1963). See 8:28–33.

58. The text reads:

On the eve of Passover they hanged Yeshu [of Nazareth] and the herald went before him for forty days saying, "[Yeshu of Nazareth] is going forth to be stoned in that he hath practiced sorcery and beguiled and led astray Israel. Let everyone knowing aught in his defense come and plead for him." But they found naught in his defense and hanged him on the eve of Passover.

quoted from Joseph Klausner, *Jesus of Nazareth: His Life, Times, and Teaching,* trans. Herbert Danby (New York: Macmillan, 1945), p. 27.

6. MATTHEW'S GOSPEL THEOLOGY

1. *The Cross: Tradition and Interpretation,* trans. Elke Jessett (Grand Rapids, Michigan: Eerdmans, 1975), p. 114.

2. On the messianic secret Jack D. Kingsbury, *The Christology of Mark's Gospel* (Philadelphia: Fortress, 1983), pp. 1–46; Christopher Tuckett, ed., *The Messianic Secret,* Issues in Religion and Theology, no. 1 (Philadelphia: Fortress, 1983), contains a series of essays on the theme of the messianic secret in Mark.

3. "The Messiah of Israel as Teacher of the Gentiles: The Setting of Matthew's Christology," *Int* 29 (1975): 27.

4. On the infancy narrative see Raymond E. Brown, *The Birth of the Messiah: A Commentary on the Infancy Narrative in Matthew and Luke* (New York: Doubleday, 1977), and Krister Stendahl, "Quis et Unde? An Analysis of Matthew 1–2," in *The Interpretation of Matthew,* ed. Graham Stanton, Issues in Religion and Theology, no. 3 (Philadelphia: Fortress, 1983), pp. 56–66.

5. See Stendahl, "Quis et Unde?" pp. 57–60.

6. *Matthew* (Philadelphia: Fortress, 1977), p. 38.

7. Not all authors agree with this division of the Gospel. For a discussion of the structure of Matthew's Gospel, see Jack D. Kingsbury, *Matthew: Structure, Christology, Kingdom,* (Philadelphia: Fortress, 1975), ch. 1; John Meier, *The Vision of Matthew: Christ, Church and Morality in the First Gospel* (New York: Paulist, 1978), ch. 1 and 2; Donald Senior, *What Are They Saying about Matthew?* (New York: Paulist, 1983), ch 2.

8. Benno Przybylski, *Righteousness in Matthew and His World of Thought,* SNTSMS, no. 41 (Cambridge: Cambridge University, 1980), p. 94.

9. On the miracles in Matthew see H.J. Held, "Matthew as Interpreter of

the Miracle Stories," in Günther Bornkamm, Gerhard Barth, Heinz Joachim Held, *Tradition and Interpretation in Matthew,* trans. Percy Scott (Philadelphia: Westminster, 1963), pp. 165–299.

10. On the title "Son of David," see Leonard Goppelt, *Theology of the New Testament,* vol. 2 *The Variety and Unity of the Apostolic Witness to Christ,* trans. John E. Alsup, ed. Jürgen Roloff (Grand Rapids, Michigan: Eerdmans, 1982), pp. 220–223; and Kingsbury, *Structure,* pp. 99–103.

11. I shall deal with the element of rejection in parts two and three of this chapter.

12. Jack D. Kingsbury, "The Figure of Jesus in Matthew's Story: A Literary-Critical Probe," *JSNT* 21 (1984): 3–36, esp 11–14.

13. See Jack D. Kingsbury, *The Parables of Jesus in Matthew 13: A Study in Redaction Criticism* (St Louis: Clayton, 1969), esp pp. 92–129.

14. Kingsbury, "The Figure of Jesus," pp. 11–14.

15. Meier, *Vision,* pp. 204–210.

16. Nils A. Dahl, "The Passion Narrative in Matthew," in *Jesus in the Memory of the Early Church* (Minneapolis: Minnesota: Augsburg, 1976), p. 49.

17. On Matthew's theology of mission, see Donald Senior and Carroll Stuhlmueller, *The Biblical Foundations for Mission* (New York: Orbis, 1983), pp. 233–254.

18. See Kingsbury, *Structure,* pp. 85–86.

19. See Kingsbury, *Matthew,* p. 96.

20. See Kingsbury, *Parables,* p. 130.

21. See Kingsbury, *Matthew,* 91.

22. See the article by Günther Bornkamm, "The Authority to 'Bind' and 'Loose' in the Church in Matthew's Gospel: The Problem of Sources in Matthew's Gospel," in *The Interpretation of Matthew,* ed. G. Stanton, pp. 85–97.

23. Wolfgang Trilling, *Das wahre Israel: Studien zur Theologie des Matthäus-evangeliums,* SANT, no. 10 (Munich: Kösel-Verlag, 1964), p.106.

24. See Raymond E. Brown and John P. Meier, *Antioch and Rome: New Testament Cradles of Catholic Christianity* (New York: Paulist, 1983), pp. 68–70.

25. Scholars disagree on whether or not "nations" includes Israel. For two different views, see D.R.A. Hare and D.J. Harrington, " 'Make Disciples of All the Gentiles' (MT 28:19)," in Daniel Harrington, *Light of All Nations: Essays on the Church in New Testament Research,* Good News Studies, no. 3 (Wilmington, Delaware: Glazier, 1982), pp. 110–123, and John Meier, "Gentiles or Nations in Matt 28:19?" *CBQ* 39 (1977): 94–102.

26. For Matthew's use of righteousness, see R.A. Guelich, *The Sermon on the Mount: A Foundation for Understanding* (Waco, Texas: Word, 1982), pp. 84–88, 102–103, 170–174; and J. Reumann, *"Righteousness" in the New Tes-*

tament: "Justification" in the *United States Lutheran-Roman Catholic Dialogue* (Philadelphia: Fortress, 1982), pp. 125–135.

27. For the Pauline notion of righteousness see Reumann, *"Righteousness,"* 41–91.

28. See Guelich, *Sermon,* pp. 86–87.

29. See Przybylski, *Righteousness in Matthew,* pp. 98–99.

30. D.R.A. Hare, *The Theme of Jewish Persecution of Christians in the Gospel According to St. Matthew,* SNTSMS, no. 6 (Cambridge: Cambridge University, 1967), p. 131, n. 1.

31. Reumann, *"Righteousness,"* p. 135.

32. Hans Conzelmann, *An Outline of the Theology of the New Testament,* trans. John Bowden (New York: Harper & Row, 1968), p. 149.

33. For a slightly different view which highlights the aspect of salvation history, see Reumann, *"Righteousness,"* pp. 132–34.

34. For a detailed explanation of 5:17–20, see Meier, *Vision,* pp. 222–239.

35. On the theme of persecution, see Hare, *The Theme of Jewish Persecution.*

7. THE PASSION ACCORDING TO LUKE: OVERVIEW

1. *From Tradition to Gospel,* trans. Bertram Lee Woolf (New York: Scribners, n.d.), p. 201.

2. The authenticity of this text is seriously questioned because it is missing from many of the earliest and best manuscripts of the New Testament. For a discussion of the problem, see Bruce M. Metzger, *A Textual Commentary on the New Testament: A Companion Volume to the United Bible Societies' Greek New Testament* (United Bible Societies, 1971), p. 180.

3. This point is persuasively made by Franz G. Untergassmair, *Kreuzweg und Kreuzigung Jesu: Ein Beitrag zur lukanischen Redaktionsgeschichte und zur Frage nach der lukanischen "Kreuzestheologie"* (Paderborn: Schoningh, 1980), pp. 156–171.

4. I am making a distinction between the historical centurion and the centurion as a literary figure in Luke's narrative. It is conceivable that the historical centurion declared that Jesus was "innocent." But the declaration that Jesus was "righteous," in the Old Testament sense of the word, can only be attributed to the centurion as a literary figure because it presupposes knowledge of Jesus' entire life, knowledge reserved to the author of the narrative. I shall deal with the translation of *dikaios* (innocent or righteous) in the next chapter.

5. I am indebted to Josef Ernst (*Das Evangelium nach Lukas,* RNT, [Regensburg: Pustet, 1977], pp. 643–644) for the listing of this data.

6. This position is espoused by Vincent Taylor (*The Passion Narrative of*

St. Luke: A Critical and Historical Investigation, ed. O. Evans, SNTSTMS, no. 19 [Cambridge: Cambridge University, 1972]), and Joachim Jeremias ("Perikopen-Umstellungen bei Lukas?" *NTS* 4 [1958]: 115–119).

7. This position was championed by J.M. Creed (*The Gospel According to St. Luke* [London: Macmillan, 1930]). In recent years it appears to have gained momentum. Marion Lloyd Soards, Jr. ("The Scope, Origin, and Purpose of the Special Lukan Passion Narrative Material in Luke 22," Unpublished Dissertation, Union Theological Seminary, New York) contends that Luke did not make use of a continous passion narrative in addition to Mark in the composition of chapter 22. Untergassmair (*Kreuzweg*) argues a similar position for chapter 23. Joseph A. Fitzmyer (*The Gospel According to Luke X-XXIV,* Anchor Bible, vol 28A [Garden City, New York: Doubleday, 1985], pp. 1365–1366) has added his authority to this position. I have defended a similar position in a brief article (Frank J. Matera, "The Death of Jesus according to Luke: A Question of Sources," *CBQ* 47 (1985): 469–485.

8. *The Gospel According to Luke,* p. 1365.

9. "The Scope, Origin, and Purpose," pp. 218–222.

10. *Ibid.,* p. 221.

8. THE PASSION ACCORDING TO LUKE: COMMENTARY

1. For a discussion of how Jesus got to the cross, see Robert J. Karris, *Luke: Artist and Theologian: Luke's Passion Account as Literature* (New York: Paulist, 1985), pp. 16–22. Karris answers that "Jesus got to the cross by being God's righteous person and by being the prophet of God's good news to the poor" (p. 16).

2. See I. Howard Marshall, *The Gospel of Luke: A Commentary on the Greek Text,* NIGTC (Grand Rapids, Michigan: Eerdmanns, 1978), pp. 786–787.

3. This point is made by Hans Conzelmann, *The Theology of Saint Luke,* trans. Geoffrey Buswell (New York: Harper & Row, 1961), pp. 28 and 199. Conzelmann thinks that the period between the temptation and the trial was a Satan-free period. For a corrective of this view see Schuyler Brown, *Apostasy and Perseverance in the Theology of Luke,* AnBib, no. 36 (Rome: Biblical Institute, 1969), esp. pp. 9–10.

4. The theme of possessions in Luke-Acts is developed by Luke T. Johnson, *The Literary Function of Possessions in Luke-Acts,* SBLDS, no. 39 (Missoula, Montana: Scholars Press, 1977).

5. For a discussion of the chronology see Joseph A. Fitzmyer, *The Gospel According to Luke X-XXIV,* Anchor Bible, vol 28A (Garden City, New York: Doubleday, 1985), pp. 1378–1382.

6. See Raymond E. Brown, *The Gospel According to John (XIII-XXI)* The

Anchor Bible, vol 29A (Garden City, New York: Doubleday, 1970), pp. 883–895.

7. For a discussion of the table talk within this chapter, see Paul S. Minear, "A Note on Luke xxii 36," *NovT* 7 (1964): 128–134. For a discussion of the meal motif which runs throughout Luke's Gospel, see Robert Karris, *Luke: Artist and Theologian,* pp. 47–78; and John Navone, *Themes of St. Luke* (Rome: Gregorian University, n.d.).

8. The thesis that Luke's version of the Last Supper follows the genre of the Farewell Discourse has been developed by X. Léon-Dufour in "Das letzte Mahl Jesu und die testamentarische Tradition nach Lk 22," *ZKT* 103 (1981): 33–55 and *Le partage du pain eucharistique selon le Nouveau Testament* (Paris: Seuil, 1982). The position has also been espoused by Marion Lloyd Soards, Jr., "The Scope, Origin, and Purpose of the Special Lukan Passion Narrative Material in Luke 22," Unpublished Dissertation, Union Theological Seminary, New York, pp. 91–96. For a discussion of the genre, see Brown, *The Gospel According to John,* pp. 597–601; and Johannes Munck, "Discours d'adieu dans le Nouveau Testament et dans la littérature biblique," *Aux sources de la tradition chrétienne: Mélanges offerts à Maurice Goquel* (Neuchatel/Paris, 1950), pp. 155–170.

9. Several authors have noted the parallels between Jesus and Paul in Luke-Acts. See Walter Radl, *Paulus und Jesus im lukanischen Doppelwerk: Untersuchungen zu Parallelmotiven im Lukasevangelium und in der Apostelgeschichte* (Bern: Herbert Lang, 1975).

10. This point is made by Jacob Jervell, *Luke and the People of God: A New Look at Luke-Acts* (Minneapolis, Minnesota: Augsburg, 1972), pp. 75–112.

11. Fitzmyer (*The Gospel According to Luke,* p. 1397) emphasizes the eschatological aspect of the meal.

12. *Ibid.,* p. 1390, for a brief description of the Passover meal.

13. For a discussion of the textual problem, see Bruce M. Metzger, *A Textual Commentary on the New Testament: A Companion Volume to the United Bible Societies' Greek New Testament* (United Bible Societies, 1971), pp. 173–177.

14. For a positive discussion of Luke's soteriology, see Joseph A. Fitzmyer, *The Gospel According to Luke I-IX,* Anchor Bible, vol 28 (Garden City, New York: Doubleday, 1981), pp. 219–226.

15. This point is made by S. Brown, *Apostasy and Perseverance,* p. 83.

16. See *ibid.,* p. 9; and John Gillman, "A Temptation to Violence: The Two Swords in Lk 22: 35–38," *Louvain Studies* 9 (1982): 142–153, esp. p.146.

17. For a discussion of this difficult text, see Gillman, "A Temptation to Violence," and Minear, "A Note on Luke xxii 36."

18. *The Gospel According to Luke,* p. 1432.

19. For a detailed study of Luke's account, see David M. Stanley, *Jesus in Gethsemane: The Early Church Reflects on the Suffering of Jesus* (New York: Paulist, 1980), pp. 188–222.

20. For this outline I am indebted to Bart D. Ehrman and Mark A. Plunkett, "The Angel and the Agony: The Textual Problem of Luke 22:43–44," *CBQ* 45 (1983): 401–416.

21. For a discussion of the text critical question see the article listed in note 20. Also, see Metzger, *A Textual Commentary*, p. 177.

22. See Marshall, *The Gospel of Luke*, p. 831.

23. André Feuillet, *L'Agonie de Gethsémani: Enquête exégétique et théologique suive d'une Étude du "Mystere de Jesus" de Pascal* (Paris: Gabalda, 1977), p. 23 disagrees. He argues that Luke does not excuse the disciples since he reprimands them in the next verse. It is true that Luke does not completely excuse the disciples, but in comparison to Mark he is more benevolent toward them.

24. S. Brown (*Apostasy and Perseverance*, p. 69) makes the point that their faith in Jesus as the Messiah is not destroyed.

25. For the important theme of prayer in Luke, see Augustin George, *Études sur l'oeuvre de Luc*, Sources Bibliques (Paris: Gabalda, 1978), pp. 395–427; P.T. O'Brien, "Prayer in Luke-Acts," *Tyndale Bulletin* 24 (1973): 111–127; and Stanley, *Jesus in Gethsemane*, pp. 189–194.

26. For a thorough discussion of this question, see Gerhard Schneider, *Verleugnung, Verspottung und Verhor Jesu nach Lukas 22,54–71. Studien zur lukanischen Darstellung der Passion*, SANT, no. 22 (Munich: Kösel, 1969).

27. Fitzmyer, *The Gospel According to Luke*, p. 1456.

28. Marshall, *The Gospel of Luke*, p. 839.

29. Schneider, *Verleugnung*, p. 170.

30. S. Brown (*Apostasy and Perseverance*, p. 70) notes, "Peter's sin will consist not in refusing to acknowledge Jesus for what he is, i.e., the Christ (cf. 12,9), but simply in falsely denying his personal acquaintance."

31. For a discussion of Luke's benevolent attitude toward the temple, see Francis D. Weinert, "Luke, the Temple, and Jesus' Saying about Jerusalem's Abandoned House (Luke 13:34–35)," *CBQ* 44 (1982): 68–76.

32. For a discussion of this scene, see Brown, *The Gospel According to John*, pp. 843–872.

33. See the remarks by Fitzmyer, *The Gospel According to Luke*, p. 1480.

34. For a comparative study of this scene in all four Gospels, see Grant R. Osborne, "Redactional Trajectories in the Crucifixion Narrative," *EvQ* 51 (1979): 80–96.

35. I have argued this position in my article, "The Death of Jesus According to Luke: A Question of Source," *CBQ* 47 (1985): 469–485.

36. See Fitzmyer, *The Gospel According to Luke,* p. 1496.

37. Jerome Neyrey, "Jesus' Address to the Women of Jerusalem (Lk. 23.27–32)," *NTS* 29 (1983), 74–86. I am indebted to Neyrey for many of the comments made in this section.

38. For a fuller explanation, see Fitzmyer, *The Gospel According to Luke,* p. 1498.

39. I consider the Pastoral Epistles to be deutero-Pauline.

40. For a discussion of the problem, see Metzger, *A Textual Commentary on the New Testament,* p. 180.

41. On the important theme of "seeing," see Karris, *Luke: Artist and Theologian,* p. 41.

42. On the meaning of paradise, see Fitzmyer, *The Gospel According to Luke,* p. 1510; and Marshall, *The Gospel of Luke,* pp. 872–873.

43. This point is made by Weinert, "Luke, the Temple, and Jesus' Saying," p. 43.

44. For a survey of opinions see Fitzmyer, *The Gospel According to Luke,* p. 1518. Fitzmyer favors the outer curtain hypothesis.

45. For a discussion of this point, see Brian E. Beck, " 'Imitatio Christi' and the Lucan Passion Narrative," in *Suffering and Martyrdom in the New Testament: Studies Presented to G.M. Styler by the Cambridge New Testament Seminar,* ed. William Horbury and Brian McNeil (Cambridge: Cambridge University, 1981), pp. 28–47; Hermann Dechent "Der Gerechte"—eine Bezeichnung für den Messias." *TST* 100 (1927–28): 438–443; Karris, *Luke: Artist and Theologian,* pp. 109–111; and Matera, "The Death of Jesus According to Luke."

46. See Karris, *Luke: Artist and Theologian,* p. 113.

9. LUKE'S GOSPEL THEOLOGY

1. For a discussion of Luke's infancy narrative, see Raymond E. Brown, *The Birth of the Messiah: A Commentary on the Infancy Narratives in Matthew and Luke* (Garden City, New York: Doubleday, 1977), pp. 235–499; and Joseph A. Fitzmyer, *The Gospel According to Luke (I-IX): Introduction, Translation, and Notes,* Anchor Bible, vol 28 (Garden City, New York: Doubleday, 1981), pp. 303–348.

2. Note that in Matthew's account of the temptation, the temptation at the pinnacle of the temple is the second of Jesus' three temptations (Mt 4:5–6). It may be that Luke has altered the original order of the temptations in order to have the final, climactic temptation occur at Jerusalem. In this way he achieves an inclusion effect for the first four chapters of his Gospel. The activity begins and ends with references to Jerusalem's temple.

3. It is true, of course, that 8:27–10:52 forms a distinctive section of Mark's Gospel during which Jesus teaches his disciples that he must suffer and die at Jerusalem. But Mark does not cast this section into a journey to Jerusalem as Luke does in 9:51—19:44. Mark does not mention the journey to Jerusalem until 10:1.

4. In 9:51–19:44 Luke appears to draw upon two sources: (a) special material known only to him, usually referred to as "L"; (b) material known to Matthew as well as Luke, usually referred to as "Q." Matthew and Luke, however, employ the Q material differently. For a listing of the Q and L passages in Luke, see Fitzmyer, *The Gospel According to Luke,* pp. 75–85.

5. The importance of the ascension for Luke's theology is stressed by Eric Franklin, *Christ the Lord: A Study in the Purpose and Theology of Luke-Acts* (Westminster: Philadelphia, 1975).

6. *Das Evangelium nach Lukas,* RNT (Regensburg: Pustet, 1977), p. 327.

7. The concept of the "reestablished Israel" is stressed by Jacob Jervell, *Luke and the People of God: A New Look at Luke–Acts* (Minneapolis, Minnesota: Augsburg, 1972), pp. 41–74.

8. *The Gospel According to Luke,* p. 241.

9. See Jack D. Kingsbury, *Jesus Christ in Matthew, Mark, and Luke* (Philadelphia: Fortress, 1981), pp. 122–124.

10. For a description of discipleship in Luke, see Fitzmyer, *The Gospel According to Luke,* pp. 235–256; and Franklin, *Christ the Lord,* pp. 145–172.

11. David Gill, "Observations on the Lukan Travel Narrative and Some Related Passages," *HTR* 63 (1970): 199–221.

12. On the theme of the rejected Prophet, see Luke T. Johnson, *The Literary Function of Possessions in Luke–Acts,* SBLDS, no. 39 (Missoula, Montana: Scholars Press, 1977), esp. pp. 38–78; and David L. Tiede, *Prophecy and History in Luke–Acts* (Philadelphia: Fortress, 1981), pp. 19–63.

13. For a discussion of the Christological importance of the category "prophet," see Oscar Cullmann, *The Christology of the New Testament,* trans. Shirley C. Guthrie and Charles A. M. Hall, rev. ed. (London: SCM, 1963), pp. 13–50.

14. For a discussion of parallels between Jesus and John in Luke's infancy narrative, see Fitzmyer, *The Gospel According to Luke,* pp. 313–316. Fitzmyer notes that Luke employs a step-parallelism, that is, a parallelism of one-upmanship. Although there are constant parallels between the events surrounding the births of John and Jesus, Jesus is always presented in a more favorable light.

15. For a good discussion of this sermon, see Tiede, *Prophecy and History,* pp. 33–55.

16. For a discussion of how Luke composed chapter 9, see Joseph A. Fitz-

myer, "The Composition of Luke, Chapter 9," *Perspectives on Luke-Acts,* ed. Charles H. Talbert, (Danville, Virginia: Association of Baptist Professors of Religion, 1978), pp. 139–152.

17. For a discussion of the prophet like Moses theme, see David P. Moessner, "Luke 9:1–50: Luke's Preview of the Journey of the Prophet Like Moses of Deuteronomy," *JBL* 102 (1983): 575–605.

18. For a discussion of the prophet theme in this chapter, see Richard J. Dillon, *From Eye-Witnesses to Ministers of the Word: Tradition and Composition in Luke 24,* AnBib, no. 82, (Rome: Biblical Institute, 1978), pp. 114–127.

19. For a discussion of the royal motif in Luke's Gospel, see Augustin George, "La royauté de Jésus," *Études sur l'oeuvre de Luc,* Sources Bibliques (Paris: Gabalda, 1978), pp. 257–282.

20. On the meaning of Son of God in the New Testament see James D.G. Dunn, *Christology in the Making: A New Testament Inquiry into the Origins of the Doctrine of the Incarnation,* trans. John Bowden (Philadelphia: Westminster, 1980), pp. 12–64; Martin Hengel, *The Son of God: The Origin of Christology and the History of Jewish-Hellenistic Religion* (Philadelphia: Fortress, 1976); and C.F.D. Moule, *The Origin of Christology* (Cambridge: Cambridge University Press, 1977).

21. On the importance of the notion of the benefactor for Luke's Christology, see Frederick W. Danker, *Luke* (Philadelphia: Fortress, 1976), pp. 6–17; and the commentary by the same author, *Jesus and the New Age According to St. Luke: A Commentary on the Third Gospel* (St. Louis, Missouri: Clayton, 1972).

22. The text can be found in *Documents for the Study of the Gospels,* ed. David R. Cartlidge and David L. Dungan (Philadelphia: Fortress, 1980), pp. 13–14.

23. For Luke's royal theology in Acts, see "The Concept of the Davidic 'Son of God' in Acts and Its Old Testament Background," *Studies in Luke–Acts,* ed. Leander E. Keck and J. Louis Martyn (Philadelphia: Fortress, 1966), pp. 186–193.

BIBLIOGRAPHY

Achtemeier, Paul J. *Mark*. Philadelphia: Fortress, 1975.

Ambrozic, Aloysius. *The Hidden Kingdom: A Redaction-Critical Study of the References to the Kingdom of God in Mark's Gospel*. Washington: CBA, 1972.

Beck, Brian E. " 'Imitatio Christi' and the Lucan Passion Narrative." *Suffering and Martyrdom in the New Testament: Studies Presented to G. M. Styler by the Cambridge New Testament Seminar*. ed. William Horbury and Brian McNeil. Cambridge: Cambridge University Press, 1981.

Best, Ernest. *Mark: The Gospel as Story*. Edinburgh: T. & T. Clark, 1983.

Blinzler, Josef. *The Trial of Jesus*. Westminster, Maryland: Newman, 1959.

Bonnard, Pierre. *L'Évangile selon Saint Matthieu*. Neuchatel: Delachaux & Niestle, 1983.

Bornkamm, Günther. "The Authority to 'Bind' and 'Loose' in the Church in Matthew's Gospel: The Problem of Sources in Matthew's Gospel." *The Interpretation of Matthew*. ed. Graham Stanton. Philadelphia: Fortress, 1983: 85–97.

Bornkamm, Günther; Barth, Gerhard; Held, Heinz J. *Tradition and Interpretation in Matthew*. Philadelphia: Westminster, 1963.

Brown, Raymond E. *The Birth of the Messiah: A Commentary on the Infancy Narrative in Matthew and Luke*. New York: Doubleday, 1977.

———— . *The Gospel According to John (XIII–XXI)*. New York: Doubleday, 1970.

Brown, Raymond E., and Meier, John P. *Antioch and Rome: New Testament Cradles of Catholic Christianity*. New York: Paulist, 1983.

Brown, Schuyler. *Apostasy and Perseverance in the Theology of Luke*. Rome: Biblical Institute, 1969.

Breytenbach, Cilliers. *Nachfolge und Zukunftserwartung nach Markus:*

Eine methodenkritische Studie. Zürich: Theologischer Verlag, 1984.

Bultmann, Rudolf. *The History of the Synoptic Tradition.* New York: Harper & Row, 1963.

Cartlidge, David, and Dungan, David L. *Documents for the Study of the Gospels.* Philadelphia: Fortress, 1980.

Charlesworth, James H. ed. *The Old Testament Pseudepigrapha, vol I, Apocalyptic Literature and Testaments.* New York: Doubleday, 1983.

Conzelmann, Hans. *An Outline of the Theology of the New Testament.* New York: Harper & Row, 1968.

Cope, Lamar O. *Matthew: A Scribe Trained for the Kingdom of Heaven.* Washington: CBA, 1976.

Creed, J.M. *The Gospel According to St. Luke.* London: Macmillan, 1930.

Cullmann, Oscar. *The Christology of the New Testament.* London: SCM, 1963.

Culpepper, R. Alan. "The Passion and Resurrection in Mark." *RevExp* 75 (1978): 583–600.

Dahl, Nils A. *The Crucified Messiah and Other Essays.* Minneapolis: Augsburg, 1974.

———. "The Passion Narrative in Matthew." *Jesus in the Memory of the Early Church.* Minneapolis: Augsburg, 1976.

Danker, Frederick. *Jesus and the New Age According to St. Luke: A Commentary on the Third Gospel.* St. Louis: Clayton, 1972.

———. *Luke.* Philadelphia: Fortress, 1976.

Descamps, Albert. "Redaction et christologie dans le recit matthéen de la Passion." *L'Évangile selon Matthieu.* ed. M. Didier. Gembloux: Éditions J. Duculot, 1972.

Dechent, Hermann. " 'Der Gerechte'—eine Bezeichnung für den Messias." *TST* 100 (1927–28): 438–443.

Dillon, Richard J. *From Eye-Witnesses to Ministers of the Word: Tradition and Composition in Luke 24.* Rome: Biblical Institute, 1978.

Donahue, John R. *Are You the Christ? The Trial Narrative in the Gospel of Mark.* Missoula, Montana: Scholars Press, 1973.

Dunn, James D.G. *Christology in the Making: A New Testament Inquiry into the Origins of the Doctrine of the Incarnation.* Philadelphia: Westminster, 1980.

Ehrman, Bart D. and Plunkett, Mark A. "The Angel and the Agony: The Textual Problem of Luke 22:43–44." *CBQ* 45 (1983): 401–416.

Ernst, Josef. *Das Evangelium nach Lukas.* Regensburg: Pustet, 1977.

————. *Das Evangelium nach Markus.* Regensburg: Pustet, 1981.

Feuillet, André. *L'Agonie de Gethsémani: Enquête Exégétique et theologique suivi d'une Étude du 'Mystere de Jesus' de Pascal.* Paris: Gabalda, 1977.

Fitzmyer, Joseph A. "Crucifixion in Ancient Palestine, Qumran Literature, and the New Testament." *CBQ* 40 (1978): 493–513.

————. "The Composition of Luke, Chapter 9." *Perspectives on Luke-Acts.* ed. Charles H. Talbert. Danville: Virginia Association of Baptist Professors of Religion, 1978.

————. *The Gospel According to Luke.* 2 vols. New York: Doubleday, 1981, 1985.

Fowler, Robert M. *Loaves and Fishes: The Function of the Feeding Stories in the Gospel of Mark.* Chico, CA: Scholars Press, 1981.

Franklin, Eric. *Christ the Lord: A Study in the Purpose of Luke-Acts.* Philadelphia: Westminster, 1975.

Gaston, Lloyd. "The Messiah of Israel as Teacher of the Gentiles: The Setting of Matthew's Christology." *Int* 29 (1975): 24–40.

George, Augustin. *Étude sur l'oeuvre de Luc.* Paris: Gabalda, 1978.

Gerhardson, Birger. "Jesus livré et abandonné d'après la Passion selon Saint Matthieu." *RB* 76 (1969): 206–227.

Gill, David. "Observations on the Lukan Travel Narrative and Some Related Passages." *HTR* 63 (1970): 199–221.

Gillman, John. "A Temptation to Violence: The Two Swords in Lk 22:35–38." *Louvain Studies* 9 (1982): 142–153.

Gnilka, Joachim. *Das Evangelium nach Markus: 2. Teilband Mk 8:27–16:20.* Zürich: Benziger, 1979.

Goppelt, Leonard. *Theology of the New Testament.* vol 2. Grand Rapids, Michigan: Eerdmans, 1982.

Guelich, Robert A. *The Sermon on the Mount: A Foundation for Understanding.* Waco, Texas: Word, 1982.

Hare, D.R.A. *The Theme of Jewish Persecution of Christians in the Gospel According to St. Matthew.* Cambridge: Cambridge University Press, 1967.

Hare, D.R.A., and Harrington, D.J. " 'Make Disciples of All the Gentiles' (MT 28:19)." Daniel Harrington. *CBQ* 37 (1975):359–369.

Harrington, Daniel, J. "A Map of Books on Mark." *BTB* 15 (1985): 12–16.

Hengel, Martin. *Crucifixion in the Ancient World and the Folly of the Message of the Cross*. Philadelphia: Fortress, 1977.

———. *The Son of God: The Origin of Christology and the History of Jewish-Hellenistic Religion*. Philadelphia: Fortress, 1976.

Hennecke, Edgar, and Schneemelcher, Wilhelm. ed. *New Testament Apocrypha: vol 1, Gospels and Related Writings*. Philadelphia: Westminster, 1963.

Hooker, Morna. *The Message of Mark*. London: Epworth, 1983.

Horsley, Richard A. "Popular Messianic Movements around the Time of Jesus." *CBQ* 46 (1984): 471–495.

Jeremias, Joachim. *New Testament Theology: The Proclamation of Jesus*. New York: Scribners, n.d.

———. "Perikopen-Umstellungen bei Lukas?" *NTS* 4 (1958): 115–119.

Jervell, Jacob. *Luke and the People of God: A New Look at Luke-Acts*. Minneapolis: Augsburg, 1972.

Johnson, Luke T. *The Literary Function of Possessions in Luke-Acts*. Missoula, Montana: Scholars Press, 1977.

Juel, Donald. *Messiah and Temple: The Trial of Jesus in the Gospel of Mark*. Missoula, Montana: Scholars Press, 1977.

Karris, Robert. *Luke: Artist and Theologian: Luke's Passion Account as Literature*. New York: Paulist, 1985.

Kee, Howard Clark. *Community in the New Age: Studies in Mark's Gospel*. Philadelphia: Westminster, 1977.

Kelber, Werner. *The Kingdom in Mark: A New Place and a New Time*. Philadelphia: Fortress, 1974.

———. *Mark's Story of Jesus*. Philadelphia: Fortress, 1976.

Kelber, Werner H. ed. *The Passion in Mark: Studies on Mark 14–16*. Philadelphia: Fortress, 1976.

Kingsbury, Jack Dean. *Matthew*. Philadelphia: Fortress, 1977.

———. *Matthew: Structure, Christology, Kingdom*. Philadelphia: Fortress, 1975.

———. *The Christology of Mark's Gospel*. Philadelphia: Fortress, 1983.

_____ . ''The Figure of Jesus in Matthew's Story: A Literary-Critical Probe.'' *JSNT* 21 (1984): 3–36.

_____ . *The Parables of Jesus in Matthew 13: A Study in Redaction Criticism*. St. Louis: Clayton, 1969.

Klausner, Joseph. *Jesus of Nazareth: His Life, Times, and Teaching*. New York: Macmillan, 1945.

Lamarche, Paul. ''La mort du Christ et le voile du temple selon Marc.'' *NRT* 106 (1974): 583–599.

Léon-Dufour, Xavier. ''Das letzte Mahl Jesu und die testamentarische Tradition nach Lk 22.'' *ZKT* 103 (1981): 33–55.

_____ . *Le partage du pain eucharistique: selon le Nouveau Testament*. Paris: Seuil, 1982.

Lindars, Barnabas. *Jesus Son of Man: A Fresh Examination of the Son of Man Sayings in the Light of Recent Research*. Grand Rapids, Michigan: Eerdmans, 1984.

Lohfink, Gerhard. *The Last Days of Jesus: An Enriching Portrayal of the Passion*. Notre Dame, Indiana: Ave Maria, 1984.

Marshall, I. H. *Last Supper and Lord's Supper*. Grand Rapids, Michigan: Eerdmans, 1980.

_____ . *The Gospel of Luke: A Commentary on the Greek Text*. Grand Rapids, Michigan: Eerdmans, 1978.

Martin, Ralph. *Mark Evangelist and Theologian*. Grand Rapids, Michigan: Zondervan, 1972.

Matera, Frank J. ''Matthew 27:11–54.'' *Int* 38 (1984): 55–59.

_____ . ''The Death of Jesus according to Luke: A Question of Sources.'' *CBQ* 47 (1985): 469–485.

_____ . *The Kingship of Jesus: Composition and Theology in Mark 15*. Chico, CA: Scholars Press, 1982.

Marxsen, Willi. *Mark the Evangelist: Studies on the Redaction of the Gospel*. New York: Abingdon, 1969.

McCaffrey, U.P. ''Psalm Quotations in the Passion Narratives of the Gospels.'' *Neotestamentica* 14 (1981): 73–89.

Meier, John. ''Gentiles or Nations in Matt 28:19?'' *CBQ* 39 (1977): 94–102.

_____ . *Matthew*. Wilmington, Delaware: Glazier, 1980.

_____ . *The Vision of Matthew: Christ, Church and Morality in the First Gospel*. New York: Paulist, 1978.

Metzger, Bruce. *A Textual Commentary on the Greek New Testament:*

A Companion Volume to the United Bible Societies' Greek New Testament. United Bible Societies, 1971.

Minear, Paul S. "A Note on Luke xxii 36." *NovT* (1964): 128–134.

Moesner, David P. "Luke 9:1–50: Luke's Preview of the Journey of the Prophet Like Moses of Deuteronomy." *JBL* 102 (1983): 575–605.

Moo, Douglas J. *The Old Testament in the Gospel Passion Narratives.* Sheffield: Almond Press, 1983.

Moule, C.F.D. *The Origin of Christology.* Cambridge: Cambridge University Press, 1977.

Munck, Johannes. "Discours d'adieu dans le Nouveau Testament et dans la littérature biblique." *Aux sources de la tradition chrétienne: Mélanges offerts à Maurice Goguel.* Neuchatel/Paris, 1950.

Navone, John. *Themes of St. Luke.* Rome: Gregorian University, n.d..

Neyrey, Jerome. "Jesus' Address to the Women of Jerusalem (Lk. 23.27–32)." *NTS* 29 (1983): 74–86.

O'Brien, P.T. "Prayer in Luke-Acts." *Tyndale Bulletin* 24 (1973): 111–127.

Osborne, Grant R. "Redactional Trajectories in the Crucifixion Narrative." *EvQ* 51 (1979): 80–96.

Perrin, Norman. "Towards an Interpretation of the Gospel of Mark." *Christology and a Modern Pilgrimage.* ed. H.D. Betz. Missoula, Montana: Scholars Press, 1974.

Pesch, Rudolf. *Das Evangelium der Urgemeinde.* Freiburg: Herder, 1979.

———. *Das Markusevangelium, II. Teil: Kommentar zu Kap. 8,27–16,20.* Freiburg: Herder, 1977.

Petersen, Norman, R. *Literary Criticism for New Testament Critics.* Philadelphia: Fortress, 1978.

Prybylski, Benno. *Righteousness in Matthew and His World of Thought.* Cambridge: Cambridge University Press, 1980.

Radl, Walter. *Paulus und Jesus im lukanischen Doppelwerk: Untersuchungen zu Parallelmotiven im Lukasevangelium und in der Apostelgeschichte.* Bern: Herbert Lang, 1975.

Rensberger, David. "The Politics of John: The Trial of Jesus in the Fourth Gospel." *JBL* 103 (1983): 395–411.

Reumann, John. *"Righteousness" in the New Testament: "Justification" in the United States Lutheran-Roman Catholic Dialogue.* Philadelphia: Fortress, 1982.

Rhoads, David, and Michie, Donald. *Mark as Story: An Introduction to the Narration of the Gospel.* Philadelphia: Fortress, 1982.

Riebl, Maria. *Auferstehung Jesu in der Stunde seines Todes? Zur Botschaft von Mt 27,51b–53.* Stuttgart: Katholisches Biblewerk, 1978.

Rivkin, Ellis. *What Crucified Jesus? The Political Execution of a Charismatic.* Nashville: Abingdon, 1984.

Sanders, E.P. *Jesus and Judaism.* Philadelphia: Fortress, 1985.

Schmidt, Karl Ludwig. *Der Rahmen der Geschichte Jesus: Literarkritische Untersuchungen zur ältesten Jesusüberlieferung.* Berlin: Trowitzsch & Sohn, 1919.

Schneider, Gerhard. *Die Passion Jesu nach den drei älteren Evangelien.* Munich: Kösel-Verlag, 1973.

––––––. *Verleugnung, Verspottung und Verhör Jesu nach Lukas 22,54–71. Studien zur lukanischen Darstellung der Passion.* Munich: Kosel-Verlag, 1969.

Schneider, J. *"stauros." Theological Dictionary of the New Testament.* Grand Rapids, Michigan: Eerdmans, 1971.

Schweitzer, Albert. *The Quest of the Historical Jesus: A Critical Study of Its Progress from Reimarus to Wrede.* New York: Macmillan, 1968.

Schweizer, Eduard. "The Concept of the Davidic 'Son of God' in Acts and Its Old Testament Background." *Studies in Luke-Acts.* ed. Leader Keck and J. Louis Martyn. Philadelphia: Fortress, 1966.

––––––. *The Good News according to Matthew.* Atlanta: John Knox, 1975.

Senior, Donald. "The Death of Jesus and the Resurrection of the Holy Ones." *CBQ* 38 (1976): 312–329.

––––––. *The Passion Narrative according to Matthew: A Redactional Study.* Louvain: Louvain University Press, 1975.

––––––. "The Passion Narrative in the Gospel of Matthew." *L'Évangile selon Matthieu.* ed. M. Didier. Gembloux: Éditions J. Duculot, 1972.

––––––. *The Passion of Jesus in the Gospel of Mark.* Wilmington, Delaware: Glazier, 1984.

––––––. *What Are They Saying About Matthew?* New York: Paulist, 1983.

Senior, Donald, and Stuhlmueller, Carroll. *The Biblical Foundations for Mission.* New York: Orbis, 1983.

Snodgrass, Klyne. *The Parable of the Wicked Tenants: An Inquiry into Parable Interpretation*. Tübingen: Mohr, 1983.

Soards, Marion Lloyd. "The Scope, Origin, and Purpose of the Special Lukan Passion Narrative Material in Luke 22." Unpublished Ph.D. dissertation. Union Theological Seminary, New York.

Stanley, David. *Jesus in Gethsemane: The Early Church's Reflection on the Suffering of Jesus*. New York: Paulist, 1980.

Stanton, Graham. "The Origin and Purpose of Matthew's Gospel: Matthean Scholarship from 1945 to 1980." *Aufstieg und Niedergang der römischen Welt II,25,3*. ed. H. Temporini and W. Haase. Berlin: de Gruyter, 1983.

Stendahl, Krister. "Quis et Unde? An Analysis of Matthew 1–2." ed. Graham Stanton. *The Interpretation of Matthew*. Philadelphia: Fortress, 1983.

Stock, Augustine. *Call to Discipleship: A Literary Study of Mark's Gospel*. Wilmington, Delaware: Glazier, 1982.

Strange, J.F. "Crucifixion." *The Interpreter's Dictionary of the Bible Supplementary Volume*. Nashville: Abingdon, 1976.

Strecker, Georg. *Der Weg der Gerechtigkeit*. Göttingen: Vandenhoeck & Ruprecht, 1971.

Strobel, August. *Die Stunde der Warheit: Untersuchungen zum Strafverfahren gegen Jesus*. Tübingen: Mohr, 1980.

Tannehill, R.C. "The Disciples in Mark: The Function of a Narrative Role." *JR* 57 (1977): 386–405.

Taylor, Vincent. *The Gospel According to Mark: The Greek Text with Introduction, Notes, and Indexes*. New York: St. Martin's Press, 1966.

——— . *The Passion Narrative of St. Luke: A Critical and Historical Investigation*. Cambridge: Cambridge University Press, 1972.

Tiede, David L. *Prophecy and History in Luke-Acts*. Philadelphia: Fortress, 1981.

Trilling, Wolfgang. *Das wahre Israel: Studien zur Theologie des Matthäus-evangeliums*. Munich: Kösel-Verlag, 1964.

Tuckett, Christopher. ed. *The Messianic Secret*. Philadelphia: Fortress, 1983.

Untergassmair, Franz G. *Kreuzweg und Kreuzigung Jesu: Ein Beitrag zur lukanischen Redaktionsgeschichte und zur Frage nach der lukanischen "Kreuzestheologie."* Paderborn: Schoningh, 1980.

Weber, Hans-Ruedi. *The Cross: Tradition and Interpretation*. Philadelphia: Fortress, 1977.

Weeden, Theodore J. *Mark: Traditions in Conflict*. Philadelphia: Fortress, 1971.

Weinert, Francis D. "Luke, the Temple, and Jesus' Saying about Jerusalem's Abandoned House (Luke 13:34–35)." *CBQ* 44 (1982): 68–76.

Winter, Paul. *On the Trial of Jesus*. Berlin: de Gruyter, 1974.

Three important works appeared after the completion of this manuscript.

Neyrey, Jerome. *The Passion according to Luke: A Redactional Study of Luke's Soteriology*. New York: Paulist, 1985.

Senior, Donald. *The Passion of Jesus in the Gospel of Matthew*. Wilmington, Delaware: Glazier, 1985.

Witherup, Ronald, D. *The Cross of Jesus: A Literary-Critical Study of Matthew 27*. Unpublished Ph.D. dissertation. Union Theological Seminary in Virginia, 1985.

INDEX